# SACRED TERROR

# SACRED TERROR

Religion and Horror on the Silver Screen

*Douglas E. Cowan*

BAYLOR UNIVERSITY PRESS

© 2008 by Baylor University Press
Waco, Texas 76798

*All Rights Reserved*. No part of this publication may be reproduced, stored in a retrieval system, or transmitted, in any form or by any means, electronic, mechanical, photocopying, recording or otherwise, without the prior permission in writing of Baylor University Press.

*Cover Design* by Grant Nellesson

The Library of Congress has cataloged the hardcover edition as follows:

Library of Congress Cataloging-in-Publication Data

Cowan, Douglas E.
  Sacred terror : religion and horror on the silver screen / Douglas E. Cowan.
  325 p. cm.
  Includes bibliographical references and index.
  ISBN 978-1-60258-018-3 (hardback : alk. paper)
  1. Horror films--History and criticism. 2. Religion in motion pictures. I. Title.
  PN1995.9.H6C69 2008
  791.43'6164--dc22
                                    2008012614

The paperback ISBN for this title is 978-1-4813-0490-0.
First paperback edition ©2015.

Printed in the United States of America on acid-free paper.

For Leith,
who knows the difference between the English and Spanish
versions . . .

# CONTENTS

| | | |
|---|---|---|
| Preface | | ix |
| 1 | Tickets, Please<br>*An Introduction to Sacred Terror* | 1 |
| 2 | Lying at the Heart of Horror<br>*Religion and Horror on the Silver Screen* | 25 |
| 3 | Angels to Some, Demons to Others<br>*Fear of Change in the Sacred Order* | 61 |
| 4 | No Sanctuary<br>*Ambivalence and the Fear of Sacred Places* | 93 |
| 5 | Stalking Life<br>*The Fear of Death and of Dying Badly* | 123 |
| 6 | Mainstreaming Satan<br>*Fear of Supernatural Evil Internalized and Externalized* | 167 |
| 7 | The Unholy Human<br>*Fear of Fanaticism and Fear of the Flesh* | 201 |
| 8 | Curtain and House Lights<br>*Possibility Persists in the World Outside the Frame* | 249 |
| Filmography | | 265 |
| Bibliography | | 277 |
| Index | | 309 |

# PREFACE

I was not a fan of scary movies as a child. I have a vivid imagination, and I tend to frighten rather easily. I devoured science fiction, though, with which horror has considerable overlap. In 1966, the salt-sucking creature in the *Star Trek* pilot, "The Man Trap," scared me, but I didn't lose sleep over it. I saw *The Exorcist* when it was released in 1973, and it affected me deeply enough that parts of the experience still haunt me whenever I screen it for a class today. I avoided *The Omen* when it was released but was completely taken with *Alien* just a few years later. As I reflected on this paradox, I realized that I avoided movies with a religious component. For some reason, they scared me at a more profound level. Thus, in many ways, I'm an unlikely candidate to write a book about cinema horror and religious belief, but in other, more significant ways, I think my tenuous relationship with this kind of scary movie has prepared me well. I want to understand my own fears as much as I do those of other people, and I think the best scholarship comes from this kind of personal investment.

*Sacred Terror* began a few years ago during a *Hellraiser* marathon a local television station was running during the Hallowe'en weekend. I'd not seen any of the films, though I had looked at their covers, if only to learn more about the iconic Pinhead. Watching the films that Saturday, though, I was hooked. As I saw the *Hellraiser* mythology unfold, rather than the scared eight-year-old watching the salt-sucker try to drain Captain Kirk, the trained sociologist of religion began to make connections. The epiphany came during the fourth film, *Hellraiser: Bloodline*, when, in what I consider the quintessence of the relationship between religion and cinema horror, Pinhead says to the main human character (and to us): "Do I look like someone who cares what God thinks?"

I thought, "No, you don't." And I began to wonder what else this film genre could tell us about our relationship with the unseen order. What could our fears reveal about our beliefs?

A number of people read all or part of the manuscript at various stages of writing, and I thank them for their support and their critiques; both are invaluable. I would like to thank John Morehead for his interest in the book long before I started writing, and for promoting it on his TheoFantastique blog. Parts of this preface have appeared there. Paul Thomas and Glenn Young read the manuscript with great care, and to Glenn I owe particular thanks for reminding me of the classic moment in *The Tingler* when fear is let loose in the theater itself.

I would like to acknowledge a seed grant from the University of Waterloo and the Social Sciences and Humanities Research Council of Canada, and to thank one of my graduate students, David Feltmate, for his work tracking down source material. Thanks are due also to Casey Blaine at Baylor University Press for her support and careful editing of the final manuscript. Though the faults of the book remain inevitably my own, *Sacred Terror* is stronger for all her efforts.

My greatest debt I owe to my wife, Joie, always my most enthusiastic reader and who learned if not to love scary movies, then at least to appreciate their value.

# 1

# TICKETS, PLEASE
## An Introduction to Sacred Terror

```
EXT. BEACH - NIGHT

                    MACHEN
11:55. Almost midnight. Enough time for
one more story, one more story before
twelve. Just to keep us warm. In five
minutes it will be the twenty-first of
April. One hundred years ago on the
twenty-first of April out in the waters
around Spivey Point a small clipper
ship drew toward land. Suddenly, out
of the night, a fog rolled in. In a
moment, they could see nothing. Not
a foot ahead of them. And then, they
saw a light. By God, it was a fire,
burning on the shore, strong enough
to penetrate the swirling mist. They
steered a course toward the light, but
it was a campfire--like this one--and
the ship crashed against the rocks. The
hull sheared in two. Masts snapped like
a twig. The wreckage sank, with all the
men aboard. At the bottom of the sea
lay the Elizabeth Dane with her crew,
```

their lungs filled with salt water, their eyes open and staring into the darkness. And above, as suddenly as it had come, the fog lifted, receded back across the ocean, and never came again.

But it is told by the fishermen and their fathers and grandfathers that when the fog returns to Antonio Bay, the men at the bottom of the sea out in the water by Spivey Point will rise up and search for the campfire that led them to their dark, icy death.

SOUND of bell-buoy...
(John Carpenter, *The Fog*)

## RELIGION APPEARING OUT OF THE FOG

Campfires are the quintessential setting for ghost stories. As the sun drops behind the hills, as daylight steals away into the trees, darkness gathers close about the camp and ghost stories just seem to appear . . . supernaturally. Shadows deepen, moving and shifting in the fire's unsteady glow. Sounds that seemed innocuous only moments before now threaten ominously from the gloom. A chill ripples through the group as campers don sweaters, pull sleeping bags tight about their shoulders, and huddle closer to the fire and to each other. A few laugh nervously, and hesitant smiles pass between friends in anticipation of the dubious but undeniable thrill to come.

"It happened," says the storyteller, peering carefully out into the dark, "not far from this very spot, not so very long ago. . . ." John Carpenter's *The Fog* begins as a ghost story told around just such a campfire. An elderly sailor, Captain Machen (John Houseman), is entertaining a group of local children. As with all good ghost stories, his are at least reputed to be true and to have happened at or near the spot where the children sit listening with rapt attention.

We, of course, are the children; we are his audience. The tale is told for our benefit; the screen is our campfire. As the film unreels, midnight on the one-hundredth anniversary of the founding of Antonio Bay brings the return of a thick, eerily glowing fog—and with it the drowned crew of the *Elizabeth Dane*. A fishing trawler disappears in the murk, power goes down inexplicably, and dogs bark for no apparent reason. As townsfolk are murdered by the vengeful revenant, the fullness of the *Elizabeth Dane* tragedy gradually emerges. Recorded in the 1880 journal of Father Patrick Malone, the grandfather of Antonio Bay's current Episcopal priest (Hal Holbrook), is the story of a small group of lepers who, led by the wealthy but similarly afflicted Mr. Blake, wanted nothing more than to found an onshore colony not far from the nascent town.

```
FR. MALONE (reading from journal)
```
'April 20. The six of us met tonight. From midnight to one o'clock, we planned the death of Blake and his comrades. I tell myself that Blake's gold will allow the church to be built and our small settlement to become a township, but it does not soothe the horror I feel being an accomplice to murder.' . . .
'April 21. The deed is done. Blake followed our false fire onshore and his ship broke apart on the rocks off Spivey Point. We were aided by an unearthly fog that rolled in as if heaven-sent, although God had no part in our actions tonight. Blake's gold will be recovered

tomorrow, but may the Lord forgive us for what we have done.'

A century after the crime, as the mysterious fog rolls in off the water once again and the enormity of the danger becomes clear, Stevie Wayne (Adrienne Barbeau), who operates a radio station from the Spivey Point lighthouse, calls the fog's approach, warning the townspeople and directing them away from the approaching horror.

>	STEVIE (V.O. RADIO)
> Richardsville Pike up to Beacon Hill is the only clear road. Up to the church! If you can get out of town, get to the old church. Now the junction at 101 is cut off. If you can get out of town, get to the old church. It's the only place left to go. Get to the old church on Beacon Hill!

Reading further in his grandfather's journal as the terrified townsfolk seek refuge in the church, Father Malone deduces the reason for the apparent curse.

>	FR. MALONE (reading from journal)
> 'My fellow conspirators believe that the confiscated fortune has been stolen from them, when in fact I am the thief and God's temple is the tomb of gold.' (Repeating) 'I am the thief and God's temple is the tomb of gold.'

*The Fog* reaches its dénouement as the ghosts of the drowned lepers smash their way through the stained glass windows and enter the ultimate site of their murder—the village church where the conspiracy was hatched. Brandishing cutlasses, knives, and cargo hooks, they advance on the descendents of their killers. Suddenly, Father Malone realizes what they want, what may finally allow them to rest. Pulling frantically at loose stones in the wall of the church basement, he removes a massive gold cross, carefully wrapped in oil cloth. Obviously cast from the bulk of Blake's treasure, it has lain hidden in the very foundation of the sanctuary for a hundred years. To discover what happens next, you'll have to rent the movie.

Though Rupert Wainwright's 2005 remake of *The Fog* eliminates virtually all religious elements from the story, Carpenter's original highlights the two questions that lie at the heart of *Sacred Terror*: "What do we fear?" and "Why religion?" That is, what are the particular fears that cinema horror reveals to us, and, with all the nonreligious sources of horror in the *real* world, why does the *reel* world continually come back to the religious as a font of inspiration for those things that frighten us? A third of those interviewed by a British horror magazine said they would rather be trapped on a desert island with the entirely fictional Freddy Krueger (of *A Nightmare on Elm Street* fame) than with former Prime Minister Margaret Thatcher. Our lives, it seems, are already populated by monsters, both real and imagined. If that is the case, then why do writers, producers, and directors of horror films so often rely on some element of religion to help them tell a scary story? And what do those stories tell us about the fears that lurk not so very far below the veneer of late modern civilization?

On one level, *The Fog* is a fairly straightforward supernatural revenge story. In all its different cultural forms, a classic component of the horror tale is that the souls of murdered men and women cannot rest until they have found either vengeance or release. Trapped between this plane of existence and the next, their conflict drives the narrative, and without it there would be no story. There are, however, a number of other dimensions in

Carpenter's original film that illustrate more particularly the intimate, multifaceted, and inextricable relationship between religion and horror that lies at the heart of this book.

First, and most obviously, there is the issue of the supernatural itself, the sine qua non of at least some definitions of religion (see, for example, James, [1902] 1999, 31; Stark and Bainbridge, 1987, 39). Whether the narrative antagonists are vampires, werewolves, ghosts, mummies, demons, or elder gods, religiously oriented cinema horror relies for much of its effect on the direct collision between nature and supernature, between what we believe to be true about the world and what we fear may be the reality of the "unseen order" (James, [1902] 1999, 61). Horror films regularly juxtapose what we expect as we go about our daily routines and what we suspect lurks just beyond the borders of our perception once those routines have been interrupted. When the mysterious fog first enshrouds the *Elizabeth Dane*, for example, it comes suddenly and without warning. It glows in a clearly unnatural way, and, when it returns a century later, it approaches Antonio Bay against the prevailing winds. Plainly, Carpenter means for us to regard it as under some kind of control that defies the accepted natural order. Or, consider the vindictive spirits themselves, searching for that which will allow their souls some final peace. All but ubiquitous in horror cinema, whether tormented, at rest, or the object of supernatural conflict, the soul is an explicitly religious concept, one that makes little sense apart from the various religious frameworks in which it comes embedded.

Next, the conspirators who led the *Elizabeth Dane* to her doom did not gather in a town hall, a saloon, or a farmhouse to plot their betrayal. They met at the church, a place of putative sanctuary, and they were led in their plan by the local minister. A century later, when Stevie Wayne tries to direct the townsfolk out of the fog's path, she tells them to "get to the old church. It's the only place left to go"—when it is, in fact, the one place they should *not* go. Instead of a sanctuary, it has become the basement in the old house behind the Bates Motel (*Psycho*), the egg repository found by the doomed crew of the *Nostromo* (*Alien*), the musty attic room through which the Cenobites pass into our world (*Hellraiser*). By this time in the movie, we know that the church is not a place of safety, but instead of the principal locus of danger, both for the passengers and crew of the *Elizabeth Dane*, and for the descendants of their murderers.

In reversing popular expectations about the clergy and the church—a process I discuss in more depth as the metataxis of horror, the inversion or reversal of accepted cultural categories—sequences such as this draw on deeply embedded cultural ambivalences about the church as a place of safety and the clergy as peerless guardians of decency and morality. Similarly, in many horror films—particularly, though not exclusively, Western vampire films—the cross represents a significant component in the technology of salvation and the successful narrative resolution of the conflict. Even when only passively deployed—worn as a pendant or created through the interplay of light and shadow—the cross protects, binds, banishes, and destroys the evil that comes against it. In *The Fog*, however, the importance and salvific power of the cross have been reversed. Rather than the symbol of divine sacrifice and benevolence, here it is the material artifact of betrayal, a golden relic of human weakness, fear, and greed. Father Malone (the elder) not only helped murder the lepers on board the *Elizabeth Dane* but also double-crossed his own coconspirators and kept most of the gold for the church. As has been so often the case throughout history, and as we will see in a number of films, church wealth is gained through deceit and betrayal, and the robes of supposedly godly men are lifted to reveal feet of clay stained with blood.

Finally, there is the larger question of the popular notion of religion as a cultural and societal good, an issue that will be discussed in more detail in chapter 2 as the ambivalence of the sacred. Put briefly, in popular discourse, "religion" is more often than not taken as a synonym for "good," "moral," and "decent." That which is immoral or indecent, that which does not have what we regard as a positive or salutary effect in society, is then, by definition, "not religious." Although there is overwhelming historical evidence that this is hardly the case, the misperception continues and provides significant grounding for cinema horror.

In his review of Rupert Wainwright's *Stigmata*, Ron Burke writes that "you do not expect to find religion and spirituality in a horror film" (1999, ¶1). On the contrary, however, cinema horror is replete with religion and always has been. From a secretive Egyptian priesthood using its occult power to ensure the return of *The Mummy's Ghost* to Amanda Donahoe's biting devotion to a pre-Christian snake god in Ken Russell's *The Lair of the White Worm*, from the cross-and-holy-water combination that ultimately defeats the vampire Baron in *The Brides of Dracula* to Steve Beck's nervy reinterpretation of the Charon myth in *Ghost Ship*, religion has proven a staple of cinematic horror since Georges Méliès brought Mephistopheles to the screen in 1896 and Frankenstein's creation first lurched in front of Thomas Edison's kinetoscope nearly fifteen years later.

When Joseph, the spoiled protagonist in Fritz Lang's monumental *Metropolis*, begins to understand the horror on which his city is built, he envisions it as Moloch, an Ammonite god to whom biblical mythistory maintains children were sacrificed in great numbers. Though imagined in any number of ways, when cinema horror brings the "end-of-the-world-as-we-know-it" to the silver screen, it just as often wraps it in the apocalyptic cloak of religious belief as the laboratory coat of secular science. "They had their two thousand years," proclaims the leader of a Satanic insurgency in Janusz Kaminski's *Lost Souls*. "Now it's our turn."

Real life horror from the jungles of Guyana (Jonestown) to the upscale suburbs of San Diego (Heaven's Gate) confronts us with the power of religion to motivate participants in ways that those of us not privy to their secrets are often at a loss to understand. In reel life, this power is reflected in films ranging from Victor Halperin's *White Zombie* to John Schlesinger's *The Believers*, and from John Llewellyn Moxey's *Horror Hotel* to Robin Hardy's *The Wicker Man*. Though few viewers might accept the existence of a three-hundred-year-old witch living with her coven in the foggy backwoods of Massachusetts (*Horror Hotel*), how many would have believed the willingness of several hundred people to commit suicide or homicide on behalf of religious convictions ranging from belief in an imminent attack by the U.S. government or the presence of an alien spacecraft hiding in the tail of the Hale-Bopp comet? Or, that audiences around the world would credence the story of three university film students lost in the fictional "Black Hills" of Maryland, allegedly victims of the Blair Witch? To this day, with over $135 million in revenue, *The Blair Witch Project* easily retains the record in cinema history for the greatest return on capital investment.

On the other hand, temptation, particularly sexual temptation, just as often reveals the powerlessness of religion in society, the fear that faith will ultimately fail and prove unable to counter the demands of the flesh. "Nunsploitation" films, for example—from Sergio Grieco's *The Sinful Nuns of St. Valentine* to Bruno Mattei's *The Other Hell*, and from Masaru Konuma's *Sister Luna's Confession* to Lucio Fulci's *Demonia*—all probe the deeply ambivalent relationship between the sacred and the profane, especially as it is negotiated among those who have set themselves apart for the religious life. In these films, when the Devil comes calling, he almost inevitably appears in the flesh.

In his introduction to *American Horrors*, film scholar Gregory Waller contends that "horror films have proven to be among the most significant documents in America's public debate over the status of the independent woman in a society still dominated by men" (1987, 5). Creatively misreading Waller for a moment, my basic argument in *Sacred Terror* is that religiously oriented cinema horror remains a significant material disclosure of deeply embedded cultural fears of the supernatural and an equally entrenched ambivalence about the place and power of religion in society as the principal means of negotiating those fears. As a pop culture exercise in sociophobics (a concept I will discuss in more detail in the next chapter), cinema horror provides a window into both the cultural stock of knowledge on which those fears depend and the various cultural discourses they support. As Stephen King writes in *Danse Macabre*, which remains one of the most insightful analyses of the horror genre, "When the horror movies wear their various sociopolitical hats—the B-picture as tabloid editorial—they often serve as an extraordinarily accurate barometer of those things that trouble the night-thoughts of a whole society" (1981, 131). Put differently, what scares us reveals important aspects of who we are, both as individuals and as a society.

Whether religion underpins the plot of a particular film, frames the narrative crisis and its resolution (or lack thereof), or simply dresses the set on which the horrific story is played, *Sacred Terror* is concerned with horror films that have distinct (and, I will argue, crucial) religious components. While slasher films (e.g., *The Texas Chain Saw Massacre* or *Saw*) and what we might loosely call "areligious" monster films (e.g., *Godzilla* or *The Creature from the Black Lagoon*) may be employed occasionally as discursive foils, they are not the central focus here. Readers who are more interested in these types of films should refer to some of the excellent studies already available (see, for example, Bellin, 2005; Clover, 1992; Grant, 1996; Halberstam, 1995; Paul, 1994; Pinedo, 1997; Tsutsui, 2004).

Rather, *Sacred Terror* asks: What roles are religion writ large, religious traditions in particular, or specific religious characters asked to play in the vast corpus of cinema horror? How are Roman Catholic priests portrayed, for example, or Protestant ministers, or Tibetan monks—religious characters drawn from traditions either familiar to or different from those that dominate in a particular culture? How do those portrayals reflect or refract the image of religion outside the cinematic frame? How is this image distorted by the director's lens, the angle from which the shot is made, or the elements of the subject that have been both included in and, perhaps more importantly, excluded from that frame? And, most importantly, what can these aspects of the film tell us about the times and the cultures in which and by which they were produced? How does what scares us comment on what we believe, or claim we don't believe?

In the universe of Roman Catholic discourse, for example, the almost sepia-toned cinematography of Kaminski's *Lost Souls* both suggests the black-and-white nature of the battle between good and evil that lies at the film's heart and, at the same time, highlights the impression that this battle is not black-and-white, that the narrative, like the cinematography, is considerably less confident about the struggle and its outcome. In films like *Lost Souls*, the religious context is obvious and provides the main stage for the narrative; in others, its presence is more subtle, requiring significant excavation for a more detailed, culturally intertextual reading of the film.

By "culturally intertextual," I mean a number of interrelated things. First, intertextuality implies a set of conventions—social norms, religious practices, artistic products, folk wisdom, different parts of the taken-for-granted information that Berger and Luckmann call "a body of transmitted recipe knowledge" (1966: 83)—that are available for filmmakers to exploit as a kind of cultural shorthand to make specific points in their work. In genre cinema, for example, whether horror, science fiction, or spy thriller a filmmaker's ability to count on particular references to resonate with his or her audience reduces the necessity to spell everything out in the film. Consider television programs that often include episodes advertised as "ripped from the headlines"—though the lead-in to the program almost inevitably includes an oxymoronic disclaimer that there is not meant to be any correlation between the show's narrative, characters, and action, and real people or real events. It's a patent falsehood, of course, because the producers are counting on precisely those events on which episodes are based to resonate with viewers in order to secure their audience share. Without this intertextual reliance, such a television series as *The X-Files*, for example, would have been considerably more difficult to produce. Because of the cultural awareness of and resonance with the concepts of unidentified flying objects, extraterrestrial intelligences, and the possibility that the American government has more knowledge of these than it is willing to share, however, Chris Carter was able to turn what could have been just another off-beat cop show into a cult TV phenomenon. A similar dependency holds for cinema horror, and the issue, to put it one way, is concision: how quickly, and with how little effort, can we convey the central sense of threat, of dread, or of danger? The less effort filmmakers have to expend setting up the background for a story—why zombies are scary, why people are afraid of ghosts, why cemeteries and abandoned churchyards are spooky—the more time they have to tell that story.

Second, many genre films are relentlessly self-referential, and that is part of the attraction for the audience. Cuban horror director Jorge Molina, for example, describes his films as "an accumulation of shots that I've liked in other films.... Cinema for me is totally referential" (Goldberg and Schneider, 2003, 90). Intertextuality allows films to comment on other films, often as a way of setting themselves apart or establishing a different character of credibility. In *John Carpenter's Vampires*, for example, vampire hunter Jack Crow (James Woods) tells a young Catholic priest, "Forget whatever you've seen in the movies. They don't turn into bats; crosses don't work." That is, this film presents vampires in a different way, but a way that is only effective because its intended audience is already familiar with films in which vampires do turn into bats and crosses do work. Without intertextuality, that particular story element is meaningless.

Finally, I am not limiting myself to those artifacts that traditionally have been labeled "texts"—books, magazines, diaries, letters, and so forth. While film can obviously be included in this more traditional understanding (and certainly has been in the history of film criticism), my argument in *Sacred Terror* turns in many ways on reading a number of cultural products as mutually intervailing texts that move in an intimate and inextricable relationship. That is, religious belief and practice, cultural sensibility, economic opportunity and exploitation, and material culture all function to inform the filmmaking effort; are informed by its products, both direct and indirect; and together form the interpretive landscape out of which a more complete understanding of the society that produced those films emerges.

Premier in this material, obviously, is the religiously oriented horror film itself. As I have noted, there is the cultural stock of "recipe knowledge" on which cinema texts depend—whether this knowledge functions as commentary on a dominant religious tradition or as a way of casting the religious Other. Much of the cinematic effect of a film like *The Exorcist*, for example, would be lost if it were either disembedded from its Roman Catholic context or screened in a culture for which that context had no meaning. On the other hand, the power of such films as Karl Freund's *The Mummy* (and its many successors) resides in the trialectic between a Western fascination with all things Egyptian (cf. Day, 2006; Irwin, 1980; Iversen, 1961; Lant, 1997; Schroeder, 2003), a relative ignorance in the West of the realities of ancient Egyptian religion, and a love for the basic elements of tragic romance that underpin most mummy films. Put differently, if vampire films can be loosely categorized as eroticism (if not softcore pornography), mummy movies are love stories, a theme that will be considered in chapter 5. Too, cultural commentary, whether professional, journalistic, or fan-based, provides an important insight into the ways in which films are received or, according to film critics, ought to be received. The advent of the Internet in the last decade makes this a particularly fruitful avenue for exploration. Finally, though to a somewhat lesser extent, there is the material culture of modern horror. While it may seem odd to include such things as movie tie-in games (especially videogames), models, and toys as part of the interpretive process, and though the religious element here is often implicit at best, I would argue that these products contribute to the meaning-making systems encoded both in the cinema horror texts themselves and the commercial culture out of which many of these texts emerge.

The film, then, is the celluloid trace, one material artifact of a very particular processual relationship between the filmmakers and the culture in which and for which they produce their films. Just as material artifacts ranging from potsherds to architectural ruins can help us understand more fully the cultures in which they were created, so too a fuller appreciation of cinematic horror can deepen our understanding of religious sensibilities that many commentators suggest have been (or ought to be) discarded by the very cultures in which these films are made.

## TICKETS, PLEASE . . .

The complex relationship between religion and cinema is important to explore if for no other reason than that the former remains one of the most pervasive cultural forces in late modern society, and the latter has emerged as one of its most visible cultural industries. Both are intervailing dialects in the lingua franca of late modernity. Before we begin a more in-depth consideration of their relationship, however, let's briefly consider a working definition of the two principal constituents in *Sacred Terror*: religion and horror.

### "The Unseen Order": Defining Religion

Scores, if not hundreds, of attempts to define "religion" have marked the study of human interaction with what some call "God" and others "gods and goddesses," what millions refer to as "the Ultimate" or "the ground of Being," and what millions more refuse to describe in any concrete terms at all. In some cases, "religion" means "my religion," and practitioners discount all other expressions of faith as false and misleading. In many countries, official designation as a "religion"—by whatever means—confers a significant level of cultural acceptance, a social legitimacy denied to groups considered suspect or illegitimate. Many of these, of course, have come to be labeled as "cults" or "sects," with all the stigma that has historically been attached to such groups. Historian of religions Jonathan Z. Smith, on the other hand, contends that "religion [as an analytic concept] is solely the creation of the scholar's study" and "has no existence apart from the academy" (1982, xii). For Smith, lived religion is rarely understood by practitioners in the same terms as by scholars. Few, for example, consider their daily devotions as a hopeless indulgence in "the opium of the people" (Marx) or as expressions of a comparatively harmless "collective neurosis" designed to preempt the manifestation of more serious personal neuroses (Freud). Indeed, these days, more and more people are choosing to deny that they are "religious" at all, preferring instead to describe themselves as "spiritual"—though what they mean by that just as often remains unclear.

For me, though, one of the most useful definitions is that proposed by William James in his famous Gifford Lectures, delivered in 1901 and 1902 at the University of Edinburgh and published as his classic text, *The Varieties of Religious Experience*. In his third lecture, "The Reality of the Unseen," James defined "the life of religion" as "the belief that there is an unseen order, and that our supreme good lies in harmoniously adjusting ourselves thereto" ([1902] 1999, 61). Though necessarily broad in scope, and obviously ignoring aspects of the phenomena that some scholars would consider essential, this definition has two principal advantages. First, by refusing to limit religion to those traditions that hold to belief in a supreme being of one kind or another, it avoids the problem that marked many early attempts to establish a working definition and allows for greatly expanded understandings of religious belief and practice. Moreover, it does not restrict religion to those groups that believe in a socially approved supreme being or spiritual path, relegating all others to the murky and indistinct world of "cults," "sects," and "false religions."

Second, and more important in the context of religion and horror, it avoids what I have called elsewhere the "good, moral, and decent fallacy" (Cowan and Bromley, 2008, 10–11), the popular misconception that religion is always (or should always be) a force for good in society, and that negative social effects somehow indicate false or inauthentic religious practices. Many critics may dismiss horror films that have at their core some depiction of religiously motivated torture or human sacrifice, for example, arguing that this does not accurately represent religion, that its depiction denigrates authentic (and, by implication, decent) religious impulses. As Smith reminds us, though, "Religion is not nice; it has been responsible for more death and suffering than any other human activity" (1982, 110). Consider the religiously motivated torture that marked the various inquisitions carried out by the Roman Catholic Church during the Middle Ages. Historians such as Henry Kamen (1997) and Edward Peters (1988) have argued compellingly that, in the effort to extract either confessions or recantations from accused heretics, torture was used only as a last resort and far less often than popular legends of the Inquisition would suggest. Still, that such extreme methods were used at all (or that people are willing to credence the more extreme versions of Inquisition history) says something significant about the nature of the unseen order to which medieval Catholics sought to "harmoniously adjust" themselves, and the lengths to which they were willing to go to realize what they regarded as their "supreme good." Or, consider that for the Aztecs, the "unseen order" was the province of a powerful war god, Huitzilopochtli, whose eternal battle with a pantheon of other gods ensured the prosperity of the people who worshipped him. To carry on his fight on their behalf, Huitzilopochtli required a steady supply of blood—thus the Aztec practice of human sacrifice. In order to maintain a harmonious adjustment to the "unseen order" as the Aztecs understood it, then, as many as twenty thousand men and women per year had their hearts cut out with an obsidian knife. While, clearly, both of these phenomena also served as mechanisms of social control, in their departures from the popular conception of religion as good, moral, and decent, both were framed in terms of a relationship to the unseen order, and both have been used to cinematic advantage in numerous horror films.

*Fear and Frisson: Defining Horror*

Compared to more complex concepts, such as religion or the supernatural, defining "horror" seems deceptively simple. Though some commentators disagree (e.g., Strinati, 2000, 82), in terms of its emotional, psychological, and physical effects, cinema horror are films designed, scripted, shot, and edited for the principal purpose of evoking a variety of fear-based responses in the audience (Carroll, 1990, 15; Freeland, 2000, 2). We watch horror, and we are fascinated by it for the *frisson*, the physical and psychological shiver it generates in us. Although many sequences in non-horror films are frightening—crimes, combat, or car chases, for example—these are generally designed to serve a different purpose in the overall narrative. When movies that we would not ordinarily consider horror films have frightening moments and produce fear responses (whether these reactions are manifest in a psychological terror or the more visceral revulsion usually associated with horror), they do so to advance narrative agendas that have something other than fear at their cores. The hunt for a serial killer has its frightening moments, to be sure, but *The Bone Collector*, about a rookie forensic investigator tracking a serial killer, is not a horror film in the same sense as *The Bone Snatcher*, which is set in the deserts of Africa and involves swarms of preternaturally intelligent ants—the *isikulu*—that assume human form in an effort to consume human flesh. Non-horror films may frighten the audience to tell their stories, but horror films tell stories to frighten the audience. In the former, fear is a side effect; in the latter, it is the object of the exercise.

In cinema horror, all the film's elements work together to evoke an ever-increasing fear response in the audience. Though a film like *The Bone Snatcher* may seem little more than a straightforward monster movie, careful attention reveals religious undertones. As we learn through Titus, the African security officer, the *isikulu* are an example of how groups supernaturalize that which they do not understand—especially if what they do not understand is dangerous—and then ritualize what they come to believe are appropriate responses to it: totemic representations, sacrifice, and the sacralization of approach, relationship, and control—all elements of harmonious adjustment to an unseen order, and all deployed in pursuit of the fear response. However well or poorly this frisson is manifest in the final product, horror films use the cinematic narrative and the film techniques that go along with it to generate, elevate, and manipulate this fear response.

Noël Carroll (1990, 17) builds on this affectively oriented definition of horror, adding the important component of audience response and how this is integrally linked to cues from the narrative itself. That is, the onscreen reactions of positive characters prompt appropriate audience reactions, reactions that, "ideally, run parallel to the emotions of characters." Arguing that "this mirroring-effect . . . is a key feature of the horror genre" (1990, 17), Carroll demonstrates that when the characters with whom audiences are meant to identify feel fear, viewers feel fear; when characters feel relief that the terror has passed, a similar sense of relief washes over the audience. Because we can investigate how the different characters respond as a way of understanding how audiences are *expected* to respond, this insight allows for a more nuanced reading of cinema horror. Not all characters, for example, respond in the same way: some may feel fear and shut down; in others fear provokes action, response, and ultimately resolution. No one would suggest that Ripley (Sigourney Weaver) in *Aliens* does not feel fear as she rescues the young girl, Newt (Carrie Henn), from the egg chamber of the alien queen and then fights her way back to the waiting dropship in an attempt to escape. Her fear, however, generates a vastly different response than that of the marine, Private Hudson (Bill Paxton), who responds to the overwhelming presence of the aliens with a simple "We're fucked! We're never getting out of here!" Thus, not only is there a range of experiences that evoke the fear response, there is also a range of onscreen responses to fear with which the audience can identify.

In his attempt to understand how the fear response can be stimulated by representations the audience knows to be fictitious, Carroll rejects the understanding of both "illusion theorists," who argue that horror fiction "so [overwhelms] us that we are deceived into believing that a monster really looms before us" (1990, 63), and "pretend theorists," who "deny that the audience's emotional responses to fiction are genuine" (1990, 68)—put differently, those who believe horror audiences are stupid, and those who argue that their responses are fraudulent. Among other things, the main problems here are: if the emotional state is illusory, what is the emotional reality during the experience? If we seem horrified or terrified, but in fact are not, then what are we? If the emotional state is inauthentic, why and how is it generated? What is the genuine emotional state during those moments? In answer to this dilemma, Carroll proposes a third way, a "thought theory of emotional response to fictions" (1990, 79–88). That is, "it is the thought of the Green Slime that generates our state of art-horror, rather than our belief that the Green Slime exists. Moreover, art-horror here is a genuine emotion, not a pretend emotion, because actual emotion can be generated by entertaining the thought of something horrible" (Carroll, 1990, 80). As James Twitchell points out, the "scariest moment" in *The Blob*—one working title of which was *The Glob that Girdled the Globe*—was "when the goo came dripping down from the projection booth and onto our surrogate selves watching a horror movie at a downtown theater" (1985, 15). Similar moments occur when theater audiences watch a tornado rip through a drive-in in *Twister* or follow a deadly *Outbreak* of the Ebola virus as it is transmitted by a sneeze in the confines of an urban movie house. In classic horror cinema, of course, there is William Castle's *The Tingler*, about a creature that lives inside each of us, feeding on our fear but controlled by our screams. Given form because of a deaf-mute's inability to scream, the creature is chased into a movie theater filled to capacity. At that moment, the screen in the real theater goes black, and a voice tells the real audience that the Tingler is in *their* midst and that *they* must scream to protect themselves. Dubbed a "gimmick picture" by *Los Angeles Times* reviewer Philip Scheuer (1959, C8), the film was released in 1959 just before Hallowe'en, and seats in selected theaters across the country were rigged with a device called a "Percepto," which was designed to vibrate at the film's "tingliest" moments.

It is also important to note that horror is both a responsive and creative continuum, not a fixed point in psychological, sociological, or cinematic space. First, it is not the case that we are either frightened or not; fear is not a predetermined state, but rather a range of responses rooted in an assortment of stimuli. As a film proceeds to its climax, skilled directors take us through various levels of frisson, alternately relaxing and tightening their grip on our fear, guided and controlled among other things by the technological limits of their craft and the explicit or implicit standards of the culture in which and for which their films are produced. Narrative foreshadowing, the quick shot and cutaway that reveals and then hides the source of our fear, cues from the onscreen action, as well as the power of what we expect to see on the screen—which is a product both of our familiarity with the genre and the almost unavoidable hype that currently surrounds many theatrically released cinematic products—all contribute to generating, elevating, and manipulating the fear response.

Second, though there are certain generic considerations to which all creators of cinema horror must attend, the simple fact is that we in the audience are not all scared by the same things. Not all stimuli produce the same level of frisson. For some, thoughts of ghosts and discarnate spiritual entities are the height of horror, while zombies leave them cold. For others, demonic possession gives them the creeps, but they remain entirely unaffected by mummy movies or slasher films. For me, snakes are interesting and enjoyable as cinema monsters (especially when they are eating annoying cast members), but spiders are virtually impossible for me to watch. Snakes generate little fear response in me, but when spiders appear onscreen, I begin looking for them offscreen, checking the corners of the room, watching the shadows carefully, and starting out of my seat when the dog's nose touches my arm and my mind screams, "Spider!"

These considerations raise important questions about how broadly construed the horror continuum should be, what films it should include or exclude, and how hybridized these films often are. Responding to and respecting the differences in the potential horror audience, different cinematic hybrids use different generic conventions to create their effects. Horror can be based on the generic premises of science fiction, the psychological or supernatural thriller, the slasher film, the monster movie, or some combination of these. Occasionally, films that were for decades locked in the horror vault try to break out and transcend their genre. Consider, for example, the various incarnations of *Dracula*. Like those in the Hammer series, most are clearly part of the horror genre and rely for their effect on a rather straightforward exploitation of the fear response. Others, such as Francis Ford Coppola's *Bram Stoker's Dracula*, do not fit quite so well into the genre because they are (or appear to be) concerned with what the writers, producers, and directors regard as more significant concerns. Subtitled *Love Never Dies*, Coppola's version is in many respects more faithful to Stoker's novel than almost all of the Hammer films, but it departs in significant ways—from the prelude, where we learn the origin of Dracula, to the conclusion, where his fate seeks to turn the film from a horror movie to a tragic love story.

Following Vivian Sobchak's argument in *Screening Space* (1987b, 25), one of the reasons that horror films are often dismissed by critics—or why filmmakers like Coppola seek to make them something other than what they are—is that there are far more "bad" horror films than "good." Low production values, poor scripts poorly delivered, and plotlines riddled with holes and non sequiturs arguably mark more horror films than not. And far fewer of those achieve the frisson, psychological or visceral, that has come to define the genre than fall short in the effort to realize the effects of terror and horror. To say that horror films are about telling scary stories is not to say that all stories horror films tell are scary or that all storytellers are equally skilled in the attempt. They are not.

To suggest, however, as many critics do, that because far more horror films are "bad" than "good" the genre itself is unworthy of attention is superficial at best, and intellectually irresponsible at worst. Cinema horror matters, if for no other reason than its ubiquity and durability as a cultural product. Furthermore, if my thesis is correct—that these films reveal the cultural bases of specific, religiously oriented, and socially reproduced fears—then to ignore them is to deny the value and validity of this most basic of human experiences.

### A Fearful Symmetry: The Beginnings of Sacred Terror

Many believers are appalled at the notion that religion and fear are related. "My god is a god of love and compassion," they say. "His perfect love casts out all fear." They are, of course, entitled to this belief, but there seems remarkably little evidence in religious history to warrant it. Indeed, fear, wrote the Roman novelist Petronius, brought the primal gods into being. While terror, angst, and existential dread are not, perhaps, the singular genesis of divine-human interaction—though sociologist Elemér Hankiss argues persuasively that they form the foundation of human culture and civilization (2001)—their part in the interplay between the unseen order and those who seek to harmoniously adjust themselves thereto cannot be denied. One of the first to explore this relationship in any systematic fashion was Rudolf Otto (1869–1937).

For generations of Western scholars and students of religion, Otto's *The Idea of the Holy* (*Das Heilige*, [1923] 1950) has been a seminal text. Debated and discussed, celebrated and criticized, it has driven the thinking of thousands of men and women seeking to understand more fully the religious impulse in humankind. As every reader of Otto or his many interlocutors knows, arguably his central concept is the *numinous*, the "holy" shorn of any ethical or rational trappings. "There no religion," he writes, "in which it does not live as the real, innermost core" ([1923] 1950, 6). It is worth remembering that Otto was, first and foremost, a Christian theologian, occupying the prestigious Chair of Theology at the University of Marburg for the last twenty years of his life, during which time he wrote *Das Heilige*. As such, he does not dispute that the idea of the holy has come to mean "goodness, absolute goodness" (Otto, [1923] 1950, 6), but he points out that it has done so only as human religious belief, practice, and, most importantly, reflection, have evolved and developed.

Rather, in the holy, he is talking about a "unique feeling response," an affect that when it "first emerges and begins its long development, all those expressions . . . mean beyond all question something quite other than 'the good'" (Otto, [1923] 1950, 6). Whatever criticism we can offer about the theological assumptions built into Otto's argument, one of the most important aspects to grasp is that the primordial religious state or experience is affective; it is a feeling, an emotion. Though, as a theologian, Otto is concerned to put the best possible face on the problem, he cannot escape the logical consequences of his inquiry. Reflecting on a "'fear' that is more than fear proper"—and citing such passages as Exodus 23:27 ("I will send my terror in front of you . . .") and Job 9:34 (". . . not let dread of him terrify me")—Otto writes that "here we have a terror fraught with an inward shuddering such as not even the most menacing and overpowering created thing can instil [*sic*]. It has something spectral to it" ([1923] 1950, 13, 14).

Tracing the various etymological attempts to describe this primordial fear—the "gruesome," the "grisly"—he concludes that "'religious dread' (or 'awe') would perhaps be a better designation. Its antecedent stage is 'daemonic dread' (cf. the horror of Pan) with its queer perversion, a sort of abortive offshoot, the 'dread of ghosts'" (Otto, [1923] 1950, 14). He continues:

> It is this feeling which, emerging in the mind of primeval man, forms the starting point for the entire religious development in

history. "Daemons" and "gods" alike spring from this root, and all the product of 'mythological apperception" or "fantasy" are nothing but different modes in which it has been objectified. (Otto, [1923] 1950, 14–15).

Whether Otto is correct in saying that human religion finds its genesis in fear, he points directly at the heart of sacred terror. Even when this primordial dread has long passed into systematic theology, ritual, dogma, and sheer fancy, it is never far from the surface of the soul. "That this is so," writes Otto, "is shown by the potent attraction again and again exercised by the element of horror and 'shudder' in ghost stories, even among persons of high, all-round education" ([1923] 1950, 16).

Since the turn of the twentieth century, cinema horror has been one of "different modes" in which this fear has been objectified. It has become our campfire, our blanket and flashlight, our haunted house, the place to which our imaginations return when we confront the dread of the unseen order. "The 'cold blood' feeling may be a symptom of ordinary, natural fear," Otto concludes, "but there is something non-natural or supernatural about the symptom of 'creeping flesh'" ([1923] 1950, 16). The chapters that follow explore a number of the ways in which scary movies have peeled away the veneer of late modern sophistication to reveal the "daemonic dread" that still lurks beneath.

# 2

# LYING AT THE HEART OF HORROR
## Religion and Horror on the Silver Screen

MAYA

If you really believed in God, Father,
why is it so inconceivable to you that
his adversary could be just as real?
(Janusz Kaminski, *Lost Souls*)

## OUTTAKES: *LOST SOULS, GHOST SHIP, DRACULA HAS RISEN FROM THE GRAVE*

There are thousands of hours of cinema horror from which we could choose to begin our consideration of the intimate relationship between religious belief and the horror film. Some of these movies are well known, others less so. Though I alluded to a few of these in the introduction, to broaden this conceptual map and to draw its contours in more detail, consider three examples: *Lost Souls, Ghost Ship*, and *Dracula Has Risen from the Grave*. As cultural outtakes, if you will, each illustrates different facets of the relationship between religion and horror cinema that will be discussed more thoroughly in the following chapters, and each reveals particular aspects of the sociophobics on which sacred terror depends. While in many films the religious referents are obvious, in others they require more careful excavation. In still others, religious elements are so patently explicit that they render the narrative almost propagandistic.

## The Obvious ... Lost Souls

Released in 2000 amidst a variety of millennial speculations, *Lost Souls* opens with an epigraph.

```
...a man born of incest
will become Satan
And the world as we know it,
will be no more.
                        Deuteronomy 17
```

The first thing an astute observer notes, however, is that this is a completely fabricated quotation. Not only is there no such passage in Deuteronomy 17—which actually concerns proper sacrifice and the organization of the Israelite tribal confederacy in Canaan—there is no such passage in the Bible at all. Though Rod Armstrong (1999), who reviewed *Lost Souls* for Reel.com, one of the most extensive movie content sites on the Internet, does recognize quite correctly that the film "shows all its cards" in this epigraph, that the hand itself is a fake seems to have escaped him and almost all his fellow critics. As I will discuss elsewhere, however, fabricated scripture—complete with bogus chapter-and-verse—is quite common in religiously oriented cinema horror. The salient question is: why? Why would a filmmaker include such an obvious sham, something so open to immediate and conclusive disconfirmation? If we agree from the beginning that writers, producers, and directors mean their work to be taken seriously—after all, as Greg Smith points out, "a Hollywood film is one of the most highly scrutinized, carefully constructed, least random works imaginable" (2001, 128) and that there are "thousands of minute decisions that consciously construct the artificial world" within the cinematic frame—why do we find such arguably cheap tricks so often? What is the cinematic power of the (pseudo-) scriptural reference?

The directorial debut of Janusz Kaminski, an Oscar-winning cinematographer who has worked for much of his career with Steven Spielberg, *Lost Souls* is not only set in an explicitly religious context—the Roman Catholic subculture of demonic possession and exorcism—it draws on a number of popular evangelical Protestant themes, including the expectation of the Antichrist and the ability of discerning Christians to predict who this person will be and when he will appear. All but universally panned—most reviewers dubbed it a tepid remake of such films such *Rosemary's Baby* and *The Exorcist*—*Lost Souls* belongs to the subfamily of horror films that deal with the "naziresis of evil." While I will take up this theme in more detail in chapter 6, briefly, these are films that present us with the possibility of a satanic legacy, the expectation of a child dedicated in some way to the Devil. As the leader of the film's Satanic cabal says to one of the main characters, "They had their two thousand years. Now it's our turn." Filmed by cinematographer Mauro Fiore, with stark contrasts and desaturated colors, the film's disturbing, often disorienting angles accent its overall gothic look. The first sequence sets the tenor for the story.

Maya Larkin (Winona Ryder) is a possession survivor whose personal experience of demonic oppression and deliverance has earned her a place on a Roman Catholic exorcism team led by the enigmatic Father Lareaux (John Hurt). The subject of this particular exorcism, a homicidal math professor named Henry Birdson (John Diehl), has requested the ritual and, though the Church's position is left unclear at this point, a secular court has granted approval. As the team arrives, Birdson is scribbling columns of numbers in a notebook. Preparation of the room itself evokes both *The Exorcist* and images popularly associated with the Inquisition. While Birdson is buckled into a wooden chair with a set of heavy leather restraints, Lareaux and his assistants vest and lay out the various implements of exorcism—crucifix, Bible, liturgical books, and holy water. All the windows are covered, nonessential personnel are asked to leave, and a tape recorder is secured to a counter with black, military-style duct tape. Not surprisingly, the exorcism goes horribly wrong. Lareaux and Birdson are left comatose; Maya barely makes it out of the room, though she escapes with Birdson's papers and the tape recorder.

28 / *Lying at the Heart of Horror*

Breaking Birdson's numerical code reveals the other agenda for Maya and her mysterious group, as well as the film's main plot: finding and stopping the human who is destined to be possessed by Satan himself and so become the Antichrist. This leads her to Peter Kelson (Ben Chaplin), a true-crime writer who rejects any notion of ultimate good and evil as "illusions." Guided by Birdson's possessed numerology, Maya comes to believe that Kelson fits "all the criteria" her group has gathered on the identity of the Antichrist—"never baptized, devoid of faith, born of incest." The problem is that the ones she most needs to convince are those least inclined to believe her.

As with many of the religiously oriented horror films we will consider in this book, *Lost Souls* turns on the fundamental problem of religious belief in the late modern period, and everyone Maya encounters has an eminently rational reason to reject the supernatural premises of the narrative. Birdson's psychiatrist (Alfre Woodard, in what many critics consider a wisely uncredited role) has diagnosed him with temporal lobe epilepsy; Kelson classifies killers of his type as "malignant narcissists"; and the church, which Maya believes ought to be most open to the possibility of demonic possession, invokes the modernist evolution of theology to dismiss the idea of Satanic interference and to reject the notion of Satan as, in Kelson's words, "a third-party bad guy pulling all the strings." Theologically speaking, though, as she tries in vain to convince the diocesan authorities of her findings, Maya poses a not-unreasonable question:

> FATHER THOMAS
> 
> Maya, the diocese has rejected your report. And I have to tell you, I agree with them. Maya, these are projections caused by your unfortunate childhood. Satan is not what you think he is.

MAYA

If you really believed in God, Father, why is it so inconceivable to you that his adversary could be just as real?

Father Thomas' disbelief notwithstanding, a few brief points are worthy of mention here. First, in many ways, *Lost Souls* is *Rosemary's Baby* all grown up, and it resembles a number of other films that build on the concept of a satanic legacy: *To The Devil . . . a Daughter*, *The Omen* cycle, *End of Days*, *Good Against Evil*, and *Day of the Beast*, to name a few. Next, though not a few Catholics have joined in the hunt as well, since the publication of such theological potboilers as Hal Lindsey's genre-defining *The Late Great Planet Earth* in 1970, the late modern search for the identity of the Antichrist has been a consistent theme among (principally) dispensationalist Protestants, those who believe that God has a set timetable for events in what are collectively known as the "End Times" (cf. Boyer, 1992; Shuck, 2005). In early 1999, for example, Jerry Falwell, Baptist televangelist and founder of the Moral Majority, announced that the Antichrist is almost certainly alive now and is a male Jew living in Israel. Though two weeks later Falwell apologized for the insensitivity of the remark—which, not surprisingly, the Anti-Defamation League of B'Nai B'rith labeled antisemitic—he did not recant his theological views on the immanence of the End Times nor the reality of the Antichrist, views shared by millions of Falwell's fellow fundamentalists.

Finally, *Lost Souls* draws on a number of popular conspiracy theories about the Roman Catholic Church. On the one hand, when Maya confronts Peter with her evidence that he is to become the Antichrist, she tells him that he fits "all the criteria that we know of"—an unsubtle hint that the Church is the ecclesial guardian of dire secrets it is unwilling to share with the rest of the world and a cultural trope that has been exploited to best-seller effect by novelist Dan Brown in both *Angels and Demons* (2000) and the hugely popular *The Da Vinci Code* (2003). On the other, perhaps more sinister hand, Kelson's own Uncle James (Philip Baker Hall) turns out to be not only Peter's natural father—making Peter a "man born of incest"—but also the leader of the satanic cabal that has raised Kelson to take his place as evil incarnate. Of particular importance here is the fact that James has posed his entire adult life as a Roman Catholic priest. He and his followers operate from within the Catholic Church itself, deep-cover agents posing as devout worshipers, a fifth column as it were, for the coming of the Antichrist. Even this theme is not drawn in a cultural vacuum. The notion of a satanic conspiracy within the church has been a staple of anti-Catholic propaganda since the Reformation and continues today among both fundamentalist Protestant opponents of the Church—see, for example, Jack Chick's tracts *The Death Cookie* (1988) and *Last Rites* (1994), countercult apologist Dave Hunt's *A Woman Rides the Beast: The Catholic Church and the Last Days* (1994), and Edmund Paris' *The Secret History of the Jesuits* (1983), which is kept in print by Chick's publishing company (though, on these, see also Cowan 2003a, 171–89; Jenkins, 2003; Lockwood, 2000; Welter, 1987)—and disgruntled Catholics, such as Malachi Martin, who are angered at post-Vatican II reforms within the Church (e.g., Martin 1987, 1996; though, see also Cuneo, 1997). As one of the principle mechanisms of horrific metataxis—the inversion or reversal of accepted cultural categories of interpretation—insurrection from within the dominant faith is a theme that will emerge again and again throughout our discussion.

## The Not-So-Obvious . . . Ghost Ship

In terms of imagery and soundtrack, Steve Beck's *Ghost Ship* could not open on a more dissimilar note than *Lost Souls*. Rising through a profusion of glittering bubbles, the establishing shot sweeps across a moonlit sea as the opening violins of Gino Paoli's classic love song "Senza fine" ("Without End") float at over the title graphic, which is rendered in pink cursive script distinctly reminiscent of the television series *The Love Boat*. Panning down the length of a luxury liner, the *Antonio Graza*, the camera hovers over the foredeck dance floor where scores of well-heeled passengers are enjoying the nightly entertainment. Encouraged by the *cantante* to "dance, everyone, dance," champagne flows and the passengers enjoy the solicitous attention of captain and crew—a perfect evening aboard ship. Suddenly, a mysterious hand reaches into the frame and pushes a lever. A winch drum begins to spin, whining in protest and drawing a thin cable taut—too taut. A turnbuckle fails under the load, and carnage ensues. A moment later, in one of the creepiest scenes of modern horror cinema, all but one of the passengers on the foredeck, a young girl (Emily Browning), are dead.

*Ghost Ship* picks up its story forty years later with a crew of professional salvors led by Murphy (Gabriel Byrne) and Epps (Julianna Margulies). While celebrating the success of their latest operation, the team is approached by an arctic weather patrol pilot named Ferriman (Desmond Harrington), who shows them photos of a large vessel—obviously the *Antonio Graza*, though the crew does not know that yet—adrift in the middle of the Bering Strait. Although Murphy points out that the vessel is "a thousand miles from the nearest shipping lane," they agree to attempt a salvage, and when they find her, she appears out of the dark and the driving rain like a ghost.

MURPHY

It's the *Antonio Graza*. Jesus Christ, she's beautiful . . . She was reported missing May 21, 1962, off the coast of Labrador. Funny thing is, there was no distress signal. No contact. She just disappeared. She was gone. So ever since that day every captain and his mother's been looking for her, hoping she hasn't gone down.

As the salvage team makes their way through the abandoned vessel—a derelict, coated with rust, battered by wind, tide, and four decades of neglect—they see clues that things are not as they seem at first: A digital watch on a main bridge console. Strange apparitions that come and go—the young girl, the ship's captain, the *cantante* and her music. A swimming pool riddled with bullet holes. A dozen rotting bodies no more than a few weeks old. And, in one of the rooms off the car hold, a number of boxes filled with unmarked gold bars. Not surprisingly, the crew decides to take the gold—worth hundreds of millions of dollars—and leave the *Antonio Graza* to drift. In good supernatural fashion, though, unseen forces prevent their escape, destroying the tugboat and stranding the crew. It soon becomes devastatingly apparent that they are not alone on the drifting hulk but are trapped in a floating graveyard with far more secrets than answers. In classic ghost story fashion, members of the crew die one by one—burned to death on the tug, fallen down a shaft and impaled on debris at the bottom, drowned in a floor-to-ceiling fish tank that has not seen water since Kennedy was president.

As the film reaches its dénouement, Epps, the salvage crew's lone survivor (whose role is remarkably similar to Sigourney Weaver's in *Alien* and delivered with similar energy), finally solves the riddle of the ghost ship. No one in the forty years the *Antonio Graza* has been adrift has ever left. It is a ship literally filled with ghosts, with the souls of those who have been marked for passage from the land of the living to the realm of the dead. And the gold the salvors found has been the bait all along, placed in the trap by the one who brought them to the ship.

"What the fuck are you?" she asks, when she finally confronts Ferriman with the truth.

FERRIMAN

```
I'm a salvager. Just like you. You
collect ships, I collect souls. And
```

> when I fill my quota, I send a boatload home. This'll make management happy. You see, it's a job. Given to me after a lifetime of sin. So if I lose this ship, management won't be happy, which is not a good thing.
>
> EPPS
>
> I want my crew back.
>
> FERRIMAN
>
> Sorry, once a passenger's marked, they're mine.

Epps succeeds in destroying the *Antonio Graza*, and all but a few of the souls who made up Ferriman's "quota" are freed. Adrift, clinging to a piece of luggage, Epps is eventually rescued by another ocean liner. As she is placed in an ambulance, however, she sees a number of large boxes being loaded up the liner's gangway, followed by a familiar face—Ferriman.

The cycle continues.

Like *The Fog*, *Ghost Ship* starts and finishes as a fairly typical ghost story. Instead of a haunted house set on a lonely hill, the action takes place on a derelict cruise liner, and the various compartments of the huge ship provide an excellent narrative space for the dark room after dark room after dark room approach to horror cinema. But what director Beck and screenwriters Mark Hanlon and John Pogue also offer us, however, is a distinctly unsettling version of the myth of Charon, the boatman who ferries the souls of the dead across the river Styx. According to Greek mythology, to pay the boatman for their passage, bodies were buried with gold coins—*obuloi*—placed under their tongues. Anyone without the fare was left to wander the banks of the river, some sources say, for a hundred years.

One of the most consistent criticisms of religiously oriented horror cinema is that it doesn't get religion "right," that it misrepresents religious belief, practice, and theology (or, in this case, mythology). For example, despite Ferriman's deceitful character and while the double entendre advertising copy for *Ghost Ship* reads "Sea Evil," Charon is not a malevolent figure in Greek mythology, and there is no indication in the mythic references that he was assigned his task as punishment. He is described as a tall, thin, irascible old man, stooped over his pole as he transports the shades of the living to the land of the dead. In the film, the *obulus*, the coin used to pay for passage on his boat, has been rewritten as the gold that Ferriman ("the ferryman") uses to attract enough living men and women to fill the quota of souls he is required to deliver. Thus, rather than simply retell the story of Charon—who plays a relatively minor role in the extant mythic texts and a decidedly comic part in Aristophanes' *The Frogs*—the filmmakers have used it as a starting point for their own horrific vision of a soul collector. Rather than misrepresent mythistory, they are, in fact, following a venerable tradition in the evolution of sacred narratives by building on and adapting what other traditions have left behind.

Though the majority of films considered in this book have some manner of Christian underpinning, whether they draw explicitly on Christian mythology and iconography or depend on its cultural resonance for their power to horrify, *Ghost Ship* demonstrates that there are other myths and other monsters that lay hidden in the cinematic vault. While Bram Stoker may be best known for *Dracula*, the film version of his last novel, *Lair of the White Worm* ([1911] 1998), invokes, among other things, the myth of St. George and the dragon, as well as a pre-Christian religion dedicated to the sacrificial worship of a beast that challenges any errant notion of religion as necessarily good, moral, and decent. From the *Mr. Vampire* franchise to a variety of horror-comedy "haunted" venues (*Haunted Cop Shop*; *Haunted Jail House*; *Haunted Karaoke*; *Haunted Mansion*), Hong Kong horror cinema is suffuse with Confucian, Buddhist, and Taoist narrative, mythology, and iconography. Back in the Americas and based (albeit very loosely) on real life ethnobotanist Wade Davis' search for the so-called "zombie drug" (Davis, 1985), *The Serpent and the Rainbow* brings Hollywood vogue to Haitian Vodou. *Q*, on the other hand, which was also released as *Winged Serpent*, turns to director Larry Cohen's vision of Aztec mythology, liberally mixed with popular fascination with (and misunderstanding of) ritual murders and ancient death cults.

*And the Oh-So-Obvious* . . . Dracula Has Risen from the Grave

Whereas the mythological influence in *Ghost Ship* is subtle at best, like *Lost Souls*, the 1968 Hammer Films production *Dracula Has Risen from the Grave* is replete with religious references and imagery, as well as considerable ambiguity about the power of traditional religion when confronted by an overwhelming supernatural challenge.

Following the opening credits, which roll in typically lurid Hammer style, the body of a young woman is discovered hanging inside the tower bell of the village church. Drained of blood, she is clearly the victim of a vampire. Though it is left unclear how the vampire was eventually destroyed, the film's action quickly shifts to "one year later" as Monsignor Ernst Müller (Rupert Davies) returns to the scene of the tragedy to pay "a visit to the little village in the valley to see that all was well." Despite the apparent destruction of the vampire, the young woman's unnatural death has led the superstitious villagers to abandon the church. In a remarkably poignant scene for a Hammer film, a year after finding the body—and presumably dispatching Dracula (Christopher Lee, in his third appearance as the Count), who has been frozen in a mountain stream—we find the village priest (Ewan Hooper) saying mass in an empty church. In pre-Vatican II style, he faces the altar, not his absent congregation, while cobwebs grow on the bell tower staircase, leaves gather on the floor, chairs are strewn haphazard, and the Tabernacle lamp remains unlit. It is mass said in a ruined sanctuary, a stark comment on the powerlessness of the Church in the face of a supernatural evil like Dracula, or at least the filmmakers' set-up of this perceived powerlessness. At the altar, the priest is served by the boy who found the body originally, and who is now mute, his affliction at least implicitly attributed to the shock of his discovery. After mass, the haunted priest goes to the tavern to drink alone—something the film suggests has become his usual practice.

When the Monsignor arrives, though, he rouses the priest and undertakes to exorcise Castle Dracula, the shadow of which still touches the church at dusk. On the way to the castle, the priest's courage fails, and he remains in the rocks below the keep. As the Monsignor reads the rite of exorcism during a raging thunderstorm, the priest slips and falls, blood from a head wound seeping into Dracula's mouth through a crack in the ice. The weakness of the Church has awakened the vampire once again. Indeed, in a quasi-reversal of the psychic enslavement of Mina (Murray) Harker when she is forced to drink the blood of Dracula in Stoker's novel, the priest is similarly enthralled when his blood inadvertently revives the vampire. Unaware of this, Monsignor Müller returns to the village, believing the evil of Dracula is finally at an end:

```
           MONSIGNOR
   It's done. The evil is destroyed
   forever. I read the service of exorcism
   and sealed the door with a cross.
   His spirit will never leave there to
   trouble you again.
```

The audience, of course, knows better, and is prepared for the film's central confrontation. Like most religiously oriented horror films, belief and unbelief are the linchpins of conflict. In many cases, however, including this one, the narrative is more complicated than simply good (the Church) versus evil (the vampire). Here, the power of the Church is confronted not only by Dracula, but also by proactive unbelief in the character of Paul (Barry Andrews), a student in love with the Monsignor's niece, Maria, played by Hammer scream queen Veronica Carlson. Meeting Maria's family for the first time at the Monsignor's home, Paul reveals the other conflict that controls the narrative:

> MONSIGNOR
>
> You don't go to church?
>
> PAUL
>
> No, sir.
>
> MONSIGNOR (suspiciously)
>
> You're not a Protestant, are you?
>
> PAUL
>
> No, sir.
>
> MONSIGNOR
>
> Thank heaven for that.
>
> PAUL
>
> I'm an atheist, sir.
>
> MONSIGNOR
>
> You mean you deny the existence of God?
>
> PAUL
>
> I don't deny it. I just don't believe it. It's my own opinion, sir.

This, of course, enrages the Monsignor, who accuses Paul of "blasphemy." Not only is Dracula a threat to the Church, but here in his own home is the arguably more insidious problem of atheist intellectualism, for the film makes clear that it is not Paul's job as a "second-class pastry cook" that has led him to deny the reality of God, but his studies, his "dreary old books." As any soldier knows, far more dangerous than the enemy without is the traitor within.

Not surprisingly, to save Maria, Paul and the religion he has rejected are thrown together in the film's penultimate sequences. At first, he uses the power of the cross to compel the enthralled priest to take him to the vampire. When he stakes Dracula in his coffin, however, the Count refuses to die unless appropriate prayers are offered as well.

                    PRIEST

Pray! You must pray!

                    PAUL

I can't!

                    PRIEST

You must! You must, or he won't die.

                    PAUL

 You pray! You're a priest! You pray! You pray!

But, the fallen cleric cannot pray any more than the avowed atheist, and, pulling the stake from his own heart, Dracula escapes. The final confrontation returns the action to Castle Dracula, where the vampire commands Maria to remove the cross with which her uncle barred the door to his home. Paul attacks the vampire and, as they struggle, Dracula falls from the parapet and is impaled on the cross. As he fights to free himself, he reaches out imploringly to the priest. Unlike the aborted staking, though, this time the priest turns his eyes to the heavens and begins to recite the Our Father in Latin. When Dracula tries to pull himself free, the cross burns his hands, and, shedding tears of blood, he dies. Church bells peal as Paul crosses himself, and the film ends with the moonlit cross standing alone—triumphant.

Although legends of creatures that feed on the blood of the living have arisen both within cultures that predate Christianity and within those where Christianity has not been a major cultural influence, in Western cinema horror the defeat of the vampire is often (though not always) associated with Christian symbols and ritual implements as the technology of salvation—the cross that drives the vampire from the room, the eucharistic wafer placed to prevent the rise of the vampire from the grave, the prayers offered by the priest that ultimately consign Dracula to oblivion. In many of these more "conventional" treatments, the character of Dracula functions as a kind of antichrist. He gathers and commands disciples, followers to whom he offers a species of eternal life. His appearance at the beginning of a film is often presented as a resurrection, while his "death" at the end just as often presages a revival in the next film. The tears of blood Dracula sheds as he dies crucified, as it were, in *Dracula Has Risen from the Grave* are reminiscent of Christ's sweat becoming "as great drops of blood" (Luke 22:44) as he prayed in the garden prior to his arrest and crucifixion.

Numerous vampire narratives, however, have departed from the Christian technology of salvation to which Stoker staked them at the end of the nineteenth century. Some vampires are extraterrestrials (*Planet of the Vampires*; *Vampirella*); others comprise a parallel race with their own religious beliefs, practices, and scriptures (the *Blade* trilogy; *Underworld* and *Underworld: Evolution*); while still others emerge either in a cultural context where Christianity has no power (*Mr. Vampire*; *Tsui Hark's Vampire Hunters*) or in a battle for dominance with Christianity (*The Brides of Dracula*). Finally, at least some vampires are presented as the very product of the church that eventually sanctions and facilitates their elimination (*John Carpenter's Vampires*; *Dracula 2000*). Because the supernatural problem of the vampire is tied to the mystery of death, our fear of dying badly, and what happens to us once we have died, religion remains a central concern of vampire tales and will be discussed more fully in chapter 5.

## EXPLAINING CINEMA HORROR: ASSORTED TALES FROM THE ACADEMIC CRYPT

Though relatively few of its products ever see widespread theatrical release, horror remains one of the most resilient and enduring of cinema genres, commanding a large and often sophisticated fan base and supported by equally sophisticated writers, artists, and filmmakers. Even film franchises that have departed from their original premises and have in some cases been repudiated by their originators (for example, the *Hellraiser* series) still continue to produce straight-to-DVD installments that are eagerly awaited by fans ready to debate hotly their relative quality.

While a number of commentators have noted the ubiquitous nature of horror in the arts writ large, their appraisal of the importance of cinema horror has been varied. Some have suggested that horror films are a profound reflection of the societal tensions within which they were created. At the beginning of the Cold War, for example, and citing literary critic Edmund Wilson, Curtis Harrington contends that "the popularity of the ghost and horror story in literature rises during times of outward stress, and certainly the vogue for this genre of film follows the same pattern" (1952, 194). Half a century later, the creatures that populate what Edward Ingebretsen (2001, 2) calls "the *lingua monstra* of media," which include but are hardly limited to cinema horror, still function as metaphors for the social problems they are used to describe—serial murderers, child rapists, cannibals, those whose crimes are too demonstrably horrific for their perpetrators to remain safely within the rubric of "human." Rick Worland (1997), on the other hand, explores how American horror films produced during the latter part of World War II were often changed to suit the needs of war-time propaganda and the political ends of the Office of War Information. Mark Jancovich (1996) argues that sci-fi horror from the 1950s illuminates post-war fears of rationalization and modernization, while Jonathan Lake Crane (1994) suggests, among other things, that they represent the fear of technologies we know have now passed beyond the limits of our control.

As I noted briefly in the previous chapter, for Gregory Waller, "horror films have proven to be among the most significant documents in America's public debate over the status of the independent woman in a society still dominated by men" (1987, 5), a position shared, according to Peter Biskind (1983, 123-36), by a number of 1950s horror filmmakers. Lucy Fisher, for example, reads Roman Polanski's *Rosemary's Baby* as horrific commentary on the processes of pregnancy, birth, and afterbirth, wondering if some women did not see in it "an odious fable of parturition," "a skewed 'documentary' of the societal and personal turmoil that has regularly attended female reproduction" (1992, 4). Though he admits that there are other possible interpretations of horror—overcoming fear or "the compulsive projection of objects of sublimated desire"—James Twitchell argues that the attraction of horror is best explained "as part of a complicated rite of passage from onanism to reproductive sexuality" (1985, 66). Paradoxically, Harry M. Benshoff interprets such "blaxploitation" horror films as *Blacula*, *Sugar Hill*, and *Abby*, as "a historically specific subgenre that potentially explores (rather than simply exploits) race and race consciousness as core structuring principles" (2000, 32). Calling *The Exorcist* "one of the most extraordinary movies ever made, and one of the great aesthetic documents of the twentieth century" (2002, 185), Darryl Jones maintains that much of the horrific effect it generates is predicated on a profound antipathy toward the body that has been deeply ingrained in Christian belief and practice for centuries. On the other hand, with its explicit grounding in the dispensational theology of fundamentalist Christianity—and despite its cinematic reliance on the aesthetics and iconography of Roman Catholicism—Jones labels *The Omen* "*The Exorcist* for Protestants" (2002, 189). Whatever films they use to support this wide variety of analysis and commentary, all contend that cinema horror functions as a significant cultural artifact that somehow reflects and embeds the prejudices and fears of the times in which it was produced.

## Cinema Horror as the Denigration of Religion

Others, however, question whether cinema horror, especially that which is religiously oriented, has any revelatory or redeeming value at all. Reviewing *The Exorcist* for *Film Quarterly*, Michael Dempsey calls it "the trash bombshell of 1973, the aesthetic equivalent of being run over by a truck" (1974, 61). Together, he continues, William Friedkin and William Peter Blatty produced "a gloating, ugly exploitation picture, a costlier cousin of those ghoulish cheapies released to drive-ins and fleapits almost weekly in American cities" (Dempsey, 1974, 61). What Dempsey fails to consider is the abundance and popularity of those "ghoulish cheapies," and the willingness of horror fans to haunt "drive-ins and fleapits" to see them. On a larger scale, the often acerbic film critic Michael Medved contends that the American film industry itself has simply "gone too far" in what it offers the movie-going public (1992, xvii), especially in terms of "the self-destructive nature of Hollywood's underlying hostility to organized religion" (1992, xviii). While he is unwilling to lay the commercial success of a light comedy like *Sister Act* on its "more affectionate attitude toward the Roman Catholic Church" or the box-office failure of the sci-fi horror film *Alien³* on its "unnecessary jab at religious traditionalists" (1992, xviii), Medved clearly regards these dynamics as important. In particular, in *Alien³* he objects to what he describes as the unflattering and uncalled-for religious description of the inmates on a desolate prison planet.

According to Medved, one inmate, Dillon (Charles S. Dutton), tells Ripley (Sigourney Weaver), "You know, we're all fundamentalist Christians here"—a glaring example of what Medved considers Hollywood's "glancing and gratuitous insults to Christian believers" (1992, xix). Interestingly, though, and not unimportant in terms of the care with which reviewers of all types often represent film content, the line as Medved quotes it is not actually in the film. To support his argument, Medved has paraphrased a very different line and even placed it in the mouth of a different character. Although Dillon, the leader of the prisoners on Fury 161, does speak about the faith community they have established and the social stability it lends their Stygian existence, he is not the one who reveals the character of those beliefs to Ripley. Rather, it is Clemens (Charles Dance), the medical officer, who does so, and in a considerably more reflective and uncertain tone than Medved suggests. "What kind of religion?" Ripley asks. "Some sort of apocalyptic, millennarian, Christian, fundamentalist...," Clemens replies, his voice trailing off in uncertainty, "I don't know." Because it illustrates the importance of accurately reading the cinematic text as it is presented on the screen, this small difference is not insignificant. Medved is, of course, entitled to his own interpretation of the film, but by misrepresenting the text in the service of his interpretive agenda, he refuses to take seriously whatever messages the text actually embodies.

Arguing that because "it offends, disgusts, frightens, and features the profane, often in gruesome and ghastly proportions," Christian missiologist Bryan Stone asserts that "other than pornography, horror is the film genre least amenable to religious sensibilities" (2001, ¶3). Not unlike some of these other critics, he concludes that "the mere fact that horror films rely heavily on symbols and stories as mere conventions to scare the hell out of us does not make a case for religious vitality in our culture; in fact, their persistence eviscerated of any deeper connection to our lived questions may be a good example of the decline of the religious in our culture" (Stone, 2001, ¶39). Even though he points out that "many of the central themes of horror films overlap with traditionally religious concerns (or at least Western religious concerns)," Stone virtually dismisses the religious underpinning of cinema horror (2001, ¶3). Instead, he argues that, although it is a frequent component in the cinematic narrative, "rarely have films treated religious faith on its own terms or explored religious values and motivations with much complexity" (2001, ¶2). Commenting on the release of such films as *Bless the Child*, *The Cell*, *Lost Souls*, *Stigmata*, *End of Days*, and the release in 2000 of *The Exorcist* director's cut, Stone contends:

> It may be too much to call this new openness to the transcendent or to the supernatural a "religious" openness, for it is not necessarily related to a renewed credibility on the part of traditional religious institutions or their belief, value, and behavioral systems. . . . And yet when Hollywood wants to point to a spiritual or transcendent dimension to evil, it does not hesitate to employ large quantities of religious symbols often splattered together with no rhyme or reason—a little Buddhism here, a little Christianity there, maybe an ancient book, or a crucifix thrown in for good measure, anything that will render a pseudo-religious feel to the portrayal. (2001, ¶13)

A number of points are worth noting. First, Stone implies an equation between "religion"—as in a "religious openness"—and "traditional religious institutions or their belief, value, and behavioral systems." Why, though, should an authentic "openness" be linked either implicitly or explicitly to anything like a "renewed credibility" in "traditional religious institutions"? There was a time, after all, when the temples of Innana were the "traditional religious institutions," and human sacrifice among the Aztecs was part of traditional "religious behavior." Second, this "new openness" is hardly new. The religious markers of cinema horror are all but ubiquitous, as Stone himself points out, but they have not resurfaced, they have never gone away. Once again, though, because they do not align with his conception of authentic religion, the explosion of new religious movements, questions, and explorations that have arisen in the past several decades are simply dismissed. Third, what evidence does Stone have that these markers are "pseudo-religious," that their presence in the film is only to lend a certain "feel" to the movie and nothing more? Finally, and most important, in making this argument Stone attributes crass commercialism to the filmmakers, writers, and producers of cinema horror, and a certain numb credulity to its consumers. While the commercial aspects of cinema can hardly be ignored—movies are, after all, products—he never considers why these symbols might be chosen as opposed to others or why they might prove so effective in establishing and maintaining the narrative frame of cinema horror. Put bluntly, he never stops to ask why they work.

For example, in reanimation films such as *Night of the Living Dead*, *Re-Animator*, *Beyond Re-Animator*, and the three *Resident Evil* films, there are no religious underpinnings at all. Romero's walking dead are reanimated by extraterrestrial radiation brought to Earth by a returning satellite, while *Re-Animator*'s Lovecraftian zombies are the result of medical experiments gone horribly wrong. In the *Resident Evil* films, Alice (Milla Jovovich) battles corpses reanimated through the bioweapons research of the sinister Umbrella Corporation. Indeed, for some films—such as *The Ghouls* or *Shaun of the Dead*—flesh-eating zombies are more than enough on their own, and no real attempt is made to explain their appearance.

In other reanimation films, however, the fear of death, of dying badly, and of not remaining dead are clearly tied to religious understandings of the relationship between life and death. Consider, for example, *White Zombie*, in which the reanimated dead labor in West Indian cane fields, or *Plague of the Zombies*, which, because the dead are being reanimated through "Haitian voodoo" to work commercially unproductive Cornish tin mines, resembles a Hammer version of Bela Lugosi's 1931 classic. If a zombie film with no religious underpinning is as potentially terrifying as one with, why do so many filmmakers opt for the latter? What is it about the religious that generates the power to terrify, to horrify? Of course, it is possible that by "pseudo-religious" Stone means that these films do not accurately represent the religious traditions, beliefs, or practices they deploy as markers. That has certainly been a consistent (and hardly unwarranted) criticism of the use of religion in horror films. The portrayal of "Ha-eetean voodoo" in *Plague of the Zombies* is hardly an accurate representation of Afro-Caribbean religion, but would British filmgoers in the mid-1960s have known that? Would they even have questioned it? Would they have cared? Popular belief in Vodou and zombies—coupled with the equally popular ignorance about the origins and realities of these practices—allowed for sufficient suspension of disbelief for the film narrative to proceed.

## Cinema Horror as Pathology and Psychology

If Medved criticizes Hollywood horror for its "hostility to organized religion," and Stone dismisses cinema horror for its "pseudo-religious feel," others have located its paradoxical appeal in, among other things, a Freudian return to narcissistic infantilism (Wexman, 1987), a psychosexual transition from masturbation to procreation (Twitchell, 1985), or the adolescent performance of stereotyped bravado and gender roles (Zillman and Weaver, 1996). Like Medved and Stone, each of these approaches rejects a priori both the cultural realities that give rise to religious aspects of cinema horror and the possibility that there may be other interpretations than the psychological for the presence of religion in horror movies.

"All of Polanski's films are about insanity," writes Virginia Wexman (1987, 33) in her discussion of *Rosemary's Baby*. Like others who have commented extensively on the film's central motif (e.g., Fisher, 1992), Wexman locates Rosemary's experience of impregnation, pregnancy, and birth in a spiral of gradually deteriorating psychological competency. As the pregnancy progresses, Rosemary (Mia Farrow) slowly loses her grip on reality, and her experience becomes framed by the dark, demonic forces she has come to believe now control the events of her life. Solicitous neighbors become a coven of Satanists intent on bringing the Antichrist into our world through her womb. Her husband (John

Cassavetes) becomes the linchpin in their diabolical plot. "The confusion between inner and outer reality engendered by 'the fantastic,'" Wexman writes, "reflects modes of experience that are psychologically infantile, recalling a narcissistic period of development in which the individual was unable to distinguish itself from the world around it" (1987, 33). True enough, perhaps, and many commentators have noted how Rosemary regresses as her pregnancy progresses, paradoxically looking less like a woman and more like an adolescent. Wexman goes further, however, arguing that "social attitudes are not at issue here so much as the more global view implied by religious conviction. Polanski's *Rosemary's Baby* speaks to the ludicrous nature of all religious beliefs, for all religions grant the world an unambiguous meaning that the film wants to deny" (1987, 39).

In contesting readings of the film such as this, I am not suggesting that the storyline in *Rosemary's Baby* should be taken at face value, or that Polanski actually believes such diabolical covens and compacts exist. Nor do I think that the psychological approach to interpretation is without value. Rather, I am arguing, on the one hand, that films such as these are part of a lengthy cinematic lineage that cannot be easily and reductively psychologized. They have a social history that those who seek psychological interpretations often ignore or proscribe. On the other hand, by approaching the film (or any film) with an a priori assumption of "the ludicrous nature of all religious beliefs," Wexman actively avoids looking for any meaning other than that which she has already set out to find and severely restricts the range of interpretations available in the film.

Similarly, in *The Naked and the Undead*, feminist philosopher Cynthia Freeland (2000) also dismisses the importance of religion. "Both Regan in *The Exorcist* and Rosemary in *Rosemary's Baby* lose control," she writes, continuing that "they are both young and female, and each film presents horror in a quasi-theological context" (2000, 10). I would suggest instead that each film presents its horror in an *explicitly theological* context, and that without these contexts each film loses much of its ability to terrify, to horrify, to *confront* in any meaningful way. In *The Exorcist*, for example, Father Damian Karras (Jason Miller) is forced to confront the reality of the supernatural despite the twin pulls of the rationalist skepticism of his profession (psychology) and theological modernism of his vocation (Jesuit priesthood). Like so many characters in cinema horror whose task is to portray the "rational," the "modern," the "reasonable"—in many ways, the audience—he comes to believe, against his own will and better judgment. Finally, terrified and horrified by his encounter with the power of the Devil manifest in the demon Pazuzu, he is thrust back into the explicitly supernatural context of his calling as a Roman Catholic priest.

*Rosemary's Baby* also takes place within an explicit theological context—whether Freeland recognizes the reality of that or not. Though there is no concrete evidence to validate the so-called "satanic panics" that have emerged over the past few decades (see, for example, Ellis, 2000; Nathan and Snedecker, 1995; Richardson, Best, and Bromley, 1991; Victor, 1993), lively religious discourses—principally fundamentalist Protestant and Roman Catholic—still exist in which these kinds of events occur with startling regularity (cf. Cuneo, 2001; Larson, 1989, 1996; Ross, 1995; Smith, 1993). Possession and exorcism are not phenomena relegated to the superstitious backwaters of the Middle Ages; indeed, complex systematic theologies have been developed to explain and resolve the issue of demonism in the late modern period. These discourses are not sealed off from the rest of society and regularly erupt into the larger culture—something both Wexman and Freeland choose to ignore or dismiss.

Communications scholars Dolf Zillman and James Weaver take a slightly different approach to the problem of cinema horror and its attractions. Rejecting as tautological many of the popular explanations that have been offered in the past—an appeal to "archetypal images of fright" or "the presumed hereditary fear of the dark . . . the unknown . . . and the future" (Zillman and Weaver,

1996, 88)—they propose that horror films provide an arena for the display, testing, and reinforcement of gender-specific responses to situations of danger.

> Male and female adolescents watch a horror movie with an opposite-gender peer, ostensibly another research participant but actually an experimental confederate, who either displayed gender-appropriate, gender-inappropriate, or no emotions; and they then ascertained enjoyment of the movie, liking of the cohort, romantic attraction to that cohort, and being intimidated by the cohort. (Zillman and Weaver, 1996, 92)

Showing their test subjects *Friday the 13th, Part 3*, Zillman and Weaver designed this elaborate experiment to test a few key hypotheses, the most important of which was that "cinematic horror . . . constitutes modern society's most convenient testing ground for the display of appropriate emotional reactions to situations posing grave danger" (1996, 85). Both their research design, however, and the assumptions that underpin it present a number of problems. First, to suggest that there is an empirically demonstrable or psychosocially defensible scale of "gender-appropriate response" to cinema horror is absurd and regressive, at best (cf. Pinedo, 1997). This is only exacerbated by their next proposition, that cinema horror "provides a forum for boys to practice and achieve the display of fearlessness and protective competence . . . [and] a forum for girls to practice and achieve the display of fearfulness and the protective need" (Zillman and Weaver, 1996, 85). Second, by using a relatively straightforward slasher film as the constant, their research design ignores both the spectrum of cinema horror and the fact that different audiences are attracted to different kinds of horror films—that is, there are both personal and social components to the horror experience. Third, how realistic is it to suggest that viewing horror films, especially in the context of an overly controlled experiment like this, constitutes anything remotely like a "situation posing grave danger," or that those viewing the film are not aware of the difference? Finally, the basic question of whether cinematic horror actually "constitutes modern society's most convenient testing ground" for the control and suppression of fear-based reactions is conjectural at best. This is so especially since the vast majority of cinema horror does not see theatrical release but is available only for home viewing, and the experiment does nothing to address the controlled effects of home video presentation (e.g., small screen; lighted viewing space; pause, fast-forward, and volume control)—all of which can considerably ameliorate the experience of fear.

Each of these approaches seeks, as it were, to explain eggs in terms of bacon. On the one hand, Wexman dismisses as "ludicrous" what is arguably the most dominant source of social legitimation and cohesion in human history—a position that does nothing to explain the continued presence and power of religion in late modern society. On the other hand, Zillman and Weaver treat both cinema horror and the vicissitudes of adolescent behavior as monoliths, as though *Friday the 13th, Part 2* can somehow stand for all cinema horror, while the notion of "boys brave, girls scared" somehow provides the basis for a reasoned analysis of adolescent socialization. Indeed, both approach the problem of horror films from a position not dissimilar to that of Stone: these films represent in some way evidence of either the ongoing secularization of society or a patent need for that secularization to be encouraged.

Secularization, of course, is the belief—some would say the ideology (Hadden, 1988)—that technologized societies are becoming less religious, less dependent on faith-based models of interpretation and action. Numerous sociologists and historians of religion, however, have challenged that notion, and *Sacred Terror* takes a similar position. We may tell ourselves that we are becoming more sophisticated in our worldview, that we have left behind the superstitions of the past, that our explanations for unexpected phenomena now account for their origin and power without reference to supernatural beings or powers, and that religion is no longer a necessary component of social life—but in North America, at least, most of the data available to us indicate otherwise. Indeed, the issue is not one of *secularization*—that cinema horror discloses to us the abandonment or minimization of religious belief in late modern society—but an overwhelming *ambivalence* toward the religious traditions, beliefs, practices, and mythistories by which we are confronted, in which we are often still deeply invested, which we are distinctly unwilling to relinquish, and which we just as often only minimally understand. It is this ambivalence, and the various fears it both evokes and embeds, that the films collected and discussed here reveal.

## THE UBIQUITY OF HORROR AND THE PERSISTENCE OF BELIEF

"Human acquiescence," intones the demonic Pinhead (Doug Bradley) in *Hellraiser: Bloodline*, "is as easily obtained by terror as by temptation." And how true this has proven to be in the religious history of humankind. While it may be overstating the case to argue that all religion is rooted in fear of the dark, of disease, of drought or flood, of the myriad terrors that threaten from the forest's edge, and, ultimately, of death, there are certainly significant cross-cultural instances in which this is manifestly the case. On his way up Mount Sinai to meet Yahweh, for example, Moses is cautioned not to look on the face of the Divine if he wants to come down from the mountain alive (Exod 33:18-23). When the Ark of the Covenant was completed, the Israelites learned not to touch it if they wanted to live (see Exod 25:12-15; Num 4:15; 2 Sam 6:1-7). When the Tabernacle was erected in the wilderness, and later the Temple in Jerusalem, only the High Priest could enter the Holy of Holies—and that only on one particular day of the year. The penalty for transgression? Death (Lev 16:2; Heb 9:7). Thousands of years later, the world of the Kwaio, who inhabit the island of Malaita in the Solomon Islands, is still bounded on all sides by a host of "unseen presences" (Keesing, 1982, 33), both benevolent and malevolent, and the taboos associated with these beings form the framework of socialization for Kwaio children and of behavior for Kwaio adults. Jeanette Southgate, a young woman in Norfolk, England, has seen ghosts for most of her life and lives in a house with a variety of haunting spirits. Moved by a range of poltergeist activities, she now keeps an online diary as part of her attempt to understand her experiences and those of the spirits with whom she believes she shares her life (Southgate, 2007).

It matters little whether we believe in the ancestral spirits of the Kwaio or the noisy ghosts that disrupt Southgate's life. They believe, and they structure their worlds and their behaviors accordingly. Similarly, it matters little whether Moses really met with Yahweh, whether the Ark really destroyed all who touched it, or whether sudden death came to those who entered the Holy of Holies unbidden by the Divine. The point is that they are remembered in the sacred narratives as though they really happened, and for hundreds of millions of Jews and Christians worldwide, they have behind them the power of memory, mythistory, and, for some, literal truth.

Whether terror is the mechanism by which the gods ensure compliance or the bedrock of belief upon which compliance is built—and whether the gods invoked want such compliance, need it, or exist at all—a common denominator in the negotiation of the unseen order is *fear*. All this is part and parcel of the *mysterium tremendum et fascinans* (Otto, [1923] 1950)—*fear* of the Lord as the beginning of wisdom, despite the fact that generations of Christian preachers have glossed the passage, insisting that it means "awe" not "fear," "worship" not "terror," and "reverence" not death, destruction, and sundry mayhem as the inevitable price for transgressing the boundaries between the sacred and the profane. The fact of the matter, however, is that fear (insert *terror*) is the thread that often holds the cloth of religion together. And we have good, solid, empirical (if mythistorical) reasons to fear the Divine—just ask the assembled residents of Sodom and Gomorrah or Noah's neighbors. Oh, wait, that's right. We can't.

They're dead, riven from the earth by fire and flood at the hands of an angry, some might argue capricious and arbitrary, deity. So Pinhead's comment is not without merit. Indeed, a 2006 national survey found that more than 30 percent of Americans believe in what the researchers called an "Authoritarian God," one who "is highly involved in their daily lives," but who "is quite angry and is capable of meting out punishment to those who are unfaithful or ungodly" (Baylor Religion Survey, 2006, 27).

Belief in the unseen order persists in other ways, as well. In a fascinating look at the plight of minority faiths in a largely Christian America, Carol Barner-Barry recounts several instances in which public school officials have disciplined children for allegedly casting spells on teachers and classmates. In Oklahoma, for example, a high school student "was suspended for 15 days when school officials accused her of hexing a teacher who fell ill" (Barner-Barry, 2005, 131). Despite exemplary attendance and performance records, she had been suspended a year earlier when Wiccan literature was discovered in her bookbag. In Baltimore, a student received a day-long suspension for spellcasting, and numerous Pagan students have been suspended, sent home, or forced to remove religious symbols, such as pentagrams (see Barner-Barry, 2005, 129–35). Indeed, in a incident reminiscent of a scene from Andrew Fleming's *The Craft*, a student was suspended for writing a poem—which was interpreted as a spell—in which she wanted a rival's hair to fall out. "The interesting thing about such cases," writes Barner-Barry, "is the readiness of school authorities to take seriously the ability of a student to cast effective spells or hex others" (2005, 132). What is important to note is that these are not historical cases—all occurred within the last decade. Unsurprising, really, since the persistence of belief in the supernatural, coupled with a growing ambivalence toward established religious institutions, has marked American society for decades.

According to the Gallup organization, 68 percent of respondents to a 2001 survey told researchers that "they believe in the

Devil," and, while such belief is slightly higher in rural areas, the study concluded that "majorities of Americans of every political inclination, region, education level, and age group said they believe in the Devil" (Robison, 2003). The importance of a finding like this cannot be overstated, for if belief in the Devil cuts across every demographic boundary, it also cuts across both the viewing audiences for cinema horror and the cultural stocks of knowledge on which the sociophobics of demonic attack and possession draw. Put simply, they are not limited to one type of religious believer. Moreover, a 2004 Gallup report indicated that 70 percent of Americans believe in hell, including 92 percent of those who declared that they attend church at least weekly and 50 percent "of those who attend church seldom or never" (Winseman, 2004a). While the first breakdown here should not surprise anyone, the author of the report editorializes the second breakdown as "just half" (Winseman, 2004a). "Just half," however, is hardly insignificant. Half of the people surveyed who said that they attend church rarely or never also reported that they still believe in Hell! Although precisely what either Gallup or the respondents mean by "hell" is not made clear, it is not unlikely that their conception is based in this instance on a three-tiered Christian cosmology, an "unseen order" in which one's transgressions on Earth are punished for eternity in the pit.

In his discussion of the nature of "superstition" in the twentieth century, Gustav Jahoda notes that very often, when "talk comes around to the supernatural, the chances are that several persons will tell stories of occult occurrences that allegedly happened either to themselves or their relatives and friends; such stories are apt to range all the way from vague premonitions to seeing ghosts" (1969, 19). What this points out is that, however many rationalist, empirical, positivist, naturalist, or secularist explanations are offered for belief in the supernatural, nearly a generation ago (i.e., at the height of the secularization hypothesis' explanatory power), Jahoda's comments were right on the mark. "Enough has been said," Jahoda continues, "to indicate that under the seemingly rational surface of modern society there is an unexpectedly widespread yearning for the mysterious and occult we are supposed to have outgrown" (1969, 23).

The key word is *yearning*. That is, there is not only an ongoing *belief* in supernatural phenomena, but an equally strong inclination *to believe*, an equally powerful desire that these things be true, that, however frightening they are, the "things that go bump in the night" really do reside outside our minds. People want near-death experiences to bear out their belief in life after death; they want spiritualists, mediums, channels, and EVP (electronic voice phenomena, the belief that the unseen order can communicate through the white noise of televisions and radios) to confirm for them the ongoing existence of their loved ones, and, by extension, themselves. Borne out by recent polling data, Jahoda's words are almost prescient. "Superstition," he argues, "is still very much with us, and it is even possible that some forms of it may be on the increase" (1969, 26). And, while "the dominant intellectual temper of nineteenth-century Europe was rationalistic, the same period saw the spectacular rise of occultism, by no means confined to the vulgar and ignorant" (Jahoda, 1969, 33).

From 1993–2002, one of the most popular series on television was Chris Carter's *The X-Files*. Each week, audiences from Sweden to Singapore tuned in to watch FBI agents Dana Scully (Gillian Anderson) and Fox Mulder (David Duchovny) face the improbable and investigate the inexplicable. Though a variety of conspiracy theories and an alien abduction subplot anchored the overall *X-Files* narrative, numerous individual episodes dealt either explicitly or implicitly with supernatural or paranormal phenomena. Though it would be too much to argue for a direct correlation—and they do not try—Gallup researchers did note an increase in popular belief in psychic phenomena over the course of the series. Between 1990 and 2001, American belief in psychic or spiritual healing, for example, went from 44 to 54 percent, while belief in ghosts or haunting spirits rose from 25 to 38 percent, and a more general belief in human ability to communicate with the dead from 18 to 28 percent (Newport and Strausberg, 2001). Moreover, while belief in demonic possession fell from 49 to 41 percent, belief in haunted houses rose from 29 to 42 percent and in witches (presumably of the "wicked" variety, though the study does not specify) from 14 to 26 percent.

Clearly, we know more now than we did once. Explanations for what have turned out to be natural phenomena; causal frameworks into which events as disparate as infant deaths, cattle disease, and volcanic eruptions; theoretical positions that claim to have the answer for everything from Vegas card-counting to flightless waterfowl—all these may have shifted belief away from the supernatural in the past couple of hundred years, and shifted even more rapidly in the past few decades, but for a great many people a frightening darkness still exists just beyond the range and sweep of our cultural headlights. However bright our beams, the dark is still the dark.

## EXPLORING OUR FEAR: THE SOCIOPHOBICS OF CINEMA HORROR

In his book *Monsters and Mad Scientists* (1989), Andrew Tudor notes that the most enduring narrative schema in the films he considered—990 British horror films released from the 1930s to the 1970s—is what he calls "supernature," a threat that comes from beyond the bounds of accepted "natural" reality—that is, the "unseen order" to which participants must adapt themselves in one way or another. Tudor divides this broader category into a "manipulative supernature," populated by wizards, witches, and magicians (which he lumps together with Satanists) who inhabit no larger religious tradition and who use their access to the supernatural for personal, often malevolent gain, and "non-manipulative supernature"—vampires, demons, werewolves, and other preternatural creatures that simply "invade" the natural order. The problem with this categorization is that it ignores precisely those larger dimensions of religious belief and practice in which many of these cinematic examples are (and are very easily) embedded, as well as the particular religious beliefs, practices, histories, and cultural stocks of knowledge on which each draws or to which it adverts. If, as I am suggesting, religiously oriented horror films are much more than the simple pornography of violence implied by such critics as Medved and Stone, and not simply the infantilistic regression or adolescent identity play argued by such scholars as Wexman, Zillman, and Weaver, what then are they?

They are sociophobic artifacts, the artistic traces of a wide variety of fears that continue to haunt us. In his introduction to *The Horror People*, journalist and novelist John Brosnan notes what a number of commentators have pointed out—that horror cinema has often been denigrated as a kind of second-rate celluloid home for faded actors and failed directors. It's the place where washed-up filmmakers go to die (again and again and again). This is, of course, not to say that there are not bad horror films out there. There are, measured by any standard one cares to name. But lousy movies are hardly the sole provenance of horror cinema. Brosnan continues, however, that horror has been "picked up" by cultural critics as a reflection of the popular fears extant at the time of production. He suggests, though, that this interpretive hand has often been overplayed by academics who insist on finding meaningful symbolism in films that are simply exploitation.

> Horror films have come to be regarded by this critical "new wave" as important works that more accurately reflect the obsessions and tensions of society than their more serious, and respectable, counterparts. In some cases such claims are justifiable, but too often it becomes ludicrous when all manner of complicated symbolism is read into a film that has obviously been designed as pure exploitation. (Brosnan, 1976, 1–2)

The problem with this—or, rather, the short-sightedness of this approach (which may have something to do with a fan's entirely reasonable desire not to have his enjoyment of horror ruined by an excess of scholarly dissection, analysis, and commentary)—is that the cultural dynamic of *exploitation* is a direct function of the audience for whom a particular film is produced. There must be something within the audience that the filmmaker can exploit. In the case of cinema horror, there must be some fear a director can tap into and bring to life on the screen, if only for a moment. The mistake made by Brosnan and other critics who critique films for their exploitative character is that they tend to stop with exploitation and neglect to ask the more significant questions: With all the potential scary things around, why do horror filmmakers return over and over to an identifiable pattern of topics, themes, and treatments? Why do we fear the dead, for example? Why do we fear that the church is not the pristine sanctuary it pretends to be or presents itself as? Why do we fear the chaogonic invasion/inversion of our world, and the apparent powerlessness (or capriciousness) of God in the face of it? In this sense, it is possible that cinema horror is one cultural means by which we confront the classic theological problem of evil. Because it speaks to the social construction of fear and fearing, it is this pool of potential exploitation that interests me.

Rather than simply the product of individual psychology, for more than two decades now sociologists, anthropologists, and cultural critics have thought about fear as a social phenomenon, an affect as conditioned by culture as it is established by personality. In his introduction to sociophobics, David Scruton writes:

> Fearing is an event that takes place in a social setting; it is performed by social animals whose lives and experiences are dominated by culture. . . . It is impossible to understand fully what human fearing is, how fears happen in the individual, how they are expressed both to self and to others, how they are received and reacted to by others in the community, and what their function in our lives is unless we treat fearing as a function of cultural experience, which people participate in because they are

members of specific societies at particular times. Fearing is thus a dimension of human social life. (1986, 9)

Put differently, our culture teaches us in a variety of ways what to fear, and through a variety of cultural products reflects and reinforces the fears we have been taught. What, then, are the religiously oriented fears that cinema horror reveals to us? Though they are hardly discrete categories, and while many films contain more than one sociophobic element, there are six basic themes explored in the following chapters: fear of change in the sacred order; fear of sacred places; fear of death, of dying badly, and of not remaining dead; fear of evil that is both externalized and internalized; fear of fanaticism and the power of religion; and, finally, fear of the flesh and the powerlessness of religion. Exploiting these fears, filmmakers make us shiver, scream, and seek comfort beneath the bedclothes.

# 3

## ANGELS TO SOME, DEMONS TO OTHERS
### Fear of Change in the Sacred Order

>
> PINHEAD
> We are explorers in the further regions
> of experience. Angels to some, demons
> to others.
>
> <div align="right">(Clive Barker, <i>Hellraiser</i>)</div>
>
> PINHEAD
> The box. You opened it. We came.
>
> <div align="right">(Clive Barker, <i>Hellraiser</i>)</div>

### OUTTAKE: *HELLRAISER: BLOODLINE*

It begins with the box. Almost always, it begins with the box. Built by Phillipe the toymaker in the dark and violent days of prerevolutionary France, and known in the *Hellraiser* mythology as the LeMarchand Configuration, it is far more than simply a child's ornate plaything: it is the key to a doorway between the seen and the unseen, the boundary along which vastly different orders of reality occasionally and violently collide. It is a means to summon the Cenobites, beings who exist in a dimension where pleasure and pain come together as one, and the all-too-thin line between the two is torn relentlessly apart.

In *Hellraiser: Bloodline*, the fourth entry in the series, we learn of the box's origin, commissioned in the eighteenth century by a

French nobleman, the Duc de L'Isle (Mickey Cottrell), and designed to his exacting specifications. A master magician and occult devotee, De L'Isle has had a young prostitute murdered and plans to use the toymaker's box to breach the boundary of the unseen world. Like a teacher with a favorite student, he watches his assistant, Jacques (Adam Scott), carefully flay the murdered girl, her skin now ready for its new tenant—the demon Angelique (Valentina Vargas), whose very name indicates an inversion of the accepted sacred order.

Phillipe, however, has remained outside, watching, a horrified voyeur to the carnage that follows. When he tries to explain what he saw to a local physician, the ubiquitous contest between the supernatural and the rational is joined. Bemused by the toymaker's story, as he casually uses a bone-saw to dismember a cadaver, Dr. Auguste lectures the younger man:

> DR. AUGUSTE
> This is the eighteenth century, Phillipe, not the Dark Ages. The world is ruled by reason! We've even gotten rid of God. And if there is no heaven, then it follows, <u>reasonably</u>, that there is no hell.

Although at the time of its release *Hellraiser: Bloodline* was regarded by fans as the weakest of the franchise, there are moments in the film that speak directly to the intimate relationship between cinema horror and religious belief in the unseen order. And, however brief, this important exchange occurs in various forms throughout religiously oriented horror movies—the doctor in *Dracula* who scoffs at Van Helsing's belief in "superstitions" about vampires; Sir John Talbot's disbelief in the legends of *The Wolf Man* despite his own son's personal experience; Father Karras' initial dismissal of the possibility that Regan could be possessed in *The Exorcist*. Like these characters, Dr. Auguste is a metonym for secularization—the sloughing of old chains and the march toward a glorious new rationalist dawn. The only thing missing in this film is his own supernatural comeuppance. He is, in fact, the Enlightenment obverse of the Duc de L'Isle, dissecting a dead body in the name of science as he talks to Phillipe, just as the Duc has enervated dead flesh in the name of occult power. He blithely continues with his bone-saw—which is no less a disgusting image than the flaying of the unfortunate prostitute—despite what Phillipe has just told him, and despite what we as the audience already know.

This is the collision between modernity (e.g., medical and psychiatric science [*Hellraiser: Bloodline* and *Dracula*]; astronomy [*The Wolf Man*]; psychiatry [*The Exorcist*]) and premodernity (superstitions about vampires, werewolves, and demonic possession), between science (or simple skepticism) and the supernatural, between those who think they know and those who know better. Each of these almost stock scenes reinforces for us that, even though we constantly tell ourselves that there are no more things that go bump in the night, few nights are altogether quiet. As the audience, and within the context of the cinematic frame, we know what Renfield discovered in Castle Dracula; like the gypsies, we know that werewolves are real; like Phillipe crouched at the window as Angelique is called into our form, we know—or at least we fear—that the demonic still exists in our world.

## UNSEEN ORDERS: CINEMA HORROR AND THE SHATTERING OF THE SACRED CANOPY

Regardless of differences in belief, doctrine, or ritual, the thread that binds religions together is the relatively simple conviction that *this is not all there is*. While the dubious accomplishment of Dr. Auguste's scientific materialism may have been to convince us that there is nothing beyond the physical—and, perhaps, the neuropsychological—the ubiquity of religious belief and practice around the world continues to argue that the mundane only masquerades as the totality of existence. For those willing to accept their reality, there are other worlds apart from our own, other realms waiting to be explored—or feared. Few religious traditions, for example, do not include provisions for some kind of communication with the other realm, the unseen order that both lies behind and underpins everyday life. These unseen orders vary, of course, both across the spectrum of religious belief and within the manifold elements of that spectrum. Though their statues populate churches around the world, devout Roman Catholics cannot actually see the saints to whom they offer prayers and novenas, yet they remain certain of their reality and hopeful of their beneficence. Often quoting Paul's letter to the church at Ephesus, millions of fundamentalist Protestants believe that they are on the front lines of a daily battle "against the spiritual forces of evil in the heavenly realms" (Eph. 6:12; cf. Larson, 1999; Lewis, 1996; Perett, 1986, 1989, 1995). Mediums and trance channels continue the tradition of nineteenth-century spiritualism, contacting the dead on behalf of the living, bridging the gap between those who have crossed over and those who remain behind.

Though all these speak to belief in an unseen order of one kind or another, each is subject to a certain instability that comes both from the relative invisibility of that order and from the constant challenges to its reality by those whose understandings differ. As Peter Berger notes in his classic text, *The Sacred Canopy*: "All socially constructed worlds are inherently precarious" (1967, 29). And, whether seen or unseen, if we want the worlds we construct to continue to have meaning for us, they require stability—in theological terms, orthodoxy. All too often, though, we realize that such stability is under constant challenge, either attacked from without or undermined from within. Belief in other gods implicitly challenges the validity of our own belief. Millions of biblical literalists contend fiercely that if we cannot believe everything in the Bible, then we have no grounds for believing anything it says. If the church, the temple, or the mosque are not places of stability and safety, what does that say about the unseen orders they represent? In all this, we fear that the unseen order is either not as we believe or subject to change in drastic ways.

Horror movies are cinematic simulations that posit the effects of alternative unseen orders, illuminating what we imagine are the manifold threats to these socially constructed worlds. What would happen if the world really worked like this? What are the consequences of opening the various boxes with which we are presented? Are demons really demons, or are they angels in disguise? Of course, cinema horror is not the only genre that does this. Comedy is predicated on the dissolution and reestablishment of social order; crime dramas similarly, though in a different narrative key. Cinema horror, however, exposes both the uncertainty of the visible order and the potential for disturbance and disintegration of the unseen order on which it depends.

John Carpenter's *In the Mouth of Madness*, for example, which is a tribute both to the power of horror in late modern society and to the works of H. P. Lovecraft in particular, demonstrates this potential clearly. John Trent (Sam Neill) is an insurance investigator drawn into the search for a missing horror novelist, Sutter Cane (Jürgen Prochnow). Part of Cane's global appeal is that his work is considered so disturbing that many of his readers experience psychotic breaks while reading it. Initially, as the film's embodiment of rationalism, its Dr. Auguste or Sir John Talbot, Trent is skeptical. As he speaks with the acquisitions editor, Linda Styles (Julie Carmen), he asks:

```
                    TRENT
     What's to be scared about? It's not
     like it's real or anything.

                    STYLES
     It's not real from your point of view,
     and right now reality shares your point
```

of view. What scares me about Cane's
work is what might happen if reality
shared his point of view.

                    TRENT
Whoa. We're not talking about reality
here. We're talking about fiction. It's
different, you know.

                    STYLES
A reality is just what we tell each
other it is. Sane and insane could
easily switch places if the insane
were to become the majority. You would
find yourself locked in a padded cell,
wondering what happened to the world.

Of course, what the audience knows from both the opening and closing sequences is that Trent *is* in a padded cell and he *does* wonder what happened to the world he thought he knew. "The sheltering quality of social order," writes Berger, "becomes especially evident if one looks at the marginal situations in the life of the individual," that is, such situations as "commonly occur in dreams and fantasy. They may appear on the horizon of consciousness as haunting suspicions that the world may have another aspect than the 'normal' one, that is, that the previously accepted definitions of reality may be fragile and even fraudulent" (1967, 22, 23).

"On a deeper level, however," Berger continues, "the sacred has another opposed category, that of chaos. The sacred cosmos emerges out of chaos and continues to confront the latter as its terrible contrary" (1967, 26). Though Berger illustrates this with the battle between cosmos and chaos in "a variety of cosmogonic myths," it is worth noting that chaos is no less a matter of perspective than cosmos. What is the established order for one group appears to others as little more than an insane amalgam of belief and practice. What to some appears on the horizon as chaos—the Israelite destruction of the Canaanite Asherah, the Christian demolition and appropriation of sacred sites across Europe and the Americas, the Taliban shelling of Buddhist statues in Afghanistan—is to those arriving the righteous imposition of a sacred cosmos.

It is this challenge to the accepted sacred order that cinema horror so often reveals. The advent of one unseen order heralds—or at least threatens—the disappearance of another. This is what I call the metataxis of horror, the shift in accepted or dominant taxonomies of the sacred. It occurs in three principal ways: inversion, invasion, and insignificance.

## MONSTROUS GODS AND THE METATAXIS OF HORROR

On the one hand, by reversing aspects of culturally dominant religions, horrific metataxis *inverts* popular categories of interpretation and expectation. In films like *Stigmata* and *John Carpenter's Vampires*, for example, the Roman Catholic Church becomes the locus of malevolence, and Church officials are the proximate agents of discord and evil. In *End of Days* and *Good Against Evil*, though, the Church is relatively helpless in the face of evil, and despite its best efforts is unable to prevent the proximate agents of discord from carrying out their diabolical plans. In Tony Mandile's *Midnight Mass*, it is both.

Culturally unfamiliar religions, on the other hand, are often *invasive*, and their aspect of horrific metataxis challenges—either explicitly or implicitly—the ability of dominant traditions to function meaningfully. The various entries into *The Mummy* franchise, for example, whether from Universal Studios in the 1930s and 1940s or Hammer Studios in the 1950s and 1960s, depend for their sense of religious invasion both on orientalist notions of ancient Egyptian religion and on popular fear of secret religious societies. Though there is rarely any direct challenge in these films to the dominance of such a tradition as Christianity, that another, powerful unseen order exists, one that implicitly denies the uniqueness and efficacy of something like Christianity, is clear.

Finally, horrific metataxis is created when a new (or newly emergent) unseen order renders the dominant tradition *insignificant*. A wide variety of ghost movies, for example, from horror (*White Noise*) to comedy (*Beetlejuice*), and from thrillers (*The Sixth Sense*) to romance/drama (*Ghost*), deals explicitly with the soul's survival after death yet makes little or no reference to established religious traditions. Even those references that are made—like the shadows that finally take the evil Carl Bruner (Tony Goldwyn) in *Ghost*—are latent at best and reflect little more than the popular karmic notion that we have to pay for our crimes eventually.

## Treachery Above and Below: The Inversion of Orthodoxy

Few who have served in the military would argue that a traitor is less dangerous than an enemy. Posing as friends and allies, those who threaten the established order from within are feared and reviled in a way that few outright enemies could imagine. For nearly two millennia, the Christian Church has been far more diligent in hunting down those who threaten it from within than defending against those who challenge from without. Like the satanic followers of Father James in *Lost Souls*, the nuns devoted to Ashtoreth in *To the Devil . . . a Daughter*, or the evil Mother Superior in *The Other Hell*, traitors gain our trust, our confidence, and often our love, trading on all of these to bring about our downfall.

Take angels, for example. Billy Graham, arguably the most prominent evangelist of the twentieth century, calls them "God's secret agents" (1975). According to a 2000 survey of more than eleven hundred Americans, 77 percent believe that "angels, that is, some kind of heavenly beings who visit Earth, in fact exist"; moreover, "belief in angelic beings cuts across almost all ranges of education, income, and lifestyle" (Shermer, 2000, 244). A 2005 study conducted by the Baylor Institute for Studies of Religion found that just over 80 percent of those surveyed answered either "Absolutely" or "Probably" to the question of whether angels exist (Baylor Religion Survey, 2006). Over the past thirty years, Canadian belief in angels has hovered around 60 percent. During its nine-season run (1994–2003), CBS' *Touched by an Angel* was one of the most popular television programs in both the United States and Canada. Each week, a trio of angels appeared in the lives of ordinary people who had ordinary (or, on occasion, extraordinary) problems and helped them out—usually with hugs, smiles, and tears at the end of the episode. Feel-good programming at its best, and, invariably, the angels involved were helpful, compassionate, beautiful, and wanted nothing more than the very best for humankind.

But, what if this is wrong? What if angels are unlike anything we might think or imagine? If the message of these pop-cultural representations is "Be not afraid," then the angelic proclamation in *The Prophecy* (and the sequels that followed) is "Be afraid. Be very afraid."

Resentful of God's loving preference for "talking monkeys" (i.e., human beings), in *The Prophecy* the angel Gabriel (Christopher Walken) leads a second war in heaven, an apocalyptic conflict to claim what he considers the rightful place of the angelic in the courts of the Almighty. Rather than help men and women in pain, he keeps them barely alive to serve him as ghouls, getaway drivers, and general go-fers. Rather than guard the souls of the righteous, he seeks the darkest soul imaginable—that of an American soldier who committed unspeakable atrocities during the Korean War—to serve him in his final conflict with God. Rather than spend eternity praising the one who created him, Gabriel follows in his brother Lucifer's footsteps, using the very powers God gave him to challenge the unseen order of the universe itself. While investigating an unusual homicide, Thomas Daggett

(Elias Koteas), a police detective and former Catholic seminarian, is drawn into the battle. At the crime scene, he finds an ancient Bible containing a chapter found in no other copy on Earth: the twenty-third chapter of the Revelation to St. John, the story of the second war in heaven.

Two levels of horrific inversion play off one another in *The Prophecy*. On the one hand, there is the surface narrative. Gabriel's attempt to overthrow the sacred order and the possibility of a second war in heaven deliberately invert the theological conception of the angelic hosts. The stability of God's order—and the unseen order believed in by one-third of humankind—is threatened when those closest to God rebel. On the other hand, while we may not credence the plausibility of an angelic insurrection, whether as a plot device or as an article of faith, the film challenges the popular conception of angels at a much deeper level by drawing the audience's attention to an entirely reasonable, if underadvertised interpretation of the Bible. That is, religious popular culture notwithstanding, angels are not necessarily what we have come to believe. Instead, we are presented with an entirely different—yet entirely reasonable—interpretation of "God's secret agents."

An authority on angels, Daggett often serves as the film's chorus, gradually revealing the central metataxon of the plot. Speaking to Katherine (Virginia Madsen), a schoolteacher in rural Arizona unwittingly caught up in the conflict, he asks:

> DAGGETT
>
> You ever read the Bible, Katherine? You ever notice how, in the Bible, when God needed to punish someone, make an example, or whenever God needed a killing, he sent an angel? Did you ever wonder what a creature like that must be like? Your whole existence spent praising your God, always with one wing dipped in blood. Would you ever really

want to see an angel?

Though executed in vastly different ways, Kevin Smith's *Dogma* and Francis Lawrence's *Constantine* raise similar questions. If *The Prophecy* franchise confronts the dominance of the unseen order from above, however, Brian Helgeland's *The Order* challenges it from below. Indeed, in this film, both the unseen order and its earthly proxy are under attack from a number of different directions.

Alex Bernier (Heath Ledger) is a priest with a troubled past. Orphaned as a small child, he was raised as a member of a tiny order known as the Carolingians. Essentially an order of exorcists, Bernier and his friend Thomas (Mark Addy) have been sent out into the world to "deal with ghosts and demons and all manner of the undead." Trained in Catholic arcana, the dark secrets that comprise so much of popular folklore about the Church, Bernier and his order represent the first attack, the first level of inversion. He still says the mass in Latin, for example, with his back to the congregation in pre-Vatican II style. Placed in a poorly attended urban parish, "because the Church doesn't know what to do with me," Bernier continues to do things "the way I was taught." "Well," replies Michael Cardinal Driscoll (Peter Weller), a major power-broker in the Roman curia, "the Church doesn't know what to do with itself. Look, I won't pretend I don't know you have certain qualifications, certain skills that set you apart from other priests." The message is plain: the medieval past still exists at the heart of the modern and even postmodern present. Just because the majority of the church has ceased to celebrate the Tridentine mass or to believe in demons does not mean that either has ceased to exist. Drawing on the supernatural power of the margins, Bernier's traditionalism and training in Catholic esoterica points to the weaknesses at the center of the modern Church. This is the first challenge to the unseen order.

The second comes in Rome, where Bernier discovers the existence of a sin-eater (Benno Fürmann) while investigating the mysterious death of his own mentor. Cardinal Driscoll responds in good cinema horror fashion: "A sin-eater, here? At the start of the new millennium?" That is, *here* at the center of Roman Catholic power, and *now*, in the age of science and technology—though an age when the church "doesn't know what to do itself," which implies, at least, that perhaps her followers should begin to look elsewhere. At this point, Driscoll becomes the chorus, intertextually linking this film to others in the genre—specifically, though not precisely, *The Exorcist*—and explaining the specific threat of the sin-eater:

> DRISCOLL
>
> A sin-eater? You couldn't have shocked the bishop more if you said you'd been possessed by some Phoenician demon and demanded an exorcism. Sin-eater, a renegade who provides a path to heaven outside of the Church, outside of our Savior. If you believe such things, he has the power to grant redemption to the unrepentant. Throw a heretical wrench into the cogs of the Catholic machine.

For much of its history, the Roman Catholic Church has been underpinned by its dogmatic assertion of a single, unassailable concept: *extra ecclesiam nulla salus*. Outside of the church there is no salvation. Whatever political intrigues, economic enterprises, or military campaigns the church has supported over the centuries, somewhere underneath lies the foundation of Catholic power and piety: it was to the successors of Peter that God gave *claves regni caelorum*, the keys to the kingdom of Heaven, and to the servants of the Church the power to grant—or, more importantly, to withhold—absolution at the moment of death, absolution as the means to salvation. Without it, a soul either burned in hell or languished in purgatory, and the narrow-mindedness of the choice has hardly been lost on the makers of cinema horror.

Searching for the sin-eater brings Bernier to the labyrinthine catacombs beneath the Eternal City—and the third level of inversion. There, the set is dressed as a pagan temple, and though the message is clear, it is hardly unambiguous. Paganism still lives and breathes beneath the cobbled streets and granite monuments of the Vatican. The pagan religions on which the church was built have not disappeared; they have simply gone underground, literally undermining the Church of Rome. Whereas the massive cathedral spaces above are brightly lit, sharply focused, with little or no shadow, the vaulted rooms of the catacombs below are swathed in shadows, their tenebrous heights obscuring both detail and dimension. Prayers and the occasional sung chant float through the sanctuaries above, while heavy metal music pounds through a nightclub near the entrance to the catacombs. On the curtains behind the bar, though, is the *chi rho*, one of the earliest cruciform symbols used by the Church, and the one chosen by the emperor Constantine as the centerpiece of his military standard and later the official imperial insignia. Whether in mockery or sincerity, the connection between the spaces above and the spaces below is never lost. Indeed, as the story develops, what goes on in the catacombs is both literally and figuratively undermining what takes place in the sanctuaries, great halls, and papal apartments of the Eternal City.

Just as the pope reigns above, a "dark pope" named Chirac presides below. Hooded, robed, and masked in black, he sits on a throne high above the temple floor and proclaims his challenge to the unseen order:

```
CHIRAC (in Latin)
```
Two crosses. The Old Testament is the Father. The New Testament is the Son. The prophecy of the Third Age states the third cross is coming. I am the Third Age.

In the film's penultimate act, Thomas confronts Chirac and learns the depths to which the Church has been betrayed. Removing his hood and mask, he reveals himself as Cardinal Driscoll and declares that through the power of the sin-eater, "I will become *Pope*. A warrior pope! Pope of a church which will reclaim its property and its sanctity and its power." What is left unclear, however, is just what kind of church Driscoll hopes to lead. Will it be a revitalized Roman Catholic Church—its lost property, sanctity, and power once again intact—or some revived pre-Christian religion grafted onto the social dominance of the See of Peter?

These, then, are the multiple threats both to the unseen divine order, and to the visible, ecclesiastical order that claims to be its sole representative on Earth. Through the implicit threat of Bernier and his Carolingian order, the two explicit threats are brought together. The sin-eater threatens the Church theologically, inverting the unseen order by arrogating to himself the power to grant absolution, while Chirac and his prophecy of the Third Age threaten the very existence of the Church itself. Its power gone, it becomes irrelevant, replaced by a newer, more powerful *ecclesia*.

In what Timothy Beal calls the "paradox of the monstrous" (2002, 4–5), Freud articulates precisely the horror invoked through the inversion of the sacred order. "The 'uncanny,'" he writes, is a category that "belongs to the realm of the frightening, of what evokes fear and dread" (Freud, [1919] 2003, 123), the defining characteristic of which is that it "goes back to what was once well known and had long been familiar" ([1919] 2003, 124). Or, put more formally, "the uncanny (*das Unheimliche*, 'the unhomely') is in some way a species of the familiar (*das Heimliche*, 'the homely')" (Freud, [1919] 2003, 134). By "homely," of course, Freud does not mean "plain" or "unattractive," nor by "unhomely" that which is beautiful. Rather, the fear and dread that is evoked in these cases are functions of familiarity, products of comfort, trust, and love that have been turned on their heads. Because we have traditionally (if somewhat gullibly) looked to places like the church for comfort and safety, and to church leaders as the guardians of our own best interests, betrayal at this level is particularly frightening. Whether a simple murder plot hatched in *The Fog*, vague hints that the church harbors more secrets than it shares, or an elaborate plan to undermine the power of Heaven itself, films such as these reveal a fundamental ambivalence about the church and those who serve it. We want to trust, but remain uncertain whether trust is warranted. Another form of fear, however, is based less on the inversion of the unseen order we have come to know than on the wholesale replacement of that order by something wholly unfamiliar.

*The Old Ones Return: H. P. Lovecraft and the Invasive Other*

Numerous films have been based on (or inspired by) the works of H. P. Lovecraft (1890–1937), one of the most influential horror writers of the twentieth century (see Migliore and Strysik, 2006). Both *The Haunted Palace* (though named for a poem by Edgar Allan Poe) and *The Resurrected* originate in Lovecraft's short novel, *The Case of Charles Dexter Ward* ([1941] 1999, 90–205), about the title character's necromantic fascination with a long-dead ancestor. Both *The Unnamable* and *The Unnamable II: The Statement of Randolph Carter* are based on Lovecraft's stories of the same names ([1925] 2004; [1920] 1999). A series of *Re-Animator* films all find their foundation in "Herbert West—Reanimator," a short story about a surgeon obsessed with the possibility of, not surprisingly, reanimating the recently deceased.

Other films, however, follow what Lovecraft aficionados call "the Cthulhu mythos," tales of elder gods and powerful supernatural beings who have been supplanted on Earth and wait impatiently to return. For Lovecraft, these are the proper subjects of the "weird tale," the apex of the horror craft. Devoted to evoking humanity's "oldest and strongest emotion," for Lovecraft, "the literature of cosmic fear" was something quite apart from stories about "mere physical fear," "the mundanely gruesome," or "the conventional or even whimsical ghost story" ([1927] 2000, 21, 22). Rather, he writes, "a certain atmosphere of breathlessness and unexplainable dread of outer, unknown forces must be present" (Lovecraft, [1927] 2000, 22).

Although, as one of Lovecraft's biographers points out, the dozen or so stories that constitute Lovecraft's contribution to the mythos "do not form a consistent whole because Lovecraft never worked out his assumptions in detail" (de Camp, 1975, 270), all have at their heart one controlling idea: this is not all there is. There is another, darker unseen order pressing in at the boundaries of our awareness. Aeons past, a race of beings called, variously, the "Great Old Ones," the "Other Gods," or the "Ancient Ones" held dominion here, in some cases before the advent of humanity, but in all cases before the gods with which we are now familiar came to power. While Beal has described Lovecraft as a "theologian without God" (2002, 182), he is more accurately understood as a theologian of different, older, and much more malevolent gods. If, as Freud wrote, "Gods become demons after the collapse of their cult" ([1919] 2003, 143) then these are the gods of the Cthulhu mythos, the two best-known films of which are *The Dunwich Horror* and *Dagon*—the invasive other denied and the invasive other triumphant.

"Single white warlock seeks beautiful blonde to join him at the altar . . . the sacrificial altar!" trumpets the cover blurb on MGM's "Midnite Movie" release of *The Dunwich Horror*, concluding that "all hell is about to break loose" in "this sinister scare-fest of satanic seduction." Its rather tawdry alliteration notwithstanding, this epitomizes advertising copy for any number of "black mass" or "Satanic mass" horror films from the 1950s through the 1970s. In it, however, few Lovecraft fans would recognize one of his most widely read stories. Described by S. T. Joshi as "a rather crude film adaptation" (2001, 409), director Daniel Haller and producer Roger Corman (with whom Haller also worked as art director on numerous films) stripped the story to its bones, adding a rib here and there. Haller's alterations reveal important aspects about the way we perceive the invasive religious Other and the way it has been represented to us in popular culture.

Published first in the April 1929 issue of *Weird Tales*, "The Dunwich Horror" is a dark, moody story about the degenerate and "decayed" Whately family and their attempts to bring back the Old Ones, both through the *hieros gamos*—the sacred marriage between the human and the divine—and their use of an ancient spellbook—"the hideous *Necronomicon* of the mad Arab Abdul Alhazrad" (Lovecraft, [1929] 2001, 219). Wilbur Whately, a "bent, goatish giant" who "seemed like the spawn of another planet or dimension" (Lovecraft, [1929] 2001, 220), attempts the ritual but is defeated in a battle of arcane chants by Henry Armitage, a librarian and leading authority on ancient manuscripts. "We have no business calling in such things from outside," Armitage says as the story ends, "and only very wicked people and very wicked cults ever try to" (Lovecraft, [1929] 2001, 245).

Rather than Lovecraft's incessant gloom and decay, Haller presents a fairly routine supernatural seduction story, in which a beautiful young woman is offered by a mysterious cult as both unwitting sacrifice and demonic *theotokos*—the one who brings God into the world. Rather than the grotesque, shambling progeny of a blasphemous union between his mother and an Old One, Wilbur Whately is played with a studied urbanity by the slight, soft-spoken, and impeccably groomed Dean Stockwell. Playing on an eroticism that has informed cinema horror for decades (and a topic to which we will turn in depth in chapter 7), Wilbur's mother is not the "slatternly, crinkly-haired albino" Lovecraft describes ([1929] 2001, 211), but a ravishing, dark-haired young woman (Joanne Moore Jordan) dressed in what could only be described as a ritual negligée. Likewise, while Wilbur does want the *Necronomicon* in order to bring the Old Ones back, he spends much of the film's first half seducing a university student named Nancy, played by the beautiful, blond Sandra Dee. A motif found in numerous horror films (the most well-known of which is *Rose-*

*mary's Baby*), the Old Ones' return will be realized through her.

As the rite peaks and the gate between the worlds begins to open, Professor Armitage (Ed Begley) arrives, and a brief battle of incantations begins. A bolt of lightning strikes the site and Wilbur bursts into flames, literally going up in smoke. The Old Ones have been driven back. "It's all over now," Armitage tells Nancy as he helps her down from the altar. "The last of the Whateleys is dead." Even as he says it, though, a subtle heartbeat takes over the soundtrack and a fetus is superimposed on her belly. Fading out on the unborn child developing in Nancy's womb, the film's message is clear: the Whateleys may be gone, but the Old Ones are still around, waiting to return.

In *Le surréalisme au cinéma*, filmmaker and critic Adonis Kyrou urges readers to "learn to look at 'bad' films, they are sometimes sublime" (1963, 276). And, in many ways, this is a "bad" film, cheapened by special effects that are poor even by 1970 standards, and hampered by Haller's somewhat plodding direction and consistent choice to ignore a principal dramatic maxim—"show, don't tell." Its sublimity, however, is arguably in the manner of adaptation, in how Haller and his screenwriters change Lovecraft's gloomy tale, with its polarities of light and dark, clean and unclean, decayed and "undecayed" ([1929] 2001, 241; cf. Douglas, 1966), adapting it to exploit a variety of popular fears both extant at the time of its release and deeply grounded in the historical consciousness of all things satanic. In the adaptation of literature to film, we often see most clearly the intrusion of economics, politics, sociology, and popular religiosity, and Haller's film illustrates both his sensitivity to and exploitation of audience sociophobics that are subtly but significantly different from those of Lovecraft's pulp horror fans.

First, there is the addition of Nancy, the principal difference between Lovecraft's story and Haller's film. In the story, Wilbur's mother is the *theotokos*, while he and his monstrous sibling are the vehicles by which the Old Ones will return. *The Dunwich Horror*, however, was made in the midst of the first of several late modern "Satanic panics," popular fears that there was a large and well-organized Satanic movement operating just below the surface of polite society (cf. Best, Richardson, and Bromley, 1991; Ellis, 2000; Medway, 2001; Victor, 1993). By adding Nancy, however, by sexualizing the relationship between her and Wilbur, and by locating the Old Ones' return in their *hieros gamos*, Haller follows rather conventional imagery of the so-called black mass that reaches back at least into the seventeenth century. The Marquis de Sade's *Justine* (de Sade, [1791] 1965), for example, includes a detailed description of the black mass, and Matthew Lewis' *The Monk* ([1796] 1998) has been interpreted as one long sexualized inversion of Christian teachings and practice. In a flurry of media attention, Anton LaVey's Church of Satan was incorporated in 1966, and his altars were regularly adorned with beautiful young women. "True occult" literature is replete with stories of women used either for breeding purposes or the satisfaction of satanic lust. Numerous horror films have used a woman's nude or nearly nude body as the altar upon which a variety of blasphemous rites are performed. Arguably the earliest image Haller draws on, though, is a woodcut depicting a black mass allegedly conducted in the early seventeenth century by the Abbé Guibourg, a disgraced cleric who confessed to performing a number of black masses for wealthy patrons (see Ravaisson-Mollien, 1975, 294–98).

Throughout Lovecraft's story, while the Whateleys are unfavorably contrasted with the Dunwich townsfolk, there is no direct conflict between religious beliefs per se, no contest between dominant and invasive traditions. In the film, though, while Armitage prevents the Old Ones' return through magic no less arcane than Wilbur's, two scenes highlight the ongoing battle against the invasive other that marks so much of religious history.

Early in their relationship, as Wilbur is showing Nancy the town of Dunwich, he points out the tree where his great-grandfather was hanged by the townsfolk, "because he didn't believe in what they believe. Because he wasn't afraid of their god." When he tells Nancy of his forebear's belief in the Old Ones and their potential return, she asks, "You mean they hanged him for that?"

                    WILBUR
          Yes. They trumped up a murder charge to
          cover it up. A girl had disappeared,
          and then, without a shred of evidence,
          they went after him. They claimed he
          used her in some sort of sacrifice.

The implication is clear: it wasn't the disappearance for which he was hanged, but his use of the girl in black magic, in the worship of what the villagers regard as false (and, therefore, evil) gods.

   Wilbur himself confronts the villagers as he attempts to bury his grandfather. At the local cemetery, old Whateley lies robed in his coffin, a ceremonial staff in his hands, a ritual tattoo on his forehead. The camera follows Wilbur as he conducts a complicated occult ritual. He is interrupted, though, by Haller's equivalent of "angry villagers with torches":

                    REEGER
          Awright, hold it! You can bury your
          trash in the county dump, not here.

                    MRS. COLE
          This is a Christian cemetery. No place
          here for your kind.

Reeger (Jack Pierce) kicks all the ritual implements into the grave, throwing the book in after. As the two men begin to struggle, the sheriff intervenes:

                SHERIFF (to WILBUR)
          What in the hell are you trying to do?

                    WILBUR
          I was trying to bury my grandfather.

MRS. COLE
We got family buried here. We don't
want no Whateleys among 'em.

Whether it is an accident of shooting or a deliberate choice on Haller's part, in both the two-shot with Reeger and Wilbur and (even more apparent) in the two-shot with Wilbur and the sheriff, a power pole in the distance commands the center of the screen. With the sun reflecting off the weathered wood and set against the darkness of the evergreens, it looks like a cross. Whether this means that in the face of the blasphemous Whateleys the Christian God is still present in Dunwich is left unclear. Just as the sheriff prevents the burial in the town cemetery, though, Armitage postpones (at least) the return of the Old Ones to our world.

Whatever its flaws, in Haller's hands, *The Dunwich Horror* becomes more than a straightforward monster story; it is a bridge between the inversive and the invasive. Although both are based on themes of ritual sacrifice and the *hieros gamos*, if *The Dunwich Horror* represents the invasive other denied, Stuart Gordon's *Dagon* presents us the spectacle of the invasive other triumphant. Adapted from Lovecraft's novella, "The Shadow over Innsmouth" ([1936] 1999), rather than the eponymous "Dagon" ([1919] 1999), Gordon and scriptwriter Dennis Paoli also transport the action from the decaying village of Innsmouth on the Massachusetts seaboard to the Pacific coast of Spain and the equally squalid village of Imboca (a rather inexact translation of the original). Unlike *The Dunwich Horror*, in which the contest between religious traditions is minimized, in *Dagon* the invasive replacement of one religion by another is placed front and center.

In the film's opening sequence, light filters down through an azure sea as a scuba diver explores a vast underwater temple. A mermaid beckons him ever deeper, and as he follows her she suddenly turns and attacks. All teeth and fury, she is a creature born of Lovecraft's darkest fears, as far from Madison in Ron Howard's *Splash* (1984) or the beloved Ariel in Disney's *The Little Mermaid*

(1989) as one can get. As it turns out, she is also part of a nightmare suffered by the film's main character, Paul (Ezra Godden). While vacationing off the coast of Spain with friends, Paul is caught on a foundering sailboat during a sudden storm. Leaving the other couple on board, Paul and his girlfriend Barbara (Raquel Meroño) go ashore in the dinghy, searching Imboca frantically for help. Rain lashes the seemingly deserted village as they run to the local church, stopping short at the name on the building: *Esoterica Orde de Dagon*, the Esoteric Order of Dagon.

In Lovecraft's novella, while it is clear that the Order had "engulfed all the orthodox churches" (Lovecraft, [1936] 1999, 277), it has not taken over a church building as its headquarters; rather, "the former Masonic Hall [is] now given over to a degraded cult" ([1936] 1999, 283). Onscreen, however, it would have little impact trying to represent a "Masonic Hall," and, set in Spain, it makes considerably more sense to have the cult of Dagon supplant the Roman Catholic Church. Not unlike Byron Haskin's 1953 *The War of the Worlds*, the film version of the literary narrative makes the story's religious component far more explicit. In the Lovecraft novella, the elder gods are present in the cult of Dagon, but there is less sense that they have actively displaced the Christian god. Dennis Paoli's screenplay, however, places this contest of supernatures squarely at the story's heart.

Trapped in the village and pursued by the Imbocans, Paul learns that all are deformed in some way—one has tentacles where fingers should be; others have piscine teeth. Their voices are no longer human. A creature with webbed tentacles for hands drags itself along the wet cobblestones like a bedraggled beggar. Running from the shambling, baying crowd, Paul encounters the film's chorus, an old man named Ezequiel (Francisco Rabal)—the lone prophetic voice left in the village.

"Long before," he tells Paul, "Imboca no like now. Imboca pueblo de Cristo. Town of God." In flashback, he continues, "I am boy, son of fisherman. But no fish in ocean. So we pray." The scene cuts to a Catholic Church, with priest in full vestments, a crucifix, and a statue of the Virgin Mary, flanked by archangels.

                    EZEQUIEL

>  But God, he no answer. Then come ...
>  Capitán Cambarro. He say, in great
>  Pacific Ocean, discover gold. He say,
>  people fools pray to God who no answer
>  prayer. He say he know god who bring
>  fish ... and more. Priest say no, but
>  Capitán say he bring great god to
>  Imboca.

    The scene shifts to Cambarro and the villagers gathered on rocks by the sea. Cambarro throws a small object into the sea—a pyramid carved with the symbol of Dagon. "I hear first time new prayer," says Ezequiel sadly. "I wish I never hear. I wish I never see. Soon, Imboca rich ... People go against God. No worship Cristo. All worship Dagon, or die." In flashback, villagers are smashing all the religious statuary in the Catholic church, and when the priest tries to stop them, Cambarro kills him with a sledgehammer. The symbol of Dagon is installed in the church, and Cambarro leads the villagers in prayer to their new god. "All Imboca pray to Dagon," mutters Ezequiel, all but his own father.

    Like many gods throughout human history, Dagon demands more than chants and adoration. He wants sacrifice, the first of which is Ezequiel's father, whose throat Cambarro slits with a ceremonial dagger at the altar in the former Catholic church. As the young Ezequiel kneels beside his dying parent, Cambarro notices a gold crucifix around the boy's neck. He lifts it so that the bloodstained dagger is juxtaposed in the shot with the shining cross, then snatches it off. "All worship Dagon, or die," says Ezequiel quietly. Unlike in *The Dunwich Horror*, the Order of Dagon is not defeated in the end. Indeed, like the main character in Lovecraft's novella, who learns that he, too, has "the Innsmouth look," Paul learns that he is actually a Cambarro, great-grandson of the Capitán and destined to be the consort of the current high priestess of Dagon, Uxia (Macarena Gómez). The invasive other triumphs; the dominant order is overthrown.

From fears of inversion and invasion, we turn now to fear of insignificance, the fear that, whatever our vision of the unseen order, it simply doesn't matter anymore.

## "Do I look like someone who cares what God thinks?" Unseen Orders and the Insignificance of God

In the *Hellraiser* films, the first of which was based on Clive Barker's 1986 novella *The Hellbound Heart* (a not-insignificant double entendre), the Cenobites are what remain of human beings when they have been imprisoned—*hellbound*—by their own attachments, whether to pleasure, to pain, or to fear itself. Not unlike many vampires, though, they cannot enter our world from theirs unless invited, specifically when the LeMarchand Configuration is solved. "The box," intones Pinhead, the Cenobite leader, in the eponymous *Hellraiser*. "You opened it. We came."

Throughout the first four films, we see what might be called an escalation of divine insignificance in the story arcs, an increasing movement to dismiss the importance of the dominant religious tradition. Though the franchise's construction of reality is clearly based on popular Western understandings of heaven and hell, with each installment, God's presence is diminished and the church is shown incapable of resisting the challenge of the Cenobites. Rather than look at one film in depth, I shall examine moments from each of the first four films that demonstrate clearly the emerging pattern of God's insignificance. Some of these moments are almost throwaways—quick shots whose significance lies in their presence in the films at all; others all but define the *Hellraiser* franchise.

Before we begin, it is worth pointing out some of the fundamental inversions represented by the Cenobites themselves.

In *Hellraiser*, for example, when the female lead, Kirsty (Ashley Laurence), first encounters them, she asks, "Who are you?" To which Pinhead replies cryptically, "We are explorers in the further regions of experience. Demons to some, angels to others." His response points once again to the central metataxon of horror—the inversion or reversal of accepted religious categories as a means of invoking the horrific. That is, are they demons, or are they angels? With his shaved head ice-pale and covered with a grid of livid scars, each intersection pierced with a golden nail, Pinhead hardly fits the image of an angel. But, then, neither does Gabriel in *The Prophecy*. Perhaps he is just one more angel we don't want to meet, one more messenger from an unseen order that cares little for the concerns of humankind.

In terms of metataxis, though, it is not insignificant that, while those who have commented on the *Hellraiser* series almost inevitably (and often, I would argue, superficially) refer to Cenobite dress as "S&M black-leather garb" (Freeland, 2000, 253), only one (Kane, 2006) has noticed that "cenobite" is an explicitly religious term. In the Roman Catholic Church, there are two monastic orders: the eremitic (those who live as hermits) and the cenobitic (those who live in religious community). The *Hellraiser* Cenobites invert a number of the characteristics of the latter. Pinhead's costume resembles a medieval cassock. An initial draft of the screenplay includes a scene in which Cenobites are seen in something resembling medieval monastic cells. Indeed, in Barker's novella, the Cenobites are introduced as "theologians of the Order of the Gash. Summoned from their experiments in the higher reaches of pleasure, to bring their ageless heads into a world of rain and failure" (1986, 4). When Frank, one of the central protagonists, has completed his ritual preparations for their arrival, Barker notes that "No cardinal, eager for the fisherman's shoes, could have been more diligent" (1986, 5). Even "the Order of the Gash" is polysemous, drawing one's attention (alternately or simultaneously) to (a) the Cenobites as a religious community; (b) the medieval religious practice of mortification; (c) the various wounds and scars the Cenobites display; and, since the process of becoming a Cenobite is one of death and horrific rebirth, (d) the British use of "gash" as slang for "vagina."

Most of the first film's action takes place in the Cotton house, the family home into which Larry (Andrew Robinson) and his new bride, Julia (Clare Higgins), are moving. Unbeknownst to them, Larry's brother Frank (Sean Chapman) solved the LeMarchand puzzle box there and was taken by the Cenobites. Throughout the film, the house itself illustrates that the dominant religion is on the wane. In the opening sequences, a statue of Christ is juxtaposed with a cockroach crawling across a carving of a couple having sex. As Larry and Julia inspect the house, they find a shrine of sorts in a downstairs bedroom—an unidentified holy figure, wearing both a halo (suggesting either a saint or an angel) and a crucifix, but holding in her hands a platter on which rests a severed head. "Don't worry," Larry assures Julia, "this stuff means nothing to me. It all goes." As Julia explores the upper floors, she passes the Christ statue, giving it a cold, bitter glance. Later, when Larry's daughter, Kirsty, arrives to help them unpack, she finds a variety of Catholic artifacts—holy cards, pictures, plates, and statuary—discarded in the front yard. Four statues of the sacred heart of Jesus are gathered beside one of the Virgin Mary as the Lady of Grace and another of Michelangelo's *Piéta*—Mary holding the body of the crucified Jesus. Two other statues flank the arrangement. One appears to be St. Ignatius Loyola, the founder of the Jesuit Order, though this statue is blindfolded; the other is a smaller version of the statue in the bedroom. Finally, in the film's dénouement sequences, as Kirsty hides from Frank—now escaped from the Cenobites, resurrected by the power of blood, and wearing his own brother's skin—a life-size statue of Jesus falls from a closet, startling her. Shaking with fear, she pushes the statue back into place and closes the door. She cannot rely on the power of God to fight either Frank or the Cenobites; she must solve the

LeMarchand Configuration on her own and return them to their own world.

In the first sequel, *Hellbound: Hellraiser II*, we learn more about the origin of the Cenobites, as they come to occupy center stage in the *Hellraiser* mythology. We learn that their hell is not the fire and brimstone the Christian Church has taught for centuries, but an endless sequence of shadowy corridors, funhouse mirrors, carnival clowns, and terrors drawn from the depths of one's own mind. We are alone in this hell with whatever scares us the most. Like the Cenobites trapped by their own desires, we make the hells we occupy. Presiding over all is the Lord of Hell—Leviathan—an enormous polyhedron from which emanates beams of pure darkness. Just as there is no pity in the hearts of the Cenobites—"No tears, please," Pinhead tells Kirsty in the previous film. "It's a waste of good suffering"—there is no power of God here. There is, however, the faintest call for the divine—a plea so subtle, it is almost subliminal. When we first see Leviathan, composer Christopher Young's soundtrack incorporates into the music a bass choir chanting the Morse code signals for G-O-D, something Paul Kane suggests is there "to counterbalance the evil" (2006, 64). Rather than a counterbalance, though, it seems to speak to the increasing sense of God's absence. A rhythmic counterpoint to the classical problem of evil, it asks where God is in the midst of great suffering. If the code is there in the soundtrack to signify God's presence then the subtlety with which the point is made only underscores God's insignificance in the face of Pinhead and his followers.

What is almost subliminal in *Hellbound* is unavoidable in *Hellraiser III: Hell on Earth*. In this film's penultimate sequences, as reporter Joey Summerskill (Terry Farrell) flees from Pinhead and his growing army of Cenobites, she seeks refuge in a large Catholic Church. A priest (Clayton Hill) tries to calm her, telling her the same thing we have heard in so many other horror movies: "Demons? Demons are not real. They're parables, metaphors."

Even as he finishes, the church doors creak open, and, backlit from the street, Pinhead appears, stark, pale, and silent.

As he stalks slowly down the aisle into the sanctuary, stained glass windows on either side implode as he passes. The priest holds up a crucifix, shouting, "How dare you?" But, because even demons can quote scripture, Pinhead replies, "Thou shalt not bow down before any graven image," and the heavy metal cross melts in the cleric's hand. Pinhead walks behind the massive altar and sweeps away the altar cross and chalice. Framed by the tall altar candles, he spreads his arms in benediction, then carefully pulls two long nails from the multitude in his head and pierces his palms with them. Raising his arms in imitation of the crucifixion, he drops his head to one side and proclaims, "I am the Way." Enraged by this blasphemy, as his church begins to fall down around them, the priest attacks, crying, "You'll burn in hell for this." "Burn?" replies the Cenobite, easily subduing the man. "Oh, such a limited imagination." Pulling off a piece of his own flesh, he tells the helpless priest, "This is my body, this is my blood. Happy are they who come to *my* supper." As Pinhead forces the priest to eat, Joey tries unsuccessfully to solve the puzzle box, the only power that can contain the Cenobites. What was implicit in the first two films is now explicit: God is no longer a factor in the plans of Hell.

In many ways, the third sequel, *Hellraiser: Bloodline*, is the most ambitious of the franchise, seeking to weave together the numerous strands of the emerging *Hellraiser* mythology and to account both for the box's origin and its future. As a result of studio interference at the post-production phase, however, director Kevin Yagher withdrew his name from the film, and the Director's Guild of America's placeholder name, Alan Smithee, was used instead. This is unfortunate, because Yagher's vision for the film held such promise.

John Merchant (Bruce Ramsay), an architect and descendant of the toymaker Phillipe, has created a building-size version of the LeMarchand Configuration, which, unknown to him, has the potential to act as a permanent doorway to the Cenobites' unseen world. Indeed, when Pinhead sees it for the first time, he declares to the demon, Angelique, that "this is not a room. This is a holocaust waiting to wake itself." Since "human acquiescence is as easily obtained by terror as by temptation," Pinhead tries to coerce Merchant into finishing his design, and when the architect meets the Cenobite for the first time, he exclaims weakly, "Oh, my God." Though many franchise fans regard *Bloodline* as the weakest of the *Hellraiser* films, the next line defines both the series and the sociophobic it discloses:

```
PINHEAD
Do I look like someone who cares what
God thinks?
```

Obviously not. But the important question here is: Why? Why don't you seem to care what God thinks? This is the challenge of insignificance, the narrative arc that has been building since the first film: the fear that the gods to whom we pray or make offerings, whose altars we adorn with service and sacrifice, whose rules we follow and to whose promises we cling, simply don't matter. A deeper question is whether their insignificance in the face of an unseen order such as the Gash, is one of impotence or absence. Are the gods powerless, or do they no longer exist? The presence of the demonic in horror films does not necessarily (or even frequently) translate into the concomitant presence of the divine. Indeed, in most of these films either God is notably absent or God's power has been decidedly usurped. Despite the fact that supernatural events and phenomena very often precipitate the films' narrative crises—circumstances that draw explicitly on the dominant Christian understanding of the unseen order— the supernatural (at least in the form of divine intervention) plays only a limited role in their resolution. Almost inevitably, humans must rely on their own resources and ingenuity to resolve these crises. They must effect their own salvation, and films that do insert some kind of deus ex machina—for example, *Bless the Child* or *Omen III: The Final Conflict*—are decried for doing so by legions of horror fans. As deity is colloquially understood in the West, God is often little more than the cultural backdrop against which the real action in horror films is played out. Even in a film like *The Exorcist*, the central resolution of which is predicated on the action of an omnipotent, omnibenevolent deity, it is not the power of the divine but the self-sacrifice of the human that ultimately frees the possessed Regan. Though we might be tempted to see in this a reflection of how Christians understand the divine sacrifice, horror films also speak to the fear that our gods have grown insignificant.

The problem here, of course, is that the demonic is a dyadic concept; it only really makes religious sense in terms of the divine. Thus, it is not unimportant that these narrative crises are predicated on a religiously oriented universe. Indeed, it may be that one of the things that makes this particular kind of horror horrifying is precisely the apparent absence of God in the face of supernatural evil—and a concomitant longing for the return of the omnipotent Divine in the face of the apparent secularization of late modern society. The comfort of God's presence has been taken away, but the terrors and hazards from which, for millennia, we believe God's presence protected us are still very much alive and kicking, slashing, rending, and brutalizing. That is, rather than a loose backdrop against which a multitude of cinematic horrors are played out, the practical absence of benevolent deity is the linchpin that allows these films to succeed as horror, as cinematic comment on the fear of secularization, not necessarily the reality of it, and the ambivalence of our ongoing attempts to retain belief in an omnipotent and omnibenevolent deity. As the German officer says to Father Merrin in *Exorcist: The Beginning*, just before shooting ten of Merrin's parishioners, "God is not here today, priest."

## THE UNSEEN ORDER AND
## THE FALLACY OF RESOLUTION

Echoing Berger, in *Religion and Its Monsters*, Beal points out that "biblical monsters . . . stand for the haunting sense of precariousness and uncertainty that looms along the edges of the world, the edges of society, the edges of consciousness, and the edges of religious understanding and faith" (2002, 57). Put thus, the unseen orders to which "religious understanding and faith" inevitably advert are like the headlights of a speeding car, sweeping along a winding roadway on an endless, moonless night—now illuminating the road, now turning, elevating, or depressing to reveal the trees, ditches, and rock walls that line the passage. With each brief illumination, patterns emerge that allow us navigation. With each pattern, however, shadows deepen, and the uncertainty of faith, the precariousness of belief, is thrown into such high relief that it demands constant maintenance and reinforcement to keep it from slipping off the road into angst and despair. Put simply, we need to tell ourselves constantly that what we believe about the world is true, that our perceptions of reality are not in vain. Without this ongoing reinforcement, the darkness closes in and we are lost. To some of these patterns we cling, desperate in our attempt to avoid the shadows by which they are formed. "Evil, supernatural forces (such as Satan)," for example, writes Rodney Stark in *One True God*, "are essential to the most rational conception of divinity" (2001, 25). That is, in the unseen order, it is the very shadows themselves that give the pattern depth and texture—that give it "reality." The angelic means little without the demonic, and vice versa.

Monsters, continues Beal, are continually "warning us to retreat into the established order of things" (2002, 161). More importantly, he notes that these demonstrations of the monstrous "are not created [in us], but awakened" (Beal, 2002, 161–62). The distinction here between "creation" and "awakening" can hardly be overstated in the context of religion and cinema horror. That is, we may have convinced ourselves that God loves everyone, that gentle Jesus is meek and mild, that angels are like divinely appointed nannies charged with looking out for a race perennially incapable of growing up, that Norse Frost Giants are simply chilly friends on whom desperate teenagers can call to deal with school-yard bullies (RavenWolf, 1998, 211), or that the Sumerian *magna mater*, Inanna, is all about motherhood and universal benevolence (Telesco, 1998; cf. Thomas, 2004), but somewhere in the primal recesses of our cultural consciousness—a significant part of which, as *homo narrans*, exists in the stories we tell ourselves in order to reinforce the way we believe the world to be—we suspect that the darkness at the edge of our headlights is still populated by far more dangerous realities.

The reawakening of the monstrous, the fearful, the horrific is only the precursor to the presentation of awakening in the audience. That which terrifies already exists, long before it comes to the screen. In the *Hellraiser* series, the Cenobites and their horrific world are not created by those who control LeMarchand's puzzle box; neither the malevolent Djinn of the *Wishmaster* series nor the explosive poltergeists of *The Amityville Horror* come into being with the granting of wishes or the purchase of haunted houses—they are always and already there, just beyond our headlights, waiting to step out of the dark. As Berger puts it, "every nomos is an area of meaning carved out of a vast mass of meaninglessness, a small clearing of lucidity in a formless, dark, always ominous jungle. Seen in the perspective of the individual"—though I am suggesting also and perhaps more deeply in the context of society—"every nomos represents the bright 'dayside' of life, tenuously held onto against the sinister shadows of the 'night'" (1967, 23). That is, the nomos is the set of headlights that brings a fleeting sense of meaning to the vast ocean of dark through which we move.

# 4

# NO SANCTUARY
## Ambivalence and the Fear of Sacred Places

> PINHEAD
> This is not a room... this is a
> holocaust waiting to wake itself.
> *(Hellraiser: Bloodline)*

### OUTTAKES: *28 DAYS LATER* AND *RESIDENT EVIL: APOCALYPSE*

Directed by Danny Boyle, a British director who came to the attention of the international cinema community in 1996 with *Trainspotting*, a hard-edged look at heroin addiction in working class Edinburgh, *28 Days Later* is both a zombie film—and not. Jimmy (Cillian Murphy) is a bicycle courier in London. After an accident, he awakens "28 days later" in a deserted hospital in the middle of a deserted city. As he wanders the streets, the fullness of the horror becomes evident. Animal rights activists have freed chimps on which, we assume, government weapons research was being performed. All we are told is that the chimps had been infected with "rage," a mysterious infection that spreads through any bodily fluid contact and manifests within seconds in the newly infected. Though not technically dead themselves, they are in a zombie state and are driven by the disease to attack the uninfected. In the typology of zombie films that will be discussed in more detail in the next chapter, these poor creatures are the product of the hubris of science run amok.

At first glance, there is little to recommend the film to a consideration of religion and cinema horror. Early on, however, as Jimmy searches the city for answers, he visits a Roman Catholic church. Entering through the nave in the shadow of the cross, he makes his way through the darkened building, on one wall of which is written: "Repent . . . the end is extremely fucking nigh." Emerging into the choir loft overlooking the sanctuary, he sees bodies strewn among the pews. He speaks, and a few of the infected—principally the parish priest—rush to attack. Barely escaping the cleric and his horrific parishioners, Jimmy flees the church for the deserted city. Like the old church on Beacon Hill in John Carpenter's *The Fog*, the church in *28 Days Later* has lost the power to provide sanctuary for its people. It has become, rather, their living tomb.

Like *28 Days Later*, neither *Resident Evil* nor its sequels, *Resident Evil: Apocalypse* and *Resident Evil: Extinction* are religiously oriented zombie films, and reanimation in these films is not the result of religious ritual or supernatural intervention. Rather, based on Sony PlayStation's best-selling videogame, the *Resident Evil* saga is another woeful tale of bioweapons research gone horribly awry. Deep beneath Racoon City is the Hive, a vast underground research laboratory in which the Umbrella Corporation has created—by design or by accident—a horde of flesh-eating zombies. And, like in *28 Days Later*, one of the first places the main characters in *Resident Evil: Apocalypse* take refuge is a church—thick stone walls, solid timbered doors, and perhaps the lingering comfort of a God who seems anything but close to hand at the moment. But there is no safety in this sanctuary either, and the survivors are hunted by mutant creatures that look eerily like the gargoyles who sit atop the church's ramparts. Horrifically inverting the eucharist, a priest keeps his infected and ravenous sister tied to a chair in his office behind the vestry, feeding her on body parts he scavenges from the street.

A horror-action vehicle for such moderately bankable stars as Milla Jovovich and Oded Fehr, *Resident Evil: Apocalypse* was a big-budget Hollywood film, costing more than five times its British counterpart, *28 Days Later*. Both directors, though, chose to use churches in the crucial first refuge sequences, establishing in this way that the social framework of safety, of sanctuary, has been irrevocably disrupted. If we take seriously the claim that feature films are among the world's most carefully plotted and minutely planned cultural products, then we must acknowledge that the choice for a church in both instances was deliberate, that it has meaning both within the context of the films and for the audiences outside the frame. And, if that's the case, then we are forced to ask what the message is.

In *Night of the Living Dead*, when George Romero's "first family" sought refuge from the hordes of zombies in a farmhouse, critics were quick to point out the cinematic allusion to the late modern assault on the nuclear family and the social ravages of racism. Later, in *Dawn of the Dead*, when the survivors barricaded themselves in a shopping mall, many claimed that this was the director's commentary on the mindless consumerism that has gripped late modern America—we are drawn like zombies to shopping centers, and no matter how much we buy, no matter how much we consume (that is, no matter how much we eat), we are never satisfied (see, for example, Paffenroth, 2006). What, then, of the choice for a church?

As a human and a social phenomenon, religion is not only cosmological story, doctrinal belief, ritual practice, and daily devotional experience. It is also very much a function of place, and, as Jonathan Z. Smith notes, "place directs attention" (1987, 103). That is, place directs *our* attention *to* something. Churches, temples, mosques, shrines, ritual sites of all kinds are places excerpted from the normal ebb and flow of life, set apart as particular loci of power, and meant to direct our attention to the reality of the unseen order. "When one enters a temple," Smith continues, "one enters marked-off space," though he is quick to point out that nothing is "inherently sacred or profane. These are not substantial categories, but situational ones. Sacrality is above all a category of emplacement" (1987, 104). That is, it is a social category, a product of agreement among those for whom that particular place has meaning.

If "place directs attention," then it is worth asking to what places cinema horror would have us pay attention, and why. Where the principal sociophobic from the previous chapter related to a change in the sacred order, this chapter considers how the architectural emplacement of that order—churches, temples, and other sites set apart for the unseen order—are portrayed in a variety of horror films. And, if a change in the sacred order is one particular fear explored by cinema horror, then fear of a change in the places sacred to that order would seem to follow logically.

## SETTING THE PLACE APART: AMBIVALENCE AND THE SOCIOPHOBICS OF SACRED SPACE

As noted briefly in chapter 2, the sacred space as place of potential terror has a long history in both religious and popular culture: Moses on his way up Mount Sinai; the Israelites and the Ark of the Covenant, the Tabernacle, and, later, the Holy of Holies in the Temple. It matters little whether these things happened historically. What is important is that they represent the fearsome potential for death, destruction, and sundry mayhem as the inevitable price of transgressing the boundaries between the sacred and the mundane.

### *The Ambivalence of Sacred Space*

Over two millennia later, our ambivalence toward sacred spaces remains. The so-called Graveyard poets, for example, forerunners of the gothic revival who flourished in the first half of the eighteenth century and represented one aspect of the rebellion against the rationalism of the Enlightenment, set their works among fog-shrouded cemeteries, ruined cathedrals, and gloomy churchyards. Indeed, Walter Kendrick argues that they should be known more correctly as the "Churchyard poets," because their dark muse took them not to burial places located far from centers of population, but to cemeteries attached specifically to chapels and churches (1991, 24–25).

Though supernatural terrors are usually explained away at the end of her work, Ann Radcliffe's gothic fiction made her one of the most popular writers of the late eighteenth century. Strongly influenced by Radcliffe's *The Mysteries of Udolpho* ([1794] 1987), Matthew Lewis' *The Monk* ([1796] 1998) sets most of its horrific action in a Capuchin monastery outside Madrid, while Mrs. Carver's *Horrors of Oakendale Abbey* ([1799] 2006) features cloister walls that drip blood and gory specters seen in church tower windows. Although he is perhaps best known as a forger of alleged Shakespeare plays, William-Henry Ireland also wrote a number of gothic novels, including *The Abbess* ([1799] 2006), which was not dissimilar to Lewis' work, and *Gondez the Monk* ([1805] 2005), in which Scotland's Robert the Bruce takes refuge in the sinister Monastery of Saint Columba. Playing on the gothic penchant for locating tales of terror in putatively sacred spaces, Jane Austen's *Northanger Abbey* ([1818] 2006) relentlessly satirized such writers as Radcliffe and Lewis. In his *Gothic Bibliography*, Montague Summers lists dozens of titles that include "abbey" or "priory." Though Kendrick points out that these "buzzwords" served as a kind of "minimal, rudimentary advertising" at the time (1991, 78), that they could function effectively in that manner speaks volumes to the sociophobics of their intended audience.

Regarded by H. P. Lovecraft as "gifted with an almost diabolical power of calling horror by gentle steps from the midst of prosaic daily life" ([1927] 2000, 69), the eminent Cambridge medievalist M. R. James often set his ghost stories in abbeys, cloisters, chapels, and cathedrals. Indeed, according to S. T. Joshi, James' own deeply held religious beliefs so informed his fiction that his stories often function as cautionary tales "on the dangers of straying from orthodoxy" (2005, xiv).

Although, in Bram Stoker's *Dracula*, the Carfax estate that Jonathan Harker purchases on behalf of the vampire "is close to an old chapel or church" ([1897] 1998, 54), by the time Universal Studios had rewritten the story (actually Hamilton Deane's stage version) for the screen in 1930, the church and the manor house had been combined into "Carfax Abbey"—a place so deeply ingrained in the cinematic mythology of the Count that many are surprised to learn that no such place exists in the novel itself. Two of Stoker's other works, however, *The Jewel of Seven Stars* ([1903] 1996) and *Lair of the White Worm* ([1911] 1998), locate their horrors explicitly in the domain of the sacred space. The former, which Hammer released in 1971 as *Blood from the Mummy's Tomb*, played on the British fascination with Egyptian tombs, telling the story of "Tera, Queen of the Egypts" (Stoker, [1903] 1996, 109) and her undead fate at the hands of jealous Egyptian priests. For his last novel, Stoker moved from the tombs of ancient Egypt to the midlands of England—the Anglo-Saxon kingdom of Mercia—and a sacred site known to the Romans as "Diana's Grove," but which, in the Mercian language, was the "lair of the white worm" ([1911] 1998, 39–40). In Ken Russell's cinematic adaptation of the novel, the ritual dénouement comes when snake-god worshipper Lady Sylvia Marsh (Amanda Donohoe) tries to sacrifice the virginal Eve Trent (Catherine Oxenberg) to the serpentine object of her devotion.

In the first decades of the twentieth century, pulp magazines specializing in the "weird" fiction of writers like Lovecraft, O. Henry, Robert E. Howard, and the prolific Seabury Quinn continued the tradition of locating sacred terror in sacred space. From the early 1920s to the rise of the Cold War, cover art for *Weird Tales* regularly depicted ritual settings—like *Lair of the White Worm,* usually involving scantily clad women and impending sacrifice. For a story in the September 1925 issue, Greye La Spina's "The Gargoyle" (subtitled "A Tale of Devil Worship"), Andrew Brosnatch painted a young blond woman prostrate on an altar as satanic acolytes prepare to do her in with a ritual dagger. Similar artwork adorns the covers for stories such as "The Peacock's Shadow" (E. Hoffmann Price, November 1926), "The Gray Killer" (Everill Worrel, November 1929), "The Druid's Shadow" (Seabury Quinn, October 1930), and "Red Nails" (Robert E. Howard, July 1936)—not to mention being replicated almost precisely in Chano Urueta's 1939 Mexican horror film, *El Signo de la Muerta*. For Henry S. Whitehead's "The People of Pan" (March 1929), C. C. Serif depicted a group of bound bodies lying beneath an enormous idol of a ram while a woman offers incense and prayers. Alluding to the kind of torture meted out by the Inquisition—and beginning a series of covers that depicted the torture of women—Serif's artwork for Quinn's "The Lost Lady" (January 1931) showed a woman bound to a post and whipped, while incense from two gold censers fills the air and a creature of indeterminate lineage chants in the background. A year later, Quinn published "The Devil's Bride" (February 1932), and Serif obliged with cover art depicting two robed figures crucifying a naked woman. Rather than scourging or crucifixion, cover art for Quinn's "Living Buddhess" (November 1937), this time by Margaret Brundage, shows a nearly naked woman dressed not unlike a Vegas showgirl in gold tiara, spider-web bra, and peacock fantail. Sitting cross-legged with her hands bound in her lap—approximating, and rather unsubtly inverting, the ritual *mudra* of Buddhist meditation—she looks up uncertainly as a man dressed in the pulp fiction version of a Tibetan Buddhist monk hovers malevolently.

"Monsters seem to be particularly fond of religious spaces and decor," notes Timothy Beal, "especially the kind that has not been modernized: decrepit graveyards full of crumbling tombstones, dusty candlelit cathedrals strewn with crosses and communion goblets. And why do these same sacred spaces so often give us moderns the creeps?" (2002, 89). Perhaps the question could be usefully rewritten as: Why do we seem so drawn to locate monsters in religious spaces? Why are we so apt to surround them with religious accoutrements? Could it be because these same "sacred spaces" that give us the creeps also give rise to the very monsters that creep about within them?

Since sacred places direct our attention to the gods to whom they are dedicated, if those gods have been challenged or overthrown, that is often reflected in the way their sites are depicted. There are two distinct aspects to this particular sociophobic: (a) fear of the sacred place itself, and (b) fear that the sacred place will be destroyed or contaminated in some way. While the former is usually a function of how we continually construct the threatening religious Other, the latter confronts us with ambiguities about the security of our own sacred places. Arguably, these have the most potential to frighten us when they occur together.

The consistent religious thread that ties together the five *Mummy* films made by Universal Pictures during the 1930s and 1940s is a Hollywood version of the ancient Egyptian religion of the XIII Dynasty (roughly 1800–1600 B.C.E.) as imagined by American filmmakers, and a secretive group, the fictional Priests of Arkam, who have guarded for millennia the tombs of the priest, Kharis, and his forbidden love, Princess Ananka. In *The Mummy's Curse*, there is some indication of a contest between an incursive religion and a nominally dominant (though significantly weakened) tradition. In a strange mix of narrative locales—ostensibly, in *The Mummy's Ghost*, Kharis took the young woman Amina, who aged into Ananka as he carried her, down into a swamp in New England—*The Mummy's Curse* begins in the swamp twenty-five years later, but it appears to have shifted to a bayou in Cajun country, and the setting now includes a ruined gothic monastery serving as a temporary home for Kharis and his Arkamite guardians. Whether it makes sense in the geographic context or not, filmmakers continue to rely on the archetypal power of a sacred place to set their tales of terror. Bernard L. Schubert's shooting script describes the setting as "once probably a chapel in the old Monastery, it is now a dim, vaulted, forbidding room with stone floor and dark walls (much like the interior of the temple in 'The Mummy's Hand')" (in Mank, 2000, 27).

As the two Arkamite priests, Ilzor (Peter Coe) and Ragheb (Martin Kosleck), raise Kharis with fluid made from the sacred tana leaves—another narrative thread consistent across the series—an old man, a sacristan, stumbles into the ruined sanctuary, torch in hand, and sees the mummy sitting up in his sarcophagus.

> SACRISTAN
>
> I am Michael, self-ordained caretaker of this monastery.
>
> RAGHEB
>
> We thought this place was abandoned...
>
> SACRISTAN
>
> This house of worship, though silent for many years, is not to be desecrated by such pagan customs. I'm afraid I shall have to ask you to take these sacrilegious things away.

Not surprisingly, the sacristan is summarily dispatched by Kharis. Once again, the dominant tradition has fallen into ruin and can no longer protect its devotees from the invasive religious Other. With the exception of an appeal to the goddess Isis in *The Mummy*, there is no overt religious technology by which Kharis is fought or defeated throughout the films; unlike various *Dracula* movies, neither crosses nor holy water can destroy him. Here the contest between competing religious traditions is played out as the sacred spaces of the one are taken over by the other.

## THE SOCIOPHOBICS OF SACRED SPACE

Numerous popular films reflect our fear of sacred places. Consider Indiana Jones barely escaping with his life as he steals the small golden idol in *Raiders of the Lost Ark*, or his near demise in the eponymous *Temple of Doom* three years later. Jackie Chan reprises *Raiders* in the opening gambit of *Operation Condor*, when he attempts to steal jewels from the body of an idol but is attacked by devotees for drinking the sacred water. In the *Highlander* universe, both the film franchise and the television series, the rules of engagement forbid the Immortals from fighting on holy ground. The enormously popular *Lara Croft: Tomb Raider* locates the second-act action sequences in an abandoned Cambodian temple, where the intrepid Lady Croft (Angelina Jolie) battles an enormous quasi-Hindu idol and hordes of its animated minions. For his adaptations of the venerable *Mummy* story (1999, 2001), Stephen Sommers set much of the occult action in the fictional Egyptian necropolis of Hamunaptra, "the City of the Dead."

Of the numerous places we set apart for cinema horror, four general locales emerge. Though these are hardly discrete categories—cemeteries are often attached to churches; what is the dedicated religious building of one faith is the pagan temple of another—they serve as a useful heuristic device for exploring the different domains of sacred terror.

## The House of God: Dedicated Religious Buildings

In the nominally Christian West, cinema horror use of dedicated religious buildings means the desecrated sanctuary in *The Exorcist* and *Hellraiser III: Hell on Earth*; the Byzantine church in *Exorcist: The Beginning*, built atop a pagan temple and buried as soon as it was finished to seal in the evil the older building contains; the devastated cathedral in which the *Children of the Damned* take refuge; decayed and defiled sanctuaries in films ranging from Mario Bava's *Black Sunday* to Tony Mandile's *Midnight Mass*, and from the tent revival of *The Visitation*'s satanic devotee to the convent of putative Catholic nuns in *To the Devil . . . a Daughter*, whose religious life is really dedicated to the worship of Astoreth.

In the "English Gothic" style, Hammer Studios' hallmark from the 1950s to the early 1970s (see Rigby, 2002), ruined and tainted churches feature prominently, nowhere more, perhaps, than when the good order established by the church is threatened by the evil of Count Dracula. As mentioned in chapter 1, the opening sequence in Freddie Francis' *Dracula Has Risen from the Grave* shows a young woman drained of blood and hanging like a clapper in the church bell. Despite the fact that Dracula (Christopher Lee), "perpetrator of these obscene evils," ostensibly has been dispatched, the malevolence he represents is not fully vanquished. When Monsignor Müller confronts the villagers about their unwillingness to attend mass, he learns that the fear of Dracula still weighs heavily on the town and manifests itself in the fear the people have of their own putative sanctuary.

VILLAGER

It's the shadow, sir.

MONSIGNOR

The shadow?

VILLAGER

The shadow of his castle, sir--

INNKEEPER

It touches the church--

VILLAGER

In the evenings, it touches it.

Between 1970 and 1974, Lee returned four times as the Count for Hammer Studios. Peter Sasdy's *Taste the Blood of Dracula*, for example, which is regarded by film critic Jonathan Rigby as the best Hammer sequel and, among other things, a "powerful attack on Edwardian double standards" (2002, 167), begins precisely where *Dracula Has Risen* leaves off. While the Count's shadow is enough to taint the sanctuary in the earlier film, in *Taste the Blood,* Sasdy and screenwriter Anthony Hinds (writing as John Elder) locate the vampire's principal resurrection sequences in the chapel crypt of an abandoned church outside London. Hammer's gothic moodiness at its best, the sanctuary features a large drawing of the Baphomet hanging behind the altar, which is itself draped in black and adorned with black candles, occult symbols, and the church's own altarware. In this film, Dracula no longer merely touches the church, he has invaded it and made it his own. Using the vampire's powdered blood from the previous film and perverting all the elements of the Eucharist, four jaded and dissolute upper-class Englishmen conduct a black mass in an attempt to resurrect the Count—a trope revisited two years later in the dismal *Dracula A.D. 1972.* As Courtley (Ralph Bates) drinks the reconstituted blood of Dracula and begins to convulse, the others panic and kill him, fleeing the church. Once again, the church's influence as a force for good is questioned—it no longer serves as a sanctuary, but rather as a shell that plays host to an unholy resurrection. Just as Dracula was defeated in the previous film when he was impaled on the cross, here he is beaten when young Paul (Anthony Higgins), the son of one of the original four, reclaims the chapel for Christ, as it were. Throwing aside the vampiric accoutrements and tearing down the Baphomet, he lays a new white altar cloth and places fresh white candles on the altar. Surrounded by crosses on all sides, Dracula tries to escape by smashing through a stained glass window high above the altar. As he does, though, he has a vision of the chapel in its glory—hymns playing, altarware gleaming, a sanctuary once again. Screaming, he falls and dies on the altar, crumbling once again to dust.

As we can see, while the conflict between good and evil is often played out in dedicated sanctuaries like these, in some films they become the site of victory over malevolent forces rather than defeat. The climax in *Bless the Child,* for example, is an explicit contest between sacred spaces—a convent chapel where nuns pray for the safety of a young girl and her guardian, and a gloomy, gothic-style church that has been taken over by Satanists and prepared for ritual sacrifice. As the church begins to burn when the sacrifice is interrupted, three brilliant beings of light appear, angels who heal one of the main characters and protect another. In the end, the Satanists flee, and their leader is killed. As the now-tainted church burns to the ground, the sacred order is restored.

In the dénouement of Terence Fisher's *The Devil Rides Out*, a similar supernatural battle rages between the Duc de Richelieu (Christopher Lee) and the evil cult leader Mocata (Charles Grey). When the contest ends and Mocata is defeated, the satanic symbols on the walls of his ritual room crumble away to reveal a simple cross and Christian sanctuary. In all these films, the message seems to be that God has spoken and either reclaimed his house or destroyed that which was beyond redemption.

## *Strange Sanctuaries: The Temples of Other Gods*

The second order of ambivalence concerns the temples of other gods, the monumental touchstones of different, often more sinister unseen orders, and highlights the socially constructed nature of religious fears. What is a sacred site to one group becomes for others the architectural symbol of the dangerous religious Other. The Temple complex of Karnak, for example, located in Thebes, 450 miles south of Cairo on the east bank of the Nile River, is the principal setting for many of Universal's *Mummy* movies—though the site became "the great god, Karnak" when Hammer entered the franchise in the late 1950s. Representing the strange and the exotic, sites such as these signify the dangerous movement from modern to premodern ways of thinking. In the original *Mummy*, Helen Grosvenor (Zita Johann) looks out at the pyramids from her hotel balcony and laments, "The real Egypt. Are we really in this dreadful Cairo?" Drawing on popular interpretations of pre-Christian religion in Great Britain, Robin Hardy's *The Wicker Man* relocates human sacrifice (in the service of better agriculture) to "Summerisle," somewhere off the coast of modern Scotland. Though it has only recently received the acclaim it deserves—like *Hellraiser: Bloodline*, it suffered considerable studio interference—*Cinefantastique* labeled *The Wicker Man* "the *Citizen Kane* of horror films" (Rigby, 2002, 210). Even late modern vampire movies, which are all but divorced from their fin-de-siècle origins, prey on our propensities to locate horror in sacred space. Premiering as a 1981 Marvel comic book, the *Blade* film trilogy has gone on to construct an elaborate unseen order, a vampire religion complete with sacred texts, unfulfilled prophecies, and a temple dedicated to the coming incarnation of the Blood God.

Like the victorious sanctuary of the dominant tradition, there are occasionally cinema horror examples in which sacred sites of the religious Other protect those who oppose evil. As the *Mummy*'s modern incarnation of the virgin priestess Anck-es-en-Amon, for example, Helen Grosvenor appeals to a statue of Isis for protection from Im-Ho-Tep (Boris Karloff), and the mummy is destroyed. In *The Prophecy*, the angel Gabriel is ultimately defeated in a Navajo hogan as the sung prayers of the "enemy ghost way" are offered for the afflicted child, Mary.

## Congregations of the Dead

We also set apart places where the dead congregate—graveyards, cemeteries, tombs, and mausolea. There, we believe, our two worlds touch. This sociophobic is reflected in such ritual celebrations as All Saint's Day, the modern Pagan Samhain, and Mexico's *Dia de los Muertos*, all of which occur when practitioners believe the veil between our world and the unseen order is the least opaque. In Victor Halperin's *White Zombie*, villagers "afraid of the men who steal dead bodies" bury their loved ones "in the middle of the road—where people pass all the time." In Dan O'Bannon's camp horror classic *The Return of the Living Dead*, a secret chemical weapon is accidentally released and raises an army of zombies from the cemetery next door. Ostensibly based on a true story, the *Poltergeist* franchise is predicated on the desecration of Native American burial grounds by greedy land developers. Though cremation grounds in India provide little fodder for reanimated corpses, the prolific Bollywood producers and directors Shyam and Tulsi Ramsay did release *Hotel* in 1981. Essentially an Indian remake of *Poltergeist*, mysterious deaths occur when a wealthy industrialist builds a hotel on an abandoned graveyard. In Hong Kong tales of terror, many of which come with a liberal dash of comedy and kung fu, the action often revolves around the *kyonsi*, or hopping corpses. Guided to their final resting place through the careful ministrations of a Taoist priest, *kyonsi* are not innately evil. When the appropriate burial rituals have not been performed, however, or the rites have been performed incorrectly or in an inauspicious place, the ghosts often turn into vampires.

In dozens of mummy movies, it is the desecration of sacred burial grounds that inevitably releases the curse. As I will suggest in the following chapter, contrary to the thinly veiled erotica of vampire films, since Boris Karloff first lurched out of his sarcophagus in 1932, mummy movies are essentially tragic love stories—lovers kept eternally apart, one often doomed to guard the tomb of the other. Indeed, as one of the theatrical trailers for Terence Fisher's *The Mummy* intones somberly:

```
He was a high priest of the great god,
Karnak, until one night he attempted
the ultimate in blasphemy. He was
condemned to guard forever the princess
he had loved, and protect her from
intruders. He who robs the graves of
Egypt dies!
```

Whereas two of cinema horror's most famous denizens—Dracula and Frankenstein's monster—have literary origins, the third finds its roots in the popular obsession with Egyptology that had existed on both sides of the Atlantic for well over a century, and with popular fears surrounding the so-called "Curse of King Tutankhamen"—the urban legend that the deaths of the archeological team that found the Boy-Pharaoh's tomb were somehow linked to the discovery. Roughly fictionalized by Hammer as *The Mummy's Shroud*, but present in films ranging from *The Mummy's Tomb* to *Blood from the Mummy's Tomb*, the trope of a curse that follows those who invade and desecrate the burial places of the Egyptian dead has animated virtually every mummy film ever made.

In brief, the story of the curse is this. Taking the throne as early as nine years of age and dying when he was only eighteen, Tutankhamen reigned briefly and unremarkably in the Eighteenth Dynasty (r. 1336–1327 B.C.E.). Within three hundred years, Egyptian politics had erased him from official memory, and the whereabouts of his tomb were long forgotten. More than three millennia after his death, archeologist Howard Carter located what he believed was Tutankhamen's tomb buried in rubble in Luxor's Valley of the Kings. Summoning his patron, Lord Carnarvon, to be there at the triumphal moment, he opened the tomb in November 1922 and exposed the treasures within. Journalists quickly sensationalized the find, even inventing a curse allegedly written beside the entrance: "Death shall come on swift wings to him that toucheth the tomb of the pharaoh" ("Dr. Lucas").

Less than six months later, though, Carnarvon was dead, victim of complications from an untreated insect bite—though a "Paris prophetess" averred that his death was due to "Oriental occultism" ("Paris Prophetess has a theory"). Within four years, five more team members had died, giving the myth of a curse all but a life of its own. Despite understandable skepticism in the archeological community, a lengthy 1923 article in the *New York Times Saturday Magazine* heightened the mystery. Entitled "Pharaoh's Curse Clings to His Tombs" and complete with illustrations, the article included this sensational passage:

> It would seem strange, indeed, if a curse, undoubtedly uttered four thousand years ago, were to be potent for evil in the twenti-

eth century. But there are high authorities who maintain this. Dr. J. C. Mardrus today stands in the first rank of Oriental scholars, and he denies that he is addicted to the occult. But he believes firmly in Egyptian magic and is "absolutely convinced" that the priests of Isis and Osiris "knew how to focus upon and around the mummy certain dynamic powers of which we possess very incomplete notions." (Wilson, 1926, 3)

Mardrus was not, in fact, "in the first rank of Oriental scholars." He was a Cairo-born French physician who is noted primarily for translating *The Book of One Thousand and One Nights* from Arabic into French. Despite the fact that the curse had been debunked as early as 1934, for years—up until Carter's death in 1939, and the death of the last principal member of the archeological team, Alfred Lucas, in 1945—speculation about the curse haunted every aspect of the discovery. Indeed, without the curse and its continual media association with the Carter-Carnarvon team, one wonders whether the cinema phenomenon of *The Mummy* might ever have come to life at all.

In Karl Freund's 1932 production, for example, it is easy to see something of Mardrus in the enigmatic Dr. Muller (Edward Van Sloan), who counsels patience when Sir Joseph Whemple (Arthur Byron) and his young assistant Ralph Norton (Bramwell Fletcher) uncover the Scroll of Thoth along with the sarcophagus of Im-Ho-Tep. Clearly drawing on the Tutankhamen curse, the dialogue could easily have been written from the *Saturday Magazine* article:

```
            WHEMPLE (reading)
    'Death, eternal punishment for anyone
    who opens this casket, in the name of
    Amun-Ra, the King of the Gods.' Good
    heavens! What a terrible curse!

                 NORTON
    Well, let's see what's inside.
```

> MULLER
> Wait! We read the curse.
>
> WHEMPLE
> We recognize your mastery of the occult sciences, Muller, but I can't permit your beliefs to interfere with my work.
>
> NORTON
> Oh, come, Dr. Muller, surely a few thousand years in the earth would take the mumbo-jumbo off any old curse.

When Muller and Whemple leave the tent to discuss the matter further, the "authority on the Egyptian occult" warns the archeologist:

> MULLER
> The gods of Egypt still live in these hills, in their ruined temples. The ancient spells are weaker, but some of them are still potent. And I believe that you have in your hut the Scroll of Thoth itself, which contains the great spell by which Isis raised Osiris from the dead.

Nearly thirty years later, when Hammer brought the *Mummy* franchise back to life with Terence Fisher's remake of Universal's *The Mummy's Hand*, the tomb's guardian, Mehemet Bey (George Pastell), confronts archeologist Stephen Banning (Felix Aylmer) with a familiar warning: "You would do well to remember the ancient saying: 'He who robs the graves of Egypt dies!'" Banning, of course, does not need the warning and opens the long-sealed tomb of the princess, Ananka (Yvonne Furneaux). The mummy

*Ambivalence and the Fear of Sacred Places* / 111

Kharis, Ananka's forbidden love and eternal guardian, is awakened, and the chase is on. Called "fast-moving pulp" by Andy Boot (1999, 93), who thought the script "an amalgam of every Universal mummy picture ever made," Fisher's film contains a key encounter in terms of the cinematic sociophobics of sacred space.

Brought to England from Egypt by Mehemet Bey, Kharis (Christopher Lee) begins to exact the measure of the curse, killing both Banning and his brother, Joseph, who was with him in Ananka's tomb. Sensing what has happened, Stephen's son, John (Peter Cushing), baits the Egyptian in an attempt to learn the mummy's whereabouts. During their verbal sparring, Bey comes off far more the reasoned (and reasonable) culturalist, whose responses make eminently more sense than the xenophobic (and implicitly racist) comments screenwriter Jimmy Sangster placed in the mouth of the British archeologist.

MEHEMET BEY

It has often puzzled me about archeologists. Has it never occurred to them that by opening the tombs of beings who are sacred, they commit an act of desecration?

JOHN BANNING

If we didn't, the history of your country, indeed of a great part of civilization, would still be an unknown.

MEHEMET BEY

Nevertheless, those tombs were sealed for all time. You are an intruder. You force your way in, you remove the remains of the long-dead kings, and send them to places like the British

Museum, where thousands of people can stare at them. Does this not trouble you at times? Your conscience, perhaps?

JOHN BANNING

No, it's my job. But it troubles you?

MEHEMET BEY

Why should it trouble me? I am a civilized man, Mr. Banning. To me, the dead are the dead. Clay.

Of course, we the audience know that the dead are anything but mere clay. For ancient Egyptians, one of the most horrific acts of vandalism was tomb desecration. Whether to rob the graves of the items placed with the dead or to recycle the stones for one's own tomb, the dead no longer have a name nor any place in the world. Their ability to reside in that place rests with their tomb and its undisturbed occupancy. Whether four years have passed or four thousand, to Mehemet Bey the "long-dead kings" occupy places set distinctly apart, sacred spaces bounded out of normal time and space. Though they pose no threat when undisturbed, they are off the map, as it were, places cursed by the gods for the protection of the gods.

## Fiction and Sacred Space

Finally, sacred spaces that take on lives of their own are the fictional places that speak most powerfully to our willingness to believe that this is not all there is. Though few fans would credence the secret ritual site in *Blade* and the massive machinery devoted to the incarnation of the Blood God, far more credence is given to the existence of ritual sacrifice and satanic orgies as they are portrayed in Hammer films such as *The Devil Rides Out*, *The Wicker Man*, *The Witches*, and *The Satanic Rites of Dracula*. These last two are particularly interesting for their inclusion in Gordon Wellesley's *Sex and the Occult*. Published in 1973 in a series entitled *Frontiers of the Unknown*, to illustrate the supposed connection between ritual sacrifice and an orgiastic black mass, Wellesley uses a still from Cyril Frankel's film *The Witches* showing the high priestess (Kay Walsh) about to sacrifice the requisite virgin schoolgirl (Ingrid Brett)—all of which takes place in a ruined church sanctuary. "Authentic detail in rites and artifacts," declares Wellesley, "lends conviction to a fictional film story" (1973, Fig. 13). To illustrate "black magic" and the "black mass," Wellesley uses three stills from *Satanic Rites*, the acknowledged nadir of Hammer's Dracula franchise and the film that drove Christopher Lee from the role forever. The third of these purports to show the "blood sacrifice," as a satanic high priestess (Barbara Yu Ling) prepares to ritually kill a black cock "over a girl's nude body." "Historically," Wellesley declares, though he offers no proof, "many children died this way" (1973, Fig. 16). In both of these we see ways in which the narrative phenomena of cinema horror becomes culturally intertextual. That is, the fictional space onscreen has both drawn upon and been used to reinforce popular beliefs about the satanic world offscreen. Indeed, the regularity with which "satanic panics" and "witchcraft scares" have emerged over the past several decades indicates how close to the cultural surface these fears remain, and how willing many of us are to believe the worst when they appear (cf. Barner-Barry, 2005; Best, Richardson, and Bromley, 1991; Nathan and Snedeker, 1995; Victor, 1993). As media theorist Gary Thompson puts it, "'entertainment texts' are among the most powerful and pervasive devices for confirming the ideas and values that underlie our culture—or its fundamental ideology, known as common sense" (1997, 344). However outlandish it may seem to others and whether supported by visions of the reel world or not, what people come to accept as common sense, as part of the cultural stock of knowledge on which they depend to make sense of their world, can have (and has had) undeniable real world consequences.

Like any other system of meaning, the process of sociophobics has certain empirical characteristics. Repetition, for example, especially the repetition of information that is not seriously challenged or questioned, or that appeals to the basic beliefs and exploits the extant prejudices of the target audience, is an important aspect in the construction of a potent social fear. If, like the curse of King Tut's tomb, the repetition of information comes in different forms, via different media, and from different voices, then so long as the basic message remains the same, the impression or perception created by the sociophobic will be reinforced. It may not be believed by all those who hear or experience it, but it will be considerably more difficult to dismiss out-of-hand. Not everyone may be convinced that there is a curse of the mummy's tomb, but the reinforcement of the sociophobic by different means keeps the darkness in sight just beyond the campfire.

"As with any folk legends," writes folklorist Jan Harold Brunvard, "urban legends gain credibility from specific details of time and place or from references to source authorities" (1981, 3). Though religiously oriented horror rarely rises to the level of urban legend—despite rumors of this disaster or that on the set, or after—they are often studded with "specific details" that are close enough to "the real thing" to fool those who know no better. Indeed, there are a number of films that have urban legends attached to them: *Rosemary's Baby*, *The Exorcist*, *Poltergeist*, *The Believers*, and *Blood from the Mummy's Tomb*, to name just a few (see Brottman, 1998; McCabe, 1999). Given the high rate of biblical awareness in North America, for example, but the relatively low rate of biblical literacy—for a devastating critique of this, see Prothero, 2007—this applies particularly to references to "source authorities" such as the Bible: the fictitious Deuteronomy quote that opens *Lost Souls* or the similarly fictitious excerpts from Ezekiel that Jules (Samuel L. Jackson) quotes in Quentin Tarantino's *Pulp Fiction* (1994). Even entirely fictitious sacred texts like Lovecraft's *The Necronomicon*, are occasionally mistaken for the real thing by zealous but misinformed commentators (see, for example, Perlmutter, 2004). The surface function of a scriptural reference—like the deployment of an identifiable sacred space—is obvious: it is meant to lend a certain *gravitas* to the narrative, to imply that it is important in some way. Beyond that, however, these references, whether real or fabricated, tap into the cultural stock of knowledge on which the filmmakers depend and to which they reflexively contribute. They provide those tangible points of real life reference that blur the line between information and entertainment.

Consider Burkittsville, Maryland, population just over two hundred. Located nearly seventy miles west of Baltimore, this tiny hamlet served as the principal location for a film that must surely contend for the "most-return-on-investment" award in the history of Hollywood cinema. For an industry in which the majority of films never recover their production costs, let alone turn significant profit, *The Blair Witch Project* is a bona fide phenomenon. Produced originally for an estimated $35,000, *Blair Witch* grossed over $36 million on its first weekend of widespread theatrical release in 1999—about the same as a putative Hollywood "blockbuster" like *Runaway Bride*, which was released the same week, cost $70 million to make, and was showing on three times as many screens. By the end of its second week, grossing more than $80 million, *Blair Witch* had earned more than the tepid comedy starring the usually bankable Richard Gere and Julia Roberts, which barely recovered its production costs in the same period.

Shot on Hi-8 video and 16mm film, both of which lack the patina of 35mm and appeal more to the look of documentary films and amateur video, its production values are as far from the gorgeously gothic *Taste the Blood of Dracula* as the Transylvanian Count is from the Blair Witch herself—and that's the point. The basic story, however, is pure Hansel and Gretel: children enter the dark forest and never return, victims of the witch who reputedly lives there. In Daniel Myrick and Eduardo Sánchez' occasionally grim update, the two children are now three university film students, the witch has acquired a name ("Ellie Kedward"), and the gingerbread house has become the "Black Hills" of Maryland. While shooting a documentary about a witch who was supposedly responsible for the deaths of over half the children in the small town of Blair more than two centuries prior, the students become disoriented and hopelessly lost. After a few nights in the woods, running low on food and good humor, they suffer night terrors, experience visitations none of them can explain, and disappear one by one.

Cut together from the "original" footage ostensibly found a year later, the film presents itself as a documentary. The jerky camerawork (most of which is seen through the video diary of the director), poor video and audio quality, and lack of coherent narrative all contribute to the impression that the audience is watching something that actually happened—a belief exploited mercilessly by both the directors and their distribution company. Special pre-release features that purported to screen "newly discovered" footage, a movie tie-in book pretentiously called a "dossier" and designed to resemble open police case files (Stern, 1999), a sophisticated Web site that blurred the distinction between fiction and reality, and ambiguous messages from the producers-directors—sometimes they stated clearly that the film is fiction, other times they were noncommittal (Breznican, 1999)—all these, plus people's *desire* to believe in the supernatural gave life to the film and the *Blair Witch* phenomenon.

In *Curse of the Blair Witch*, a "mockumentary" produced for the Sci-Fi Channel as a prelude to widespread release of *The Blair Witch Project*, we meet "Dottie Fulcher," allegedly a member of the volunteer search party who looked for the three students, and who suspects that this is much more than a simple disappearance—that the government has covered up evidence in the case.

```
                    DOTTIE
     They don't tell me anything. That's why
     there's this feeling that I have that
     they know more than they're willing
```

> to talk about. I think--I think that
> they don't want to admit that they saw
> her, and that she's there. You know,
> Ellie is not very far from any of us at
> any time, and she chooses her time to
> appear. And, um, they just don't want
> to acknowledge that.

Sociophobics of this kind are always helped along by a good conspiracy theory. Heightened by six years of *The X-Files* at this point, popular culture was thoroughly saturated with the notion that the absence of explanation for any phenomenon was likely evidence of a government conspiracy to keep important information from the public. This impression, of course, is reinforced when, time and again, it is revealed that the government has lied to the populace, that it has engaged in illegal and immoral activities on behalf of its own murky agenda, that the people it has been elected to serve have been used as pawns in power games over which they have no control. It becomes more and more difficult to locate precisely where the rabbit hole begins and ends. According to one AP report, a fan of the film wrote to Myrick and Sánchez complaining about their portrayal of certain parts of "the legend"—despite the fact that there is no such legend beyond the film.

> "That letter started out, 'It's all a lie. It's a big hoax,'" said Myrick, 35. "And I thought, 'Well, this guy figured it out.' Then he went on to say, 'You had it wrong. Here's the real way they were found.'" Some believers have organized search parties to look for the fictional documentary crew. (Breznican, 1999)

Response to *The Blair Witch Project* highlights important aspects of the technological mediation of particular sociophobics. Most obviously, it would have been extremely difficult to generate the kind of exposure and folkloric interest without the multiple sources of information in which it came packaged, most specifically, perhaps, the Internet, and the well-placed questions about the "reality" of the story it raised. Before the advent of mass media technology, folkloric warnings like the "Blair Witch" were localized, and those who encountered them entered what we might call the "folkloric zone"—for example, travelers lost on a road in the dark (e.g., the hilariously camp *Rocky Horror Picture Show*) or students who seek out the source of folk tales and folk warnings (e.g., John Llewellyn Moxey's classic *Horror Hotel*). With mass media, on the other hand, folklore and folk warnings become dispersed and can draw larger numbers who are attracted as part of a more diffuse, less organized hunt for the reality of the story. For a time, Burkittsville itself was overrun by film fans seeking what they believed was the truth. The local cemetery was vandalized, town signs were stolen, and local law enforcement put in more overtime in a few months than they had in as many years.

Much of this is depicted—and exploited—in the *Blair Witch* sequel, *Book of Shadows: Blair Witch 2*, which opens with the epigraph, "The following is a fictionalized reenactment of events that occurred after the release of *The Blair Witch Project*." A key moment in the film comes when one of the main characters expresses skepticism about paranormal phenomena, a comment that sums up the creation of dangerous spaces populated by unseen orders of existence.

> STEVEN
>
> The Bermuda Triangle. It's a place
> in the world that's been created by
> hysteria, by people's own psychology,
> by their own ideas of the place.

## AMBIVALENCE AND THE SACRED SPACE

Sacred spaces are not only touchstones of power, contact points between our world and the unseen order; they also represent the ongoing establishment of order in our world. "God's in his heaven—All's right with the world," sings the little girl, Pippa, in Robert Browning's "Pippa Passes." But, what if God's *not* in his heaven, what if all's *not* right with the world? What if the social order our sacred spaces are meant to instantiate has, in fact, been demolished—the abandoned abbey, the derelict church, the tainted sanctuary—or at the very least been diminished?

Demographic data are conflicted on how constituencies in Great Britain and the United States—the two principal producers of the cinema horror we have considered in this chapter—regard religion. In the United States, for example, data indicate that such things as belief in God, religious preference, and the importance of religion have remained relatively stable over the last couple of decades. Over 95 percent consistently respond that they believe in God, yet over that same time period, those who claim to belong to particular religious denominations have decreased. Confidence in religious organizations (which tends to run 20 points or more behind those who believe in God) has wavered, and opinions on institutional religion's ability to address a range of social problem varies widely (World Values Survey, 2006b). In Britain, the trends are slightly different: between 1981 and 1999, belief in God dropped from 82 percent to 71 percent, while those with confidence in religious institutions fell from 49 percent to just under 35 percent. Fewer than 30 percent of Britons believe the church has the ability to address significant social issues (World Values Survey, 2006a). Data gathered by the Gallup organization since 1973 indicate similar volatility (see, for example, Gallup, 2003, 2004; Winseman, 2004b). Not surprisingly, both Gallup and Winseman attribute significant downturns in public confidence in religious institutions to revelations, for example, about sexual abuse in the Roman Catholic church or moral and financial scandals among Protestant televangelists. Confidence wanes, that is, when our sanctuaries are no longer considered safe.

Though it was made years before many of these data were collected, one film in particular speaks—subconsciously, perhaps—to the ambivalence many have toward organized religion and the sacred places that architecturally embody it. Anton Leader's 1963 *Children of the Damned* is the sequel to Wolf Rilla's critically acclaimed *Village of the Damned*. Based loosely on the circumstances of John Wyndham's novel, *The Midwich Cuckoos*, six exceptional children have been gathered in London from around the world. They are "miracle children," in a way, parthenogenetic, exceptionally intelligent, and capable of extraordinary feats of telepathy, telekinesis, mind control, and healing—at the dénouement, they even restore one of their own (Rashid) to life after he has been shot. They are also, however, capable of great cruelty—controlling their parents, and committing (or compelling) murder when they feel threatened. Indeed, their abilities seem at times almost supernatural. While scientists hope to study them, not surprisingly their various governments want to use them as weapons.

Clearly a morality play about the dangers of the Cold War, the film also embeds a complex set of allusions that highlight our ambivalence about the sacred spaces in our midst. Where the children in the first film sought refuge in a village schoolhouse, in the sequel, they gather together in a tenth-century church in the middle of London. Bombed out presumably during the Second World War, the church has not been rebuilt; its vaulted sanctuary and apse are littered with debris, its massive pipe organ in ruins, its galleries and choir loft devastated. A sign posted beside the boarded-up entrance reads: "Danger. No trespassing." The structure has been deemed unsafe, yet it is here that the six smartest children in the history of humankind choose to take refuge. Eventually, the children are revealed as an evolutionary anomaly—humankind advanced a million years. The implication, of course, is that this is the future of human evolution: to communicate telepathically, to operate at an intellectual level that we cannot begin to comprehend, even to raise the dead through the power of the mind.

A number of questions emerge, but the film provides few

answers. Resisting any definitive reading, *Children of the Damned* highlights only the ambivalence with which we view the sacred spaces around us. Three aspects, though, suggest that the ruined church stands both as an icon of religious belief whose place in the world is crumbling and as the architectural embodiment of a faith that stubbornly refuses to disappear.

First, there is the simple shock value of the church itself. There are no buildings so iconic on the English landscape as the village church and city cathedral, symbols of community security and protection for a thousand years. The film was produced less than two decades after the Second World War, and the images of the shattered sanctuary would have sent shivers down the spines of those who lived through the bombings. Men, women, and children emerged from the underground to find their houses of worship in ruins and realized that those buildings had lost forever the ability to protect them.

Next, self-sufficient in ways we can only imagine, the children lack any attachment to parental or caregiver figures beyond using them to procure the basic necessities. Their powers suggest that they have evolved beyond the need for religion, yet they seek sanctuary in a bombed-out church when they could as easily commandeer a school, a factory, a hospital, or a hotel. That the political and military forces arrayed against them are so quick to regard the cathedral as nothing more than a building reinforces our concerns about the church's ongoing ability to provide sanctuary.

Finally, what does the destruction of the church and the massacre of the children mean—especially since the assault begins by accident and takes place almost immediately after Rashid's "resurrection"? In terms of our potential evolution, the children represent a hope for humanity as yet undreamed of—a salvation, perhaps, if only we had eyes to see. Fearing that which we do not understand, though, leads us to turn even on those we are called to care for most—the children. Indeed, who are the "damned"? The parents—parthenogenetically saddled with children they can neither understand nor control? Humankind—damned to wage its petty wars while all around the hope that such institutions as the church are meant to represent lie in ruins? Damned because they could not see that "a little child will lead them" (Isa 11:6)? We do not know, because the children of the damned are dead, their putative sanctuary a tomb.

Religious sanctuaries, and the graveyards, cemeteries, crypts, and tombs that surround them and that they serve to protect, are the quintessential liminal spaces between life and death, between the known world of the living and the unknown realm of the dead. It is to this liminal space, and to the sociophobics that inhabit it, that we now turn.

# 5

# STALKING LIFE
## The Fear of Death and of Dying Badly

```
            PINHEAD
   We'll tear your soul apart!
```
(*Hellraiser*)

*... what we call death is in the first place the consciousness we have of it.*
(Georges Bataille, *Erotism*)

## OUTTAKE: *MARY SHELLEY'S FRANKENSTEIN*

The story of Frankenstein's monster (or Frankenstein *as* monster, depending on your perspective) needs no introduction. A favorite among connoisseurs of "weird" fiction, it has never been out of print since first appearing in 1818. Within five years, in fact, it had been adapted for the stage and opened at the English Opera House in London. Though picketed by Christians outraged that what would become the famed Lyceum Theatre should present "so impious a work" (Mank, 1981, 12), Mary Shelley is said to have enjoyed it immensely. Today, *Frankenstein* is required reading in any number of college and university courses on the gothic in English literature. It has been filmed or brought to the stage countless times in dozens of languages. Wearing Jack Pierce's archetypal makeup, though, it was Boris Karloff's 1931 portrayal that raised Mary Shelley's creation to iconic status. Rather than simply a rampaging monster, Karloff's interpretation and James Whale's direction presented the "monster" as a somber, pathetic, indeed tragic character—something that has more often than not been lost in the many remakes and reinterpretations since.

Many of those who are only familiar with *Frankenstein* through cinema are perhaps unaware that Shelley's creation is not the mute, lumbering creature made so famous by Karloff, nor do they know that Victor Frankenstein learns the story of his own creation's life outside the laboratory during their confrontation in a lonely cave deep in the Mer de Glace the "sea of ice" on the northern slopes of Mont Blanc. This pivotal encounter has been recovered in Kenneth Branagh's 1994 version of the story. There in the ice cave, as they sit across the fire from one another, the creature (Robert De Niro) challenges the creator (Branagh), posing what is arguably one of the pivotal questions of human existence, and one that drives the various sociophobics encountered in this chapter:

CREATURE

> What of my soul? Do I have one? Or was that a part you left out?

"What of my soul?" he asks, plaintively, accusingly. In Shelley's novel, this is not even a question. Confronting his creator, the creature tells Frankenstein of living in a woodsman's hovel, sharing his meager fare, playing with his children, learning about—and learning to fear—the society of humankind. "Believe me, Frankenstein," he says, "I was benevolent; my soul glowed with love and humanity: but am I not alone, miserably alone?" (Shelley, [1818] 1996, 66). Those who would dismiss cinema horror as retrograde and juvenile would do well to heed the creature's question, to consider the soul—an inextricably religious concept, one linked to our hope for a life beyond this one, our uncertainty and ambivalence about the efficacy of that hope, and our belief in the value of our souls regardless of our inability to define precisely what they are.

In *The Devil and Daniel Webster*, for example, a Faustian bargain film based on Stephen Vincent Benét's short story (1937), the Devil haggles for a poor farmer's soul, arguing that he will, in fact, never really miss it. "A soul?" asks Mr. Scratch (Walter Huston) of Jabez Stone (James Craig). "A soul is nothing. Can you see it? Smell it? Touch it? No." This same ploy appears in another Faustian movie, Stanley Donen's 1967 *Bedazzled* (amusingly remade a generation later by former *Ghostbuster* Harold Ramis). In the original, after an unsuccessful suicide attempt, Stanley Moon (Dudley Moore) is offered seven wishes in return for "the exclusive, global, and universal rights" to his soul. When he wonders whether losing his soul will hurt—indeed, "I don't know where it is, or how to get hold of it," he says—the Devil (Peter Cook) reassures him that the operation is painless and without any real consequence:

```
THE DEVIL
You see, your soul is rather like your
appendix--totally expendable. There was
a time when it did have a function,
but, nowadays, the vast majority of
people never use it.
```

Although both *The Devil and Daniel Webster* and *Bedazzled* are at best comedy-horror, cinematic hybrids we will consider only briefly throughout this book, they do point to an important aspect of the sociophobics of death: our uncertainty about the soul, but our unwillingness to relinquish it. In both films, the Devil asks whether the intended victim has any idea what the soul actually is—not an unreasonable question—and neither really knows. Yet, both understand its importance in terms of a human being's relation to the unseen order.

"Though we know at any moment that we must die," wrote sociologist Kurt Reizler more than half a century ago, "we do not fear death all the time, except in some remote or dark corner of our mind" (1944, 490). In terms of our fear of death, of dying badly (which is the real proximate fear in the death process), and of not remaining dead (that is, of the soul not moving on to whatever afterlife our religious convictions propound), it is this "remote or dark corner of our mind" that cinema horror explores in detail. We may not contemplate death at every moment—down that road surely lies madness—but part of cinema horror's agenda is to remind us, not only of the reality of death, but of the various fears that surround it.

For many scholars, human religious consciousness begins with death, with our awareness of mortality, with our ability to imagine a world in which we are . . . not. The brute fact is that death is a constant in human life, and fear surrounds death in one way or another. Religion is a primary means by which we face that fact and negotiate that fear. Recall the working definition of religion that informs our discussion: belief in an unseen order, and that our supreme good lies in harmoniously adjusting ourselves thereto.

Cinema horror yields four principal archetypes for the fear of death: entrapment and the inability to move on (ghost stories); condemnation and the requirement to remain (vampire narratives); bondage and the eternally lost love (mummy movies); and reanimation and the need to feed (zombie tales).

## NEARLY DEPARTED: ENTRAPMENT AND THE INABILITY TO MOVE ON

Few cultures in the world lack ghost stories—whether myths and sacred narratives, songs, poems and plays, fireside tales, urban legends, news reports, or, for our purposes, cinema horror. At the turn of the nineteenth century, for example, a Bengali man reported that his wife and her entire family had become *bhūts*, or malignant spirits, after his father-in-law died of cholera. With no one to perform the required funerary rites on his behalf, he then killed other members of his family until the curse of the *bhūt* was broken (Crooke, 1902). On the Western Front during the drawn-out trench warfare of 1915, a *Times* correspondent reported a German soldier "buried face downward. You know why. If he began digging his way out he would only go deeper" (Collectanea, 1916, 225). In Egypt, villagers placated the spirit of a man killed by a train by making a clay image of him and leaving it exposed outside. "As it wasted away with the weather, the haunting grew weaker and eventually ceased" (Hornblower, 1931, 164). In Taiwan, Taoist priests use talismans and amulets to maintain harmony among the *kyonsi*, or "hopping corpses," while among the Chinese in Singapore they often broker ghost marriages, which take place for reasons as varied as providing grandchildren for a son who has died to appeasing the spirit of an unmarried elder brother so that a living younger brother may marry (Topley, 1955, 1956).

Although vampires, mummies, and zombies are arguably more recognizable in Western cinema horror, ghost movies have haunted theaters around the world for decades. In 1934, Fernando de Fuentes released *El Fantasma del Convento*, about a group of travelers who seek shelter at a haunted monastery in Mexico (Rhodes, 2003). Nonzee Nimibutr's 1999 ghost film, *Nang Nak*, draws on Thai folklore and fascination with the supernatural to raise the question of whether we always know when we encounter the dead. A tremendous success in southeast Asia, it was comparable there, wrote one commentator, to James Cameron's *Titanic* (Davis, 2003, 61). Shirley Jackson's novel *The Haunting of Hill House* ([1959] 2006) has been filmed twice as *The Haunting*, by Robert Wise (1963) and by Jan de Bont (1999), while Stephen King's *The Shining* has been released both as a film and as a television miniseries. William Castle's *13 Ghosts*, about a family who moves into a haunted house and finds a special pair of goggles that allows them to see their ghostly tenants, was remade more than a generation later by *Ghost Ship*'s Steve Beck. Hundreds more examples from around the world could easily be assembled, all of which speak to the inexhaustible belief in the unseen order and those who reside just on the other side of death. Indeed, for North

American audiences, some of the most popular ghost stories are what I call "caught dead" films, movies that turn on whether the deceased actually realizes he or she has died, and the process by which such realization occurs. Though they all employ this same narrative convention—and often speak to belief in life after death quite apart from any particular religious understanding—these "caught dead" films cross genres and include horror (*Carnival of Souls*), comedy (*Beetlejuice*), drama/love story (*Ghost*), and thriller (*The Sixth Sense*).

Whether from India, China, Korea, or Japan, Asian horror has a long and robust history of ghost cinema (see Black, 2003; Kalat, 2007; O'Brien, 2003). In Korea, for example, audiences were enthralled by such films as *Yeogo goedam* (*Whispering Corridors*), about the vengeful spirit of a student who died in what Art Black describes as that country's "unimaginably oppressive girls' high schools" (2003, 185), and a year later by its sequel, released internationally as *Memento Mori*. In Hong Kong, Danny and Oxide Pang's *Gin Gwai* (*The Eye*), about a woman who is able to see ghosts following a corneal transplant, was immediately optioned for an American remake by Tom Cruise (Davis, 2003, 62). And, in Japan, Hideo Nakata's *Honogurai mizu no soko kara* joined the flood of so-called "J-horror" and was remade for American audiences as *Dark Water*. Indeed, Nakata's *Ring*, the official English title of which is *Ringu*, a "borrow word" that does not actually exist in Japanese, has seen numerous remakes and spin-offs (including Gore Verbinski's *The Ring*), won a number of awards, and remains one of Japanese cinema's most successful horror films.

Like *Ring*, another of the most popular Japanese ghost movies to appear in the past few decades is Takashi Shimizu's *Ju-on*, and its American remake, *The Grudge*, which Shimizu also directed. Like *Ring*, *Ju-on* is a vengeful revenant story, arguably the most common kind of cinema horror ghost narrative, and firmly anchored in the cultural fears of angry ghosts that are still very much alive throughout Asia. Though both the Japanese and American versions of each film tell essentially the same story, each tells it in a way that reflects the particular sociophobic of its intended audience. For one audience, ghosts are an accepted part of the world in which we live; they are, as Freud would say, *Heimlich*, familiar if often dangerous and unpredictable. For the other, they are *Unheimlich*, what we might call well-known strangers, intruders that populate the margins of our cultural consciousness, but that appear only under the most extreme circumstances.

H. P. Lovecraft may have been ambivalent about cinema in general, but I think he would have liked *Ju-on*. With its "atmosphere of breathless and unexplainable dread," it epitomizes what he considered the sine qua non of the true horror story ([1927] 2000, 23). The basic plot is simple. In an ordinary house in Tokyo, on an otherwise ordinary day, a young woman and her son die—badly. Wrongfully accused of adultery and brutally murdered by her husband, Kayako (Takako Fuji) feels such a powerful rage as she bleeds out on her bedroom floor that her anger manifests as a curse that traps all who enter the house where she and six-year-old Toshio (Ryôta Koyama) died. From the detective who investigated the crime to the family that moves in years after the tragedy to the coworker of a young woman assigned as a home care assistant, all who encounter the curse encounter Kayako—and die badly.

While *Ju-on* and *The Grudge* were made by the same director, only a year apart and using many of the same Tokyo locations and sets, the films are significantly different and illustrate clearly the different sociophobics for which they were produced. On the one hand, *Ju-on* is episodic, nonlinear in its narrative approach, each vignette connected only by the curse of Kayako's rage and the vengeance she wreaks. With her sunken eyes, long black hair hanging over her face, pale dress, and corpse-white skin, Kayako is the very icon of the Japanese wrathful spirit, an image that has haunted Japanese art and imagination for centuries, especially in images from the nineteenth century (see Addiss, 1985; Iwasaka and Toelken, 1994). Drawing on this vast and readily available cultural reservoir, Shimizu feels no need to explain either the presence of the ghost or the persistence of the curse in the lives of those who enter the house.

*The Grudge*, on the other hand, does a number of things that American audiences tend to require for a movie to make sense, things that place the supernatural problem of the curse in more proper sociophobic perspective for them. Although the film's structure is still essentially nonlinear, there is a slightly more coherent narrative, something American audiences are used to and have come to expect in their movies. Though the initial victims—Kayako and Toshio—remain the same, many of the subsequent victims are Americans: an American family living and working in Tokyo; an American exchange student and his girlfriend, who volunteers part-time for a home care center; an American university professor who was the object of Kayako's earthly obsession, and, though innocent, is the indirect cause of her murder. In *Ju-on*, we barely meet the various people who enter the house and we know little of their lives; they are sketched in only as the potential victims of Kayako's rage. The narrative focus is on the ghost and the curse, well-known topics in Japan. In *The Grudge* we learn more about these characters; they are fleshed out, as it were, and we are invited to identify with them, to see ourselves in their situation. Like us, they are foreigners negotiating a land not their own—both naturally and supernaturally. As they pass a cemetery, for example, Karen (Sarah Michelle Geller) points out to her boyfriend (Jason Behr) how people regularly offer incense at the graves of their loved ones "to help them find peace," an expository gloss that would be entirely unnecessary for a Japanese audience, but that serves to alert American viewers to the ongoing relationship the living have with the dead in Japan. A dispirited Jennifer Williams (Clea DuVall), on the other hand, struggles to adjust to her new environment. "I went for a walk yesterday, just to explore" she tells her husband, shortly after they move into Kayako's house. "And I got so lost. And I couldn't find anyone who spoke English, who could help me." Earlier in the film (though later in the story), we watch as Karen subtly bridges this gap for the viewer. A series of long and medium-long shots follow her through the crowded streets of Tokyo as she searches for the Williams' home, struggles to understand the subway map, and uses her few words of Japanese to ask directions to the house. A woman points her in the right direction, but as Karen smiles down at the woman's small child, the little girl quickly hides behind her mother's skirt.

Unlike *Ju-on*, everything about the perspective from which *The Grudge* is shot suggests strangeness and unfamiliarity, things that are out of the ordinary, that are, in a word, *Unheimlich*. There are streets, but they are not our streets; language, but not our language; food, but not our food. More importantly, comparing the two films highlights the sociophobic aspects that determine in large measure whether or not a particular type of cinema horror film will succeed with an audience. One American reviewer opined simply that *Ju-on* "doesn't make a lot of sense and offers uncertain dramatic rewards" (Russell, 2004, 33), while a reviewer for the *Boston Globe* sums up the threat as "some odd curse that leaps from victim to victim" (Morris, 2004, C8). Considerably less comfortable with ambivalence and ambiguity, American viewers require resolution, answers, explicit causality, an end to the horror—at least until the sequel appears (which it did in 2006). Reviewing *Ju-on* for the *Houston Chronicle*, film critic Bruce Westbrook writes that "the fragmented tale is a tangled mess, and the actors have no characterizations to play, apart from shrieking cowardice. The plot—rather, the situation—has an unexplained, infectious rage haunting a house" (2004, 3). What Westbrook and these other critics fail to understand in the Japanese version is precisely what Shimizu supplied when he remade the film for American audiences.

For the Japanese, Kayako's rage requires no explanation; the dead are much closer to the living than they are in American culture. It would make as much sense to explain rain during a typhoon. Though we are, perhaps, inclined to think of Japan as the quintessential late modern technological state, the Japanese have an ongoing relationship with the dead that most Westerners would find quite foreign, even disturbing. "Nearly every festival," write Michiko Iwasaka and Barre Toelken in *Ghosts and the Japanese*, "every custom is bound up in some way with relationships between the living and the dead" (1994, 6). According to Japanese belief, some spirits are trapped on Earth, unable to move on, to reincarnate: those who have been neglected by their descendants—recall Karen's graveside gloss—and, like Kayako, those who die in the grip of anger or rage. Indeed, one of the most popular rituals over the last several decades, and one that is all but omnipresent in late modern Japan, is *mizuko kuyō*, a ceremony conducted to placate the spirit of an aborted fetus or a stillborn child and prevent its return as an angry ghost (Hardacre, 1997; LaFleur, 1994; Wilson, 2008). While its meaning has shifted significantly as the ritual has migrated across the Pacific to America, the number one reason for *mizuko kuyō* in Japan remains fear of attack by a vengeful spirit (Wilson, 2008).

In America, on the other hand, death is a taboo topic, avoided in everyday conversation as if its very mention will invite disaster. Talk of wills or funeral arrangements is considered morbid and out of place, and though about 40 percent of Americans believe in ghosts, haunting spirits occupy the background, not the foreground, of popular consciousness. Their presence in one's life is the exception rather than the rule. Further, while Christianity, as the dominant tradition in the West, does not categorically deny the existence of ghosts and discarnate spirits, unlike Buddhism, Taoism, and Shinto there is no official place for them within the framework of Christian doctrine and practice. Ghosts exist, in the sense that tens of millions of people believe in them, but they have no real place in the day-to-day understanding of life and death in the West. Here, funerals are for the living—to help deal with the grief of loss, to lay the deceased to rest in the minds of those who remain, to "let go" and "get on with life." The Japanese, on the other hand, do not let go, but hold to "a worldview in which the realms of the living and the dead interpenetrate in a system of mutual responsibility" (Iwasaka and Toelken, 1994,

8). Kayako's curse is the inevitable result of a breakdown in that responsibility.

## UNDEAD ORIGINS: CONDEMNATION AND THE REQUIREMENT TO REMAIN

For many, the legend of the vampire begins with Bram Stoker's *Dracula*, though some may be familiar with John Polidori's *The Vampyre* ([1819] 1990), a story that had its origins in the same 1816 vacation trip that produced Mary Shelley's *Frankenstein*. Concern that the (un)dead were rising from their graves and feeding on the blood of the living, however, far predates both Polidori and Stoker. Katharina Wilson notes, for example, that a number of serious philosophic treatises on the problem of vampirism emerged in the mid-eighteenth century, while nearly a century before that, Paul Rycaut, a British diplomat serving in Turkey, described belief in vampirism "as a superstition resulting from the reproachable overuse of excommunication in the Greek church" (Wilson, 1985, 580). Indeed, in Greek folklore, "those who do not receive the full and due rites of burial," "who die under the ban of the Church, that is to say, excommunicate," and "who die unbaptised or apostate" are just a few of the unlucky souls in danger of becoming vampires (du Boulay, 1982, 221). That said, though, as folklorist Alan Dundes points out, the ultimate origin of the vampire figure is lost to us. "We do not even know for certain where in the world the vampire first appeared" (Dundes, 1998a, 160).

This is not the place for a detailed consideration of vampiric origins and folklore (for that, see Barber, 1988; Dundes, 1998b; Melton, 1999; Summers, [1928] 1960). I am more interested in the undead origins offered by cinema horror. Where do scary movies tell us vampires come from, and what are some of the things we can learn from that?

Many vampire films simply assume the existence of the creature and concern themselves with little more than the manner of vampiric transmission (the bite) and the method of eradication (the stake). Others, though, do try to provide some kind of backstory to buttress the plot. In a number of science fiction-horror hybrids, such as *Lifeforce, Plan 9 from Outer Space, Planet of Blood, Planet of the Vampires*, and *Vampirella*, vampires are aliens, extraterrestrials appearing on our planet because their home worlds have been ravaged by a variety of undisclosed catastrophes. Dr. Robert Morgan (Vincent Price), on the other hand, becomes *The Last Man on Earth* when a devastating plague turns the rest of humankind into vampires. In *Underworld* and its sequel, *Underworld: Evolution*, both vampires and werewolves are the result of a plague that ravaged eastern Europe in the fifth century. Though the relatively low-budget *Midnight Mass* opens with news of a similar plague sweeping the planet, the story quickly makes clear that vampires have always existed alongside humankind, but their numbers were so small they were relegated to folklore and myth. Similarly, while the popular *Blade* trilogy does not reveal the vampire's ultimate origin, but also accepts them as a different species, it develops vampire society more fully through its use of a vampire-specific religion, including sacred texts, apocalyptic prophecies, religious ritual, and the incarnation of the dread Blood God.

In Hong Kong vampire horror, such as *Mr. Vampire, Mr. Vampire IV*, and *Tsui Hark's Vampire Hunters*—films that liberally mix broad comedy, kung fu, Taoist magic, hopping corpses, and seductively predatory female ghosts—the emergence of the undead is often the result of improper burial rites, incorrect feng shui, and inattention to the details of the complex relationship between the living and the dead. Similar to *Ju-on* and *The Grudge*, the differences between films based on a Christian worldview or a Taoist illustrate the difference in sociophobics surrounding the unseen order. Even as vampires, the dead are much closer to the living in Chinese society than in Western cultures. They speak less to an invasion from beyond the grave than to an imbalance in the harmonious relations between those who have crossed over and those who remain behind.

In terms of Western sociophobics of sacred terror, on the other hand, a number of recent vampire films posit explicitly Christian origins for the undead. As we saw in *Dracula Has Risen from the Grave*, for example, it is the blood of the weak and wounded priest that resurrects the Count from his watery grave. Condemned to walk between the worlds of the living and the dead, never able to partake fully in either, hung between heaven and hell, as it were, vampires are the sine qua non of the unseen order. Indeed, in some of these films, as is implied by much of the folklore surrounding vampires offscreen, it is the Christian Church—as holder of the keys to heaven and hell—that gives rise to the vampire in the first place. The ambivalence we encountered in the fears of a change in the sacred order and of sacred places continues here. Though they take place at different times in the narrative, each of the following three films includes a specific didactic moment, an explanatory scene that functions as a chorus and allows the filmmaker to let the audience in on the secret of the vampire's origin.

In Stoker's novel, the vampire's origin is left vague, the only real clue coming in Van Helsing's exposition in chapter 18 when he explains that, centuries before, the "scions" of the Dracula clan were said "to have had dealings with the Evil One" ([1897] 1998, 280). In Coppola's version, *Bram Stoker's Dracula*, which is in many ways more faithful to the novel than previous adaptations, a crucial prelude sequence (voiced-over by the Van Helsing character [Anthony Hopkins]) departs significantly from Stoker's storyline to disclose the origin of the vampire. After resisting the Mongol Turks' invasion of Romania, Vlad Dracul (Gary Oldman) returns to his castle to find that his bride, Elisabeta (Winona Ryder, in a dual role as Mina Murray), fearing him dead, has committed suicide. When the orthodox priests rigidly refuse her burial in consecrated ground, telling the stricken prince, "She is damned," Vlad forsakes God, vowing, "I will rise from my own death to avenge hers with all the powers of darkness." Rather than excommunication by the

Church, and not unlike the rage that surrounded Kayako's death in *Ju-on*, it is Dracula's violent renunciation of God that creates the vampire.

*John Carpenter's Vampires*, on the other hand, places the didactic moment midway through the film. In an amusing case of film commenting on film, vampire hunter Jack Crow (James Woods) tells the young Catholic priest who has just joined his team, "Forget whatever you've seen in the movies. They don't turn into bats; crosses don't work." Indeed, in this film, which departs significantly from the novel on which it is based (Steakley, 1990), the cross is central to the creation of the vampire, whose origins are explicitly religious and linked to what is presented as the arcane power of the Catholic Church. Originally a Bohemian priest who turned against the Church to lead a peasant uprising, Jan Valek (Thomas Ian Griffith) was tried for heresy and burned at the stake in 1340. But his story, obviously, does not end there, as young Father Adam (Tim Guinee), in turn, explains to Jack Crow:

> FATHER ADAM
> 
> Valek is looking for an ancient relic--
> the cross of Berzier. After his trial,
> the Church declared Valek was possessed
> by demons ... An exorcism was performed
> using an ancient, forbidden form of
> the ceremony. It was long and very
> brutal--then something went wrong.
> The accounts are confused, but they
> refer to an inverse exorcism. The body
> is destroyed, but the possessed soul
> remains. The exorcism transformed Valek
> into a creature whose body is dead ...
> a vampire.

Here again we have the ambiguity of the Church's power—the creation of the vampire through a liturgical mistake—as well as its ability to ensure the vampire's ongoing power through a blasphemous reversal of its own rites. Not only is he unafraid of the cross, Valek is actually seeking the Berzier cross in order to have the ritual performed in full, something he believes will complete his transformation and allow him to walk in the daylight, immortal and unstoppable. Not unlike Cardinal Driscoll in *The Order*, the Cardinal in charge of Crow's vampire hunting team is willing to use his own power as a prince of the Church to perform the ritual. "As one grows old," Cardinal Alba (Maximillian Schell) tells Crow, "as death approaches, we begin to question our faith, and I have found mine lacking. Is there a heaven? Is there a God? I can no longer say for certain." Rather than take the chance, in his own version of the Faustian bargain, Alba has agreed to complete the Berzier ritual on Valek's behalf in return for the undead immortality of the vampire. In this film, not only does the cross provide no protection from vampires, it becomes the instrument through which the vampire's power is increased immeasurably and the means through which the undead leader becomes an anti-Christ, offering eternal life in return for the devotion of his followers.

Finally, Patrick Lussier's *Dracula 2000* gives the didactic moment to the vampire himself (Gerard Butler) and locates it at the film's dénouement. Despite moments of camp—Simon (Jonny Lee Miller) telling the vampire Marcus (Omar Epps), "Never, ever fuck with an antiques dealer!" or TV-reporter-turned-Dracula's-bride Valerie Sharpe (Jeri Ryan) asking Simon just before she bites him, "Ever make it with a TV star?"—this is arguably the most inventive reading of the Dracula legend, and one that tries to account for most of the Christian technology of salvation by which the master vampire can be destroyed. Presenting the *ur*-vampire as the epitome of religious betrayal, Dracula is actually the latest incarnation of Judas Iscariot, who died by suicide but was resurrected to an immortal half-life as punishment for his betrayal of Jesus. This is meant to explain his fear of crosses, holy water, and silver, as well as his paradoxical penchant for Christian churches and graveyards. Along with a plethora of explicitly

Christian icono-cinematography, *Dracula 2000* and its two sequels, *Dracula II: Ascension* and *Dracula III: Legacy*, include an explicitly Christian message of forgiveness and redemption. Despite all that has happened, forgiveness is available even to the most despicable of sinners.

Two questions arise from these three films: what is the point of invoking explicitly religious origins for vampires, and why implicate the Church in those origins?

"Originally," wrote Sigmund Freud, citing philologist Rudolf Kleinpaul, "*all* of the dead were vampires, all of them had a grudge against the living and sought to injure them and rob them of their lives. It was from corpses that the concept of evil spirits first arose" ([1913] 1950, 59). As denizens of the unseen order, vampires present another aspect of the problem of the soul. If wrathful spirits, such as Kayako, seek little more than vengeance for the manner in which they died, vampires raise the stakes, as it were, claiming their victims and denying them the peace of the grave. They represent not only the fear of those who will not remain dead but also the fear that we might be condemned to a similar fate. If the hope of the Christian is to move on from this life to an eternal life with God, then the prospect of remaining caught between the worlds could be terrifying indeed.

While we might not go so far as to call them Christian allegories, that the power of Christianity triumphs in the end of many vampire films is not in doubt. Indeed, from the pages of Stoker's novel onward, the cross has been the preeminent instrument for defeating Western vampires. What does it say, then, when these later films implicate the Church in the creation of the vampire? If the Church is responsible for the existence of vampires, of what use is it for protection from them? Once again, we are back to the issue of ambivalence—belief in the Church as a force for good, but fear that it guards secrets more terrible than we can imagine. For hundreds of millions of Christians, the Church is the mediator between the seen and the unseen orders, the guarantor of salvation. Priests serve as guardians/mediators of God's grace, and the belief persists that without their blessing that grace is withheld. Like so many religious figures in cinema horror, they are revealed as either intractable or ineffectual—something that speaks to the ambivalence with which people regard religious officials—and these films present a much more ambiguous Church, one more than willing to compromise with the powers of darkness it professes to keep at bay.

## BURIED ALIVE: BONDAGE AND THE ETERNALLY LOST LOVE

"Stranger than Dracula!" began the theatrical trailer for Karl Freund's 1932 *The Mummy*. "More fantastic than Frankenstein! . . . The Mummy! Is it dead or alive, human or inhuman? You'll know, you'll see, you'll feel the awful creeping, crawling terror that stands your hair on end and brings a scream to your lips!" Cue Ralph Norton (Bramwell Fletcher) screaming in horror as the mummy returns to life before his eyes. Though the *New York Times* reviewer thought Freund's film a "costume melodrama for the children," he did allow that the "moment when the tape is drawn across [Im-Ho-Tep's] mouth and nose, leaving only his wide eyes staring out of the coffin, is one of decided horror" (A.D.S., 1933, 11).

"It looks as though he died in some sensationally unpleasant manner," opines Ralph amiably, as he and two elder archeologists examine the mummy in Universal's first entry into the field. Indeed, in each of the eponymous *Mummy* movies (1932; 1959; 1999), the title unfortunate suffers a similar fate. In Freund's film, when his forbidden love, Anck-es-en-Amon, dies prematurely, the high priest Im-Ho-Tep attempts to resurrect her using equally forbidden rituals from the Scroll of Thoth. Taken before he can read the last, all-important spell, however, he is condemned to "the nameless death." Solemn priests bind him in linen wrappings and place him in a sarcophagus from which all insignia have been removed and "the sacred spells which protect the soul in its journey to the underworld have been chipped off." He is then carried deep into the desert and buried in an unmarked grave. Since the place of one's tomb and the manner of one's burial were of paramount importance to the ancient Egyptians, Muller tells us that "Im-Ho-Tep was sentenced to death not only in this world, but in the next." Nearly thirty years later, when Hammer Studios remade *The Mummy's Hand* as *The Mummy*, a similar fate ensued, this time for the high priest Kharis and his love, the princess Ananka. Attempting to bring her back with rituals from the "Scroll of Life," allegedly written by "the hand of the god Karnak himself," he breaks her tomb's sacred seal and dares the wrath of the gods. For this "ultimate in blasphemy," his tongue is cut out "so that the cries he would utter during the fate that awaited him should not offend the ears of the gods," and he is entombed alive, sentenced to guard forever Ananka's resting place.

In Stephen Sommers' remake of the Universal original, Anck-su-Namun (Patricia Velasquez) is not a priestess, but Pharaoh's haughty mistress, whom no other man was permitted to touch. Discovered in their forbidden love, she and Imhotep (Arnold Vosloo) murder the Pharaoh. While Imhotep escapes the Pharaoh's guards, Anck-su-Namun takes her own life rather than submit to the fate that inevitably awaits her for regicide. Captured trying to resurrect her, Imhotep is condemned to suffer the "Hom-dai, the worst of all ancient curses." Like Hammer's Kharis—his tongue cut out and his body wrapped tightly in linen—Imhotep is placed alive in a sarcophagus. At this point, however, Sommers introduces a particularly gruesome aspect to the proceedings. As if being entombed alive were not enough, thousands of allegedly flesh-eating scarab beetles are poured into the coffin just before the lid is closed.

While not nearly as popular as either ghost stories or vampire narratives, mummy movies have a solid place in both the history of cinema horror and the sociophobics of death and dying badly. Indeed, our fears of haunting spirits and vampiric entities pale in comparison to the root fear underpinning most mummy movies—taphophobia, the fear of being buried alive. Beyond what Jan Bondeson (2001) calls this "primal fear," though, three tangents and two paradoxes meet in the cinematic sarcophagus of mummy films. Tangentially, the films bring together Egyptian conceptions of the afterlife and the central place of the body in preparation for it, the aesthetic appeal of tragic romance that dooms lovers across the sands of time, and the British and American obsession with Egyptian antiquity that goes back more than two centuries. Paradoxically, though, in the midst of that obsession, they reveal both onscreen and off the ongoing creation of the dangerous religious Other.

As noted in chapter 4, tomb desecration constituted one of the most horrifying acts of vandalism among the ancient Egyptians. In order for an Egyptian to pass beyond the gates of death and take up full and complete residence in the afterlife, elaborate rituals had to be performed, complicated spells from *The Book of Coming-Forth by Day* (often translated as *The Egyptian Book of the Dead*) were copied out and included in the sarcophagus, and the body was carefully preserved through mummification and entombed according to elaborate ceremonial dictate (see, for example, Faulkner, 1985, 11–16; Lehner, 1997, 22–33). Failure at any point in this lengthy process could jeopardize the position of the deceased in the afterlife. Unlike both Western and east Asian conceptions of death, in which the body is treated as a vessel from which the essential element—call it a soul, a spirit, one's *kon* (Shinto), *ch'i* (Taoism), or *ti bon ange* (Vodou)—has now passed, in ancient Egypt the body remained an integral component of the individual after death. Mummification itself took seventy days and was carried out according to strict ritual and procedural standards. Because ancient Egyptians were terrified of decay and putrefaction, parts of the body that were subject to short-term necrosis—the viscera and the brain, particularly—were extracted first. The various organs were preserved in funerary vases known as canopic jars, while the brain was discarded. The rest of the body was then carefully desiccated, wrapped in linen, and entombed along with a wide

142 / *Stalking Life*

variety of things loved ones believed the deceased would require in the afterlife. Not unlike other societies, though, as archeologist Mark Lehner points out, the ritual preparation and disposition of the body served a two-fold purpose, and was, in a way, paradoxical. Although the ritual preparations were designed to allow the deceased to move on to the afterlife, they also functioned to incapacitate the dead and prevent their return as haunting spirits. "Egyptians," writes Lehner (1997, 23), "wanted the spirits of their departed to be bound to the mortal remains—but confined to the other side of the tomb." What happens, though, when the spirits remain bound to this side of the tomb? Entombed alive, rather than technically mummified, the poor creatures are caught forever between the land of the living and the happy abode of the dead, a circumstance that leads almost inevitably to the curse that plays out the principal narrative in the films.

In many mummy films (certainly those that have been most successful commercially), the mummy is as much the victim of his own passion and hubris as of the rigid requirements surrounding the preparation and burial or entombment of a corpse. Rather than the simple monster movies suggested by such taglines as "Beware the beat of the cloth-wrapped feet" (*The Mummy's Shroud*), whatever else ensues in the narrative, lost love of one kind or another lies at the heart of the mummy's story. They are tragic romances. While this may draw snorts of derision from some horror fans, consider the basic plot to which most mummy movies are ultimately tied. In both Universal versions, it is Im-Ho-Tep's love for Anck-es-en-Amon and his willingness to risk everything and read the forbidden "spell that raises the dead" that sets the stage for their eternal bondage and separation. Whether she is a virginal priestess of Isis or Pharoah's mistress, their love is doomed from the beginning. Similarly, in Universal's four sequels (*The Mummy's Hand*; *The Mummy's Tomb*; *The Mummy's Curse*; *The Mummy's Ghost*), all of which shamelessly recycle stock footage from earlier films, Kharis and the princess Ananka, who is also a high priestess, dare to love each other against the will of the gods. In Hammer's remake,

[margin note: reminds me of *Lovely Bones*]

which blends the two traditions, Kharis as well has become a high priest. In *The Mummy's Shroud*, on the other hand, which takes much of its narrative from fanciful aspects of the Carter-Carnarvon expedition to find the tomb of Tutankhamen, the mummy is Prem (Dickie Owen), the faithful servant of Kah-to-Bey (Toolsie Persaud), a child prince forced into exile by a palace coup. In each case, when awakened by whatever means—the reading of the Scroll of Thoth, the "fluid from the sacred tana leaves," or through secret incantations passed down through a family of erstwhile guardians—what the reanimated corpse desires more than anything is the love he was either denied or sworn to protect in life.

Finally, extending back more than two centuries, is the American and British obsession with Egyptian antiquities and ancient culture. Freemasonry and ritual magic lodges, such as the Hermetic Order of the Golden Dawn, are suffuse with references to ancient Egypt. Joseph Smith, the founder and first prophet of the Church of Jesus Christ of Latter-day Saints, claimed to have translated *The Book of Mormon* from "reformed Egyptian hieroglyphics," and, today, Church members believe that another of their scriptures, *The Pearl of Great Price*, contains "The Book of Abraham," which Smith allegedly purchased in papyrus form (along with four intact mummies) from a traveling dealer in Egyptian antiquities. In unmistakable Egyptian style, Facsimile 1 in the book depicts a man lying on a table while another hovers over him, brandishing a long knife. While the Mormon interpretation is that this depicts the abortive "sacrifice of Abraham" by an "idolatrous priest of Elkanah," clearly the picture refers to the process of mummification. Beneath the table on which the body lies, for example, stand the four canopic jars ready to receive the viscera—though the Latter-day Saint reading is that these are idols representing a variety of pagan gods.

Egyptian hieroglyphics, artifacts, and alleged arcana feature prominently in nineteenth-century literature. In Edgar Allen Poe's short story "Some Words with a Mummy," for example, the title character offers a very different version of mummification. Named somewhat waggishly "Count Allamistakeo," the mummy tells the dumbfounded men who revived him that it was common practice among his particular people to remove neither the viscera nor the brain before proceeding with mummification, and, as a result, "all the Scarabæi embalmed accidentally while alive, are alive" today (Poe, [1845] 1975, 543).

In addition to mummies, the wonder of Egyptian hieroglyphics—both before and after Jean-François Champollion's work with the Rosetta stone in the early nineteenth century—has fascinated writers, artists, poets, and architects on both sides of the Atlantic (see Day, 2006; Irwin, 1980; Iverson, 1961). It influenced architecture, religion, and popular culture to an extent rivaled by few ancient civilizations. As film historian David Skal notes in *Mummy Dearest*, his documentary tribute to mummy movies, "mystical egyptian décor" was all the rage "in movie palaces of the 1920s" (1999). In the early 1990s, less than sixty miles northwest of Las Vegas, and twenty miles from the mysterious, heavily guarded, and officially unacknowledged military base known around the world as Area 51, a modern Pagan named Genevieve Vaughan (1998) erected a temple to Sekhmet, the lion-headed Egyptian goddess of destruction and destructive potential. And, while the great detective of Baker Street never faced a mummy in any of the adventures written for him by Sir Arthur Conan Doyle, videogame sleuths can play Sherlock Holmes and solve "The Mystery of the Mummy" on their personal computers.

If these are among the tangents that mummy movies bring together, the paradox they disclose is that while exploiting the romantic fascination with Egyptian antiquities and exploration of ancient Egyptian ritual sites, they consistently represent the (alleged) beliefs and practices that underpin the films as a ludicrous and often dangerous religious Other. First, this onscreen creation of the religious Other is recreated offscreen in the figure of the mummy itself. In the West, we assume that the mummy is a mummy because (usually) he is wrapped in linen and plods around seeking whom he may destroy. In this sense, cinema horror has created for us the popular representation of what a mummy is, despite the fact that, the various storylines notwithstanding, none of the principal characters are actually mummies. As should be clear by now, there is a fundamental difference between being buried (or entombed) alive and mummification. For their part in the plot to raise Anck-su-Namun, for example, in Sommers' *The Mummy* the priests of Imhotep were condemned to be "mummified alive"—a technical impossibility since one of the first parts of the mummification process is evisceration. The four Universal sequels from the 1940s add a unique, even more horrific twist to the story. Rather than bring the mummy back to life through the Scroll of Thoth or various spells to raise and reanimate the dead, Kharis has been kept alive in perpetuity by the secretive priests of Arkam, who use fluid from "the sacred [and sometimes forbidden] tana leaves" to keep the poor man's heart beating through the millennia. However abhorrent the thought of being entombed alive with no possibility of reaching the promised afterlife, at least death would end one's physical suffering. How much more terrible to be kept both alive and dead, bound in linen wrappings, entombed for millennia, yet forbidden to die, to ever finally die.

While there is no indication that this change in plot device was meant to circumvent the logical problem of mummification, the Universal sequels introduce the second, arguably more insidious aspect of the paradox: that the religion presented onscreen comes to represent ancient Egyptian religion for audiences off-screen. Recall, for example, the willingness of readers around the world to credence the reality of a curse on the Carter-Carnarvon expedition following their entry into Tutankhamen's tomb, and the subcultural conspiracy theories that still circulate about the reality of the curse (Day, 2006, 48–64 *passim*). More than just newspapers and gossip, however, had prepared audiences to accept this (mis)representation of Egyptian religion. In addition to the tales of Poe, Stoker, and such racist potboilers as Ambrose Pratt's *The Living Mummy* (1910), such silent films as *The Vengeance of Egypt* and *The Eyes of the Mummy*, as well as the horror pulps of the 1920s and 1930s prepared the ground. As I noted in the previous chapter, pulp fiction magazines delighted in bringing the dangerous religious Other to eager audiences each month. In *Weird Tales*, cover stories such as Otis Adelbert Kline's "The Bride of Osiris" (August 1927), Seabury Quinn's "The Jewel of Seven Stones" (April 1928) and "The Dust of Egypt" (April 1930), and Thomas Kelley's "I Found Cleopatra" (November 1938) all feature artwork exploiting the popular obsession with Egyptian antiquity. Interest in Egypt did not die post-war. In the years leading up to Hammer's interest in mummy cinema, *Fantastic Adventures* offered cover stories such as William Hamling's "Shadow of the Sphinx" (November 1946) and Geoff St. Reynard's "The Sword of Ra" (February 1951).

Following Skal (1994), Rick Worland points out that horror films in the 1930s "metaphorically embodied the widespread fears and disillusionment that followed economic collapse" (1997, 47). Some horror films made during what many critics regard as the imaginative wasteland of the 1940s, on the other hand, "were revised to meet the national needs of wartime" (Worland, 1997, 48). *The Mummy's Ghost* is an interesting example. Quoting from an Office of War Information (OWI) critique of the original script, Worland points out that the "B[ureau of] M[otion] P[icture]'s analyst denounced the story's portrayal of the religion, culture, and peoples of contemporary Egypt and the Middle East" (1997, 54). The critique continues:

> How would Egyptians (or the many people who look to that country as the leader in the Arab-Moslem world) react to this presentation of the cult of Karnak, which is an actual part of their history? . . . Could they infer that Amina's reference to Egypt, as a place of "dark tombs and passages . . . rot, decay and death" is representative of American attitudes toward their country? . . . The script should definitely be checked by OWI

authorities on the Middle East before any recommendation is made by this office, to avoid any misrepresentation which could prove offensive to our allies in this strategic war theater. (As quoted in Worland, 1997, 54)

Good questions, but they do not address more basic concerns about why the original script was written this way in the first place. The fact that there is no "cult of Karnak" notwithstanding, why portray Egyptian religion so poorly, as so much the dangerous outsider? As a pop cultural product building on the cultural stock of knowledge established by other such products, American filmmakers were no less subject to contemporary prejudices against the various peoples of the Middle East than anyone else. For them, it *was* the dangerous religious Other. Indeed, would the Bureau of Motion Pictures have been so concerned about the accurate portrayal of Egyptian history and religion were the United States not in the midst of a war, and were Egypt not an ally "in this strategic war theater"? If we go to the original film in the Universal franchise, for example, or to those made prior to the United States' entry into the war (e.g., *The Mummy's Hand*) or after 1945 (e.g., *The Mummy*; *The Curse of the Mummy's Tomb*), would we find similarly disparaging representations of Egyptians?

Not surprisingly, we do. Of course, as Worland points out, OWI's objections had much to do with Egypt's strategic role in the North African campaign. If this is the case—and it seems likely—then their objections ring a wee bit hollow. Recall, for example, the scene from Terence Fisher's *The Mummy* introduced in chapter 4, in which John Banning confronts Mehemet Bey about the existence of the mummy, Kharis. Though Banning comes off in the scene as something of a xenophobe—by the time the film was made, after all, the sun had effectively set on the British Empire—he continues to ridicule the Egyptian's religion. Because it illustrates the problem of cinema horror's representation of the religious Other so well, I quote the dialogue here at some length.

                    BANNING

I remember the opening of Princess
Ananka's tomb. She was high priestess
to a pagan god, Karnak. We have reason
to believe that over a hundred people
were put to death during her funeral
rites.

                  MEHEMET BEY

Most probably.

                    BANNING

And Karnak wasn't a particularly
important deity. A third-rate god.

                  MEHEMET BEY

Not to those who believed in him.

                    BANNING

Perhaps not. But their standard of
intelligence must have been remarkably
low.

                  MEHEMET BEY

Why do you say that?

                    BANNING

He was insignificant. He had nothing
to commend him to anyone with the
slightest degree of intelligence.

                  MEHEMET BEY

But surely you are assuming a great
deal.

                    BANNING

I don't think so. I've made an
extensive study of this so-called
religion. It's based upon artificial
creeds and beliefs, some of them
ludicrous in the extreme.

                  MEHEMET BEY

Did it ever occur to you that beneath
the superficial you've learned about
there could be a great and passionate
devotion to this god?

                    BANNING

It occurred to me, but I dismissed it.

                  MEHEMET BEY

You're intolerant, Mr. Banning.

                    BANNING

Not intolerant. Just practical.

                  MEHEMET BEY

Intolerant. Because you are unable to
experience the greatness of a deity,
you dismiss it as of no consequence.
But, believe me, to those who worship
and serve Karnak, he is all-powerful.

                    BANNING

Surely there can't be people who still
have such beliefs?

### MEHEMET BEY

> Now you talk about something of which you know nothing. You've scratched only the surface and you know nothing. You assume the right to disturb the everlasting peace of the gods. You pry and meddle with unclean hands and eyes. Profanity, blasphemy, religious desecration. All these you are guilty of. But the powers with which you have meddled do not rest easy. I think you will not go unpunished.

This dialogue highlights an important reality pervading not only cinema horror but offscreen religious interaction as well. Put simply, what is to one group of people a deep and abiding faith is patent absurdity to any number of others. One person's gods and goddesses are another person's idols and demons; one person's prayers and rituals, another's magic and mumbo-jumbo. Indeed, rather than merely a bit of Hammeresque melodrama—which, on one level, it surely is—this interchange reflects the basic paradox of Western relationships with Egyptian antiquity: fascination and contempt, a simultaneous obsession with and reinscription of the dangerous religious Other.

Describing some of the magical acts attributed to Egyptian priests in E. A. Wallis Budge's *Egyptian Religion* ([1900] 1959) and *Egyptian Magic* ([1899] 1971), for example, British author Colin Wilson writes in *The Occult* (one edition of which is subtitled "The ultimate book for those who would walk with the Gods") that "quite obviously, these people were absurdly credulous; their state of mind was the kind that can still be found in many country villages today" (1971, 220). That is to say, credulously superstitious. Wilson's credulously superficial interpretation of Egyptian society, culture, and religion, however, continues and reveals clearly the ongoing prejudices of the Western (in this case, British) mind—a mind not unlike that displayed by John Banning in this scene. "Their culture was almost accidental," Wilson writes, and "the Egyptians were lazy, and averse to serious thinking" (1971, 222, 223):

> Their science was almost nonexistent, their mathematics remained crude. Like the Chinese, they tended to respect antiquity for its own sake, and so their medicine was a mixture of up-to-date observation and old wives' remedies out of ancient books. Their religion suffered from the same confusion, due to an aversion to discarding any link with the past. They were highly sexed, and the sexual exploits of their gods were nearly as disgraceful as those of the Greeks. (Wilson, 1971, 223)

Their massive engineering feats—including the pyramids and the temple complexes at Karnak and Luxor—get not a mention in this very long book; they are not even listed in the index.

Why spend time on Wilson, who clearly has no use for the achievements or inherent fascination of ancient Egyptian culture? Because, since his emergence in the 1950s as one of "the angry young men," writers who actively challenged the dominant literary culture in Britain, Wilson has been one of the most widely read and oft-cited members of Britain's literary community. His voice both carries a certain amount of weight in the arena of public perception and reflects a very particular form of pseudo-intellectual orientalism that is often directed not only at the cultures and religions of those countries that have been cast as the "Orient," but at religious beliefs in general when they differ from the West.

While they are brought into the present by cinema horror and popular interest, and despite the efforts of small new religious movements to reinvigorate (or reinvent) ancient Egyptian religious belief and practice (see, for example, Almond and Seddon, 2004; Clark, 2003; Krogh and Pillifant, 2004), for the vast majority of people those beliefs and practices remain securely buried in the past. Not so the final theme of this chapter, which offers another cinema horror representation of the dangerous religious Other—the zombie.

## THE DEAD DESIRE THE LIVING: REANIMATION AND THE DANGEROUS RELIGIOUS OTHER

Those with only a passing familiarity with cinema horror could be forgiven for thinking there is only one type of zombie—the mindless, ravenous revenant made famous by such filmmakers as George Romero (*Night of the Living Dead*; *Dawn of the Dead*; *Day of the Dead*; *Land of the Dead*), Lucio Fulci (*City of the Living Dead*; *The Beyond*; *The House by the Cemetery*), and a horde of imitators. Although there are obvious subtypes (e.g., *Revolt of the Zombies*, in which the evil Colonel Mazovia [Roy D'Arcy] reanimates corpses to serve in his army, or *War of the Zombies*, about a group of Roman legionnaires doing battle with the undead legions of High Priest Aderbad [John Drew Barrymore]), two basic species of zombie shamble about the vaults of cinema horror: undead servants and undead predators. Pointing out that the release of Romero's *Night of the Living Dead* in 1968 marks a watershed between these two groups, most commentators concentrate on the latter—ravening hordes seeking little more than their next meal of human flesh—and devote relatively little attention to the former (see, for example, Greene and Mohammad, 2006; Paffenroth, 2006; Russell, 2005; Slater, 2002; Waller, 1986). Since the majority of critique has focused on the development and/or the meaning of zombie films in the post-Romero period, here I will consider those elements of zombie cinema that more clearly disclose the cinematic production (and social reinforcement) of the dangerous religious Other.

In his excellent history of zombie movies, Jamie Russell (2005, 9) notes that the word "zombie" makes its first appearance in English through the writings of Lafcadio Hearn, a world traveler and prolific author perhaps best known for his collections of Chinese and Japanese ghost stories (Hearn, 1887; 1899; 1904; McNeil, 1978). The first threat of the reanimated dead, however, is arguably several thousand years older than that, dating to the dawn of recorded mythistory. Preserved in cuneiform, an Akkadian myth from Mesopotamia (the area now covered by parts of Syria, Iraq,

Iran, and southern Turkey) describes the descent of the goddess Ishtar into the netherworld. Seeking an audience with her sister, Ereshkigal, Queen of the Underworld, Ishtar warns the gatekeeper to the land of the dead:

> If thou openest not the gates so that I cannot enter,
> I will smash the door, I will shatter the bolt,
> I will smash the doorpost, I will move the doors,
> I will raise up the dead, eating the living,
> So that the dead will outnumber the living.
> (Pritchard, 1958, 81)

While this may be something of a stretch when talking about zombie films in the late twentieth century and beyond, it certainly demonstrates that fear of the revenant dead is deeply embedded in human religious consciousness.

Wondering why zombie films are as popular as they are, though, James Twitchell points out that "the very mindlessness of the zombie, the insupportable boredom of his personality, tends to mitigate any conflict that could exist between monster and victim" (1985, 266). That is, they are slow-moving, often sluggish in their attack, and not terribly difficult to kill (again). They lack the vampire's potential eroticism, the mummy's obvious pathos, and the haunting spirit's pancultural reality. Indeed, rather than monsters per se, they are our friends and neighbors, our family, sometimes even our pets. The zombies are us, as any number of commentators have pointed out.

Often shot by amateurs on videotape—a medium Russell derides as "the modern equivalent of doodling paper for any idiot with a few hundred bucks and a lot of spare time on their hands" (2005, 269)—on the surface, most zombie movies appear to have little to do with religious belief or practice. Indeed, in his introduction to a wide-ranging collection of reviews of Italian zombie and cannibal films, film critic Jay Slater notes that while many films make "blunt satirical attacks on religion," "where a religious element exists, it's largely a matter of style rather than intentional content" (2002, 17). Here, though, we are back to the original question with which I began the book: if it is merely stylistic convention, then why include it in the film at all? What is the significance of the religious component in these films, especially when so many other zombie films get along just fine without it? To what unseen order do these films advert? What gives rise to the walking dead, and what fears do they exploit and reinforce? Because long-established cultural and religious practice requires cremation, for example, zombie films make no sense to an Indian audience, and Bollywood has made few attempts to reanimate the dead this way. Not so Western cinema horror.

One way to distinguish the variety of zombie films that compete for a share of horror fans is to consider their various myths of origin. Besides the overt fear of the revenant dead—and the derivative horror that we may soon join them in their endless, shambling quest for food—origins often betray our deeply buried ambivalences about the relationships between life and death, between science and nature, between our world and the myriad unseen orders that exist just beyond the light. Where do zombies come from? In one sense, any cause serves as a plot device to introduce the gore and mayhem so beloved by fans of zombie cinema. But zombie origins do more than that. While Kim Paffenroth suggests that "the plausibility of an explanation" for the appearance of zombies is "irrelevant," and that the purpose of these films is to explicate the response of the embattled survivors (2006, 3), ignoring the genesis of the walking dead avoids the larger social and cultural issues these origins unearth. It may be, for example, that the zombies in *Dawn of the Dead* represent the mindless consumerism that has covered the Earth like a plague, but it ignores where that urge originated and why.

Of the more than three hundred films Russell lists in his zombie filmography (2005, 233–309), roughly one third of his précis gives some definite indication of the undead origins. This is not an exhaustive survey, but it does yield impressionistic data about the patterns of zombie origin in cinema horror. Broadly speaking, lurching between the worlds of the living and the dead, we find the horrific instrumentalities of nature (both terrestrial and extraterrestrial), science (both human and alien), and supernature.

Natural zombies, as it were, come in two basic forms: terrestrial and extraterrestrial. In *The Alien Dead*, *Night of the Comet*, *Night of the Creeps*, *Quatermass 2*, and *Undead*, for example, meteorite showers and cometary near-misses release a variety of extraterrestrial toxins that turn significant portions of humanity into the living dead. In other films, hitherto unknown parts of our own natural world have a similar effect. Peter Jackson's *Braindead*—released in North America as *Dead Alive*—relies on a monkey's bite to start the infection. Viral outbreaks of unknown origin, on the other hand, impart a semblance of life to *Dead Creatures* and *The Dead Next Door*, while necrotizing fasciitis (the "flesh-eating disease") gives the *Dead Life* in William Schotten's contribution to the genre.

Films like *Night of the Living Dead* and *28 Days Later* bridge the categories of nature and science. Though the contagion that reanimates the corpses of the recently dead and instills in them a need to feed on the bodies of the living is radiation in the former and an experimental virus in the latter, in both cases human scientific research serves as the delivery system. Indeed, the hubris of science—and the fear that it has spun out of all moral and technological control—arguably animates more zombie movies than any other specific myth of origin. The question in these films is: did it happen by accident or by design? Toxic chemical spills (*Ghoul School*; *The Living Dead Girl*; *The Revenge of the Living Dead Girls*), nuclear radiation leaks (*The Children*; *I Was a Teenage Zombie*), and even an untested AIDS vaccine (*Zombie 90: Extreme Pestilence*) have all raised the dead in one cinematic outing or another. Building on fears associated with such chemical catastrophes as Agent Orange, DDT, and the 1984 disaster at the Union Carbide plant in

Bhopal, India, pesticides have also figured prominently in zombie myths of origin. Films ranging from *The Grapes of Death* and *The Living Dead at Manchester Morgue* to *Toxic Zombies* and *The Return of the Living Dead* hold up to harsh criticism science's willingness to do what it can simply because it can. Indeed, the *Return of the Living Dead* franchise, which went through five installments from 1985 to 2005, is built on the combined premises of scientific carelessness, bureaucratic mismanagement, military hubris, and social collapse.

Though it has some older antecedents (for example, Victor Halperin's *Revolt of the Zombies*), another common post-Romero myth of zombie origin is the deliberate scientific attempt to create the living dead. Though the *Resident Evil* franchise opens with an accident at the vast laboratory underneath Raccoon City, as the two sequels make clear, the zombies were only accidentally released, not accidentally created. In *Bio Cops*, a CIA plan to create an army of super-soldiers goes awry, while in *Bio-Zombie* and *Biohazardous*, biological weapons unleash the undead. Based on H. P. Lovecraft's short story, the *Re-Animator* series takes the zombie movie in socially critical (if often hilarious) directions. Recalling the fear that enemy soldiers might dig themselves out of their graves if not buried face down, and the revelations of real life horror that went on in the so-called medical wards of the death camps, a number of films build on the theme of secret Nazi experiments to give life to the dead. *Maplewoods* carries this fear of military experimentation even further; whereas the Nazis were unable to create zombie soldiers, the Americans took over at the end of the war, eventually succeeding where the Germans failed. Similar themes animate such films as *Shock Waves*, *Mutation* (and its sequels), *Night of the Zombies* (which features both American and German zombie troops keeping themselves "alive" after the war has ended), and *Revenge of the Zombies* (released at the height of the Second World War).

Often hailed as one of the worst movies ever made—a distinction that virtually ensures its enduring popularity—Ed Wood's

*Plan 9 from Outer Space* introduces the possibility that zombies might not work for the government—at least not any government of this planet. Released in 1960, Phil Tucker's *Cape Canaveral Monsters* plays on fears of Communist infiltration into the U. S. space program, while the student-made *I Was a Zombie for the F.B.I.* attempts to address Cold War paranoia nearly a generation later. Both Edward Cahn's *Invisible Invaders* and Terence Fisher's *The Earth Dies Screaming* mix the standard alien invasion narrative with fears of enemy collaboration—in each case, rather than waste their own troops, the extraterrestrials reanimate human dead for use in their janissary armies.

Finally, there is the supernatural, and its hybrid derivatives. In *City of the Living Dead*, for example, the first of Fulci's zombie trilogy, the suicide of a Catholic priest opens a portal to Hell, allowing the dead to rise and prey on the living. Ancient curses (*Messiah of Evil*), spells unwittingly cast (*Children Shouldn't Play with Dead Things*), ancient ritual texts (*Lord of the Dead*), and even the revenge of the fallen angel (*Prince of Darkness*) have all appeared as cinematic myths of zombie origin. However, where some manner of supernaturalism is invoked in the creation of the living dead, Haitian Vodou is overwhelmingly implicated and continues to reanimate cultural fears of the dangerous religious Other.

Despite the fact that zombification plays only a minor role in Vodou, the two are inextricably linked in popular consciousness, largely through cinema horror. From *The Dead Don't Die* and *The House on Skull Mountain* to *Isle of the Snake People* and *Ouanga* (which was also released as *Crime of Voodoo*), from *Dead Men Don't Die* and *I Walked with a Zombie* to *Voodoo Dawn* and *Sugar Hill*, the original blaxploitation zombie film, zombies and the cinema version of Vodou have become inseparable. Similar to the connection between mummy movies and the cinematic representation of ancient Egyptian religion, zombie films have drawn upon (and reinforced) popular conceptions about Vodou, centuries-old traditions that combine elements of African religions brought to the Caribbean by slaves with the Roman Catholicism they were forced to accept upon arrival in the West Indies. In doing so, many of these films constantly recreate a dangerous religious Other that has barely a passing resemblance to its offscreen source but that highlights yet again the ambivalence and fear with which we regard religion generally and religions other than our own specifically.

As historian Laurent Dubois points out, "during the U.S. occupation of Haiti from 1915 to 1934, images of Haitian Vodou as a terrain of demonic possession, absurd superstition, and zombis proliferated in the United States" (2001, 92; see also Brown, 2001; Dayan, 1995; Desmangles, 1992; Métraux, [1959] 1972; Olmos and Paravisini-Gebert, 1997). Indeed, nearly a generation before American Marines landed on Haiti, sensational accounts of what William Seabrook would later popularize as *The Magic Island* appeared. In 1888, for example, the first issue of the *Journal of American Folklore* contained a lengthy article by anthropologist William Wells Newell on "Myths of Voodoo Worship and Child Sacrifice in Hayti [*sic*]" (1888) a contribution he followed up with "Reports of Voodoo Worship in Hayti and Louisiana" (1889). Although Newell "discredited" the existence of what he called "Voodoo worship," practices he regarded as "probably imaginary" (1889, 45), he did allow "that charms and spells supposed to possess magical efficacy are employed in Hayti and elsewhere under that name" (1888, 30). It seems that for rationalist academics of the nineteenth century, Vodou did not exist . . . unless it did. And it certainly did for many Americans of the time.

"Voodooism is the devil worship of the African ancestors of its present practitioners," begins one lengthy *New York Times* article written in 1893 (W.H.R.), while a 1909 piece from the *Saturday Magazine* purports to describe a "famous voodoo feast whose climax of horror only one man has seen" (Bonsal, 1909, 8). Complete with line drawings that render the practitioners in the most racist way possible, Stephen Bonsal's *Saturday Magazine* article presents the practice of Vodou as an unmitigated evil, its leaders "the devil's priests," its followers as likely to die of poisoning as anything else. Striving, though, for a moment of what I'm sure he considered manifest objectivity, Bonsal writes that "there is only one thing to be said in favor of the voodoo practitioners, and in fairness I think I should say it. They do not kill all the people they are reported to kill, though the toll of their victims is heavy enough" (1909, 8). Concluding his article with solemn counsel, he warns his readers to drink nothing offered to them while ashore on Haiti. "The prospect of waiting four months or even six to know whether you have been poisoned or not is far from being a pleasant one" (Bonsal, 1909, 8). Bonsal's article intimates that the horrific ritual that no one had witnessed—but which he was certain existed—was child sacrifice, something vehemently denied by scholars like William Newell.

Far more people, however, read the *New York Times* and its *Saturday Magazine* than the *Journal of American Folklore*, and this was the milieu into which Seabrook offered the first popular treatment of Haiti and its religious culture. Called "an important contribution to anthropology" by one academic reviewer (Dawson, 1929, 198) and simply "notorious" by another (Bourguignon, 1959, 39), *The Magic Island* influenced early pop cultural representations of Haitian Vodou and zombiism more than any other single source. Well reviewed by the *New York Times*—one writer pointing out charitably that Seabrook's Haiti "is far more than a nest of benighted heathen" (Duffus, 1929, 70)—Seabrook's works are sensationalistic, though fast paced and well written. They contain a wealth of color and detail that quickly found its way into a variety of other pop culture products—notably cinema horror and pulp fiction. Two years after *The Magic Island*'s appearance, for example, a 1931 issue of *Weird Tales*, arguably the most popular of the era's fantasy pulps, published Henry Whitehead's "Passing of a God," a story based entirely on Seabrook's book. Although one character points out that much of *The Magic Island* "was an old story to me," he allows that it was "a very fine piece of work, however, the thing clicks all the way through—an honest and thorough piece of investigation" (Whitehead, [1931] 1990, 116).

A year later, Victor and Edward Halperin released *White Zombie*, which is one of the earliest walking dead movies, and which, like Whitehead's story, relies directly on Seabrook's work. Though tepidly reviewed in the *New York Times*, it is still well regarded among cinema horror fans. The basic plot is simple enough. A young couple, Neil Parker (John Harron) and Madeleine Short (Madge Bellamy), are engaged to be married, and she is traveled to meet him in Haiti where he works in a Port-au-Prince bank. Riding in a carriage one night shortly after her arrival, they come upon a group of Haitians chanting, singing, and performing some kind of ritual in the middle of the road:

```
            DRIVER
It's a funeral, m'amselle. They're
afraid of the men who steal dead
bodies, so they dig the graves in the
middle of the road where people pass
all the time.
```

This is taken directly from Seabrook's initial conversation about zombies with his principal Haitian informant, a farmer named Constant Polynice. "Why, so often," Seabrook asks, "do you see a tomb or grave set close beside a busy road or footpath where people are always passing?" "It is to assure the poor unhappy dead such protection as we can," Polynice answers ([1929] 1989, 94). To prevent exhumation and zombification, graves are dug in the front yards of family homes or beside busy roadways, or are covered over with massive slabs of stone or mortar. Sometimes the dead are killed again—stabbed or beheaded—to ensure they remain in the tomb. For four nights, Polynice tells Seabrook, he even stood armed watch over his own brother's grave to deter those who would steal his fresh corpse.

In the next sequence, Neil and Madge encounter "Murder" Legendre (Bela Lugosi) and his entourage of zombies—enemies who crossed him in life, but who now serve him in living death.

Frightened, the driver lashes his horses frantically and quickly delivers the young couple to their destination.

                    NEIL
```
Why did you drive like that, you fool!
We might have been killed!
```

                    DRIVER
```
Worse than that, m'sieur, we might have
been caught . . . zombies, the living
dead, corpses taken from their graves
to work the sugar mills and fields at
night.
```

Again, based almost entirely on Seabrook's account, this is the zombie as undead servant, a haunting cultural and cinematic reminder of the slavery to which Africans were sentenced on arrival in the so-called New World. Exhumed before the body can safely rot "and endowed by sorcery with a mechanical semblance of life," Seabrook writes that zombies are no more than slaves, used "occasionally for the commission of some crime, more often simply as a drudge around the habitation or the farm" ([1929] 1989, 93).

    Rather than the farm or the sugar mill, however, Neil's erstwhile benefactor, Charles Beaumont (Robert Frazer), has paid Legendre to turn Madge into a zombie when she spurns his offer of marriage. Thus, what begins as a supernatural tale of the living dead becomes a lovers' triangle set against popular superstitions (both Western and West Indian) about the line between life and death. Poisoned by Legendre and taken from her crypt, Madge sits at the piano in Legendre's cliff-top castle, staring blankly, while Beaumont tries to animate her with diamonds and sweet nothings. Meanwhile, desperate for an explanation, Neil seeks out Dr. Bruner (Joseph Cawthorn), a Christian missionary who has spent his life in Haiti and who serves as both expository chorus and comic relief throughout the film. At this point, Western fear of the supernatural and the dangerous religious Other gives way to Western rationalism in a way that it does not in most mummy, vampire, or haunting spirit films. Once again drawing explicitly on Seabrook, Bruner explains that the dead are not really dead, but only poisoned and revived later with little or no will of their own. "There's been lots of people," he tells Neil, "that's been pronounced dead that came alive again and lived for years. Now, if nature can play pranks like that, why isn't it possible to play pranks with nature?" Quoting parts of Haiti's *Code Pénal* verbatim from Seabrook ([1929] 1989, 103), Bruner points out that "the law, the law of Haiti recognizes the possibility of being buried alive":

> BRUNER
>
> Article 749 [249 in Seabrook]: The use of drugs or other practices which produce lethargic coma or lifeless sleep shall be considered attempted murder . . . If the person has been buried alive, the act shall be considered murder no matter what result follows.

In the end, Madge is cured and reunited with Neil. Both Legendre and Beaumont are dead, and the poor slaves the former kept between life and death are finally allowed the relative peace of the grave. As Seabrook tells Polynice, and Halperin implies in the film, "it is a fixed rule of reasoning in America that we will never accept the possibility of a thing's being 'supernatural' so long as any natural explanation, however far-fetched, seems adequate" ([1929] 1989, 102). Rather than mitigate the reliance on the dangerous religious Other, however, the film's rationalist explanation only reinforces what white Western audiences must still have seen as Haiti's "benighted heathen" and their rank superstitions.

Only a few years after *White Zombie* was released, novelist and anthropologist Zora Neale Hurston published her enormously influential *Tell My Horse* ([1938] 1966), from which one reviewer gleaned that "zombies really exist in Haiti. And the dreadful creation of these 'living dead' fastens 'with Haitian variations' to 'old European belief in selling one's self to the devil'" ("Lore of Haiti," 1938). Commenting on the post-war tourist appeal of Haiti, psychiatrist Louis Mars opines that vacationers "believe that they will be able to see Zombis roaming through the villages" (1945, 38), while the current online BBC profile of Haiti virtually reinforces the continuing belief that its "history and culture [is] epitomised by voodoo" (BBC News, 2007).

If *Night of the Living Dead* bridges nature and science, later zombie films, such as Wes Craven's *The Serpent and the Rainbow*, bring together nature and supernature. In this horror adaptation of Wade Davis' account of his search for the so-called "zombie drug," not only are we presented with the possible pharmacological bases of the poison used to create zombies—something about which anthropologists, ethnologists, and ethnobotanists have wondered for decades (see, for example, Ackermann and Gauthier, 1991; Cannon, 1942; Davis, 1985, 1988; Lex, 1974; Mars, 1945; Métraux, [1959] 1972)—but we are also confronted once again by a vast oversimplification of Haitian Vodou, a reductionism to which cinema horror has now contributed for more than seventy years. In the same way that Wicca and modern Witchcraft struggle to overcome centuries of prejudice linking magical belief and practice with Satanism (a topic explored in chapter 6), the complex Afro-Caribbean religion of Vodou remains firmly linked to the appearance of zombies. Another example of the exploitation of a general cultural ignorance of religious traditions other than our own, it represents the ongoing use of cinema horror to represent the dangerous religious Other.

## STRAINING CREDULITY: THE DANGEROUS RELIGIOUS OTHER OFFSCREEN

Calling *White Zombie* "one of the most extraordinary photoplays of the day," an unidentified writer for the Sunday edition of the *Hartford Courant* opined a week before Halperin's film began its run:

> For there are devil worshippers in America today, and, although the black mass is not practiced, the swamp lands of the Carolinas still ring on moonlit nights with the chant of the devil worshippers, while in the bayous of Louisiana frequently are heard the incantations of the doctors, or voodoo sorcerers who owe allegiance only to Satan. ("White Zombie is Coming to the Capitol," 1932, A7).

Illustrated with a decidedly satanic-looking Bela Lugosi centered on the page, the article is less a preview of the film than a brief homily on the dangerous religious Other that it reveals. Rather than the complex religious system Seabrook presents, however sensationally, we are back to the "benighted heathen" of popular imagination. The *Courant*'s actual review is decidedly less sanguine about *White Zombie*, calling it "a gripping, fantastic story of sorcery as it is believed to be practiced on the island of Hayti [*sic*]," but one that puts "a very obvious strain on the credulity of the audience" ("Film, 'White Zombie,' On Capitol Bill," 1932, 16). Strain the credulity of post-Depression audiences it may have, but films that purport to be based on actual events and practices continue to draw on and reinforce popular sociophobics. The dangerous religious Other, the threatening unseen order continues to lurk just beyond the glow of our lights. "For the flash of a second I had a sickening, almost panicky lapse in which I thought, or rather felt," writes Seabrook, thinking, "'Great God, maybe this stuff is really true, and if it is true, it is rather awful, for it upsets everything.' By 'everything,' I meant the natural fixed laws and processes on which all modern human thought and actions are based" ([1929] 1989, 101). Caught between the supernaturalism of his experience and the rationalism of his explanation, Seabrook epitomizes the metataxis of horror that so many of these films present.

Each of the categories of undead considered in this chapter violates in some way the boundary between life and death. Violation breaks the rules, breaches boundaries, and transgresses taboos. For the time the film takes to unreel, at least, it holds the breach in tension, allowing questions about the nature of good and evil to float ambiguously on the surface of our horror. Indeed, if only while the film rolls—though, in some cases, far beyond that—violation, inversion, and metataxis ask whether the rules by which we think we live any longer apply.

# 6

## MAINSTREAMING SATAN
### Fear of Supernatural Evil Internalized and Externalized

<pre>
            LT. KESSEL
 God is not here today, priest.
</pre>
      (Renny Harlin, *Exorcist: The Beginning*)

*I really firmly believe that the Devil didn't want us to make the film.*
      (Harvey Bernhard, *The Omen Legacy*)

*To a far greater degree than most of us could have imagined fifteen or so years ago, a favorable climate for the occurrence of demonic Possession has developed as the normal condition of our lives.*
      (Malachi Martin, *Hostage to the Devil*)

### OUTTAKE: *THE EXORCIST*

I saw *The Exorcist* when I was fifteen, and I still remember the smell of the E. W. Bickle theater in Courtenay, British Columbia. I remember its old carpet, its creaky velvet-upholstered seats, the watered-down Tang passed off as orange drink. I even remember where I sat, though like so many who saw it in 1973 I spent a good portion of the film wandering back and forth in the lobby, caught between my own personal Scylla and Charybdis: the intense desire to run, to put as much physical and conceptual distance as I could between me and what was happening on the screen, but knowing that I would then be walking home alone, in the dark, with the Devil now fully aware that I was aware. In retrospect, it was not so much what was happening on the screen that bothered me; it was my own deeply embedded cultural fear that such things might actually happen.

Many readers are likely familiar with the plot. An ancient evil is released from an archeological dig in northern Iraq and finds its way to Georgetown, in Washington, D.C. There, apparently through the auspices of an Ouija board and a mysterious entity named "Captain Howdy," it infects young Regan MacNeil (Linda Blair), daughter of a prominent actress. The house in which she lives is suddenly plagued with poltergeist phenomena, while Regan and those around her are drawn further and further into the experience of demonic possession. To help her daughter, Chris MacNeil (Ellen Burstyn) looks first to modern medicine, to psychologists, psychiatrists, and neurologists—all of whom are unable either to explain or to alleviate Regan's symptoms. In a key scene, a desperate Chris seeks the counsel of a troubled Jesuit psychiatrist, Father Damien Karras, asking abruptly about possession and exorcism:

                    CHRIS

And, uh, how do you go about getting an exorcism?

                    FATHER DAMIEN

I beg your pardon?

                    CHRIS

If a, uh, a person's, you know, possessed by a demon or something. How do they--how do they get an exorcism?

                    FATHER DAMIEN

Well, the first thing, I'd have to get

them into a time machine and get them
back to the sixteenth century.

                    CHRIS

I didn't get you?

                    FATHER DAMIEN

Well, it just doesn't happen anymore,
Miss MacNeil.

                    CHRIS

Oh, yeah, since when?

                    FATHER DAMIEN

Well, since we learned about mental
illness, paranoia, schizophrenia, all
those things they taught me at Harvard.
Miss MacNeil, since the day I joined
the Jesuits, I've never met one priest
who has performed an exorcism, not one.

As we all know, of course, Regan is possessed, and this brings Father Karras not only to a crisis of profession but of faith—a significant portion of what he has learned since joining the Jesuits is suddenly wrong. Demons do exist, the Devil is real, and in this case he must turn to the *Roman Ritual* not the *Diagnostic and Statistical Manual* if he wants to help the girl. As the possession deepens, and an experienced exorcist, Father Lankester Merrin (Max von Sydow), takes over, the scenes for which the film is best remembered unreel: Regan levitating off her bed, projectile vomiting, physically transforming from a beautiful young girl into a hideous monster, twisting her head around 360 degrees, masturbating with a crucifix, and taunting the priests with increasingly vile language. Although the demon is defeated in the end—imitating the divine sacrifice, Karras invites the demon into himself, and in his last moment of lucidity hurls himself through the window—it is clear that the war between God and the Devil is far from over.

Later, I spent the night at my friend's house. He'd sat through the entire thing and couldn't imagine what all the fuss was about. I remember watching him fall blithely asleep as though he hadn't a care in the world, secure in his delusion that the Devil remained safely locked on celluloid. I, on the other hand, sweated in fear, knowing, certain, appallingly secure in my knowledge that now the Devil knew that I knew, and the jig was definitely up.

Now, more than thirty years later, things in the world of cinema horror have changed rather dramatically. I learned this first when I watched an undergraduate class watch *The Exorcist* during a course on "Religion and the Problem of Evil." Though few of my students were born when the film was released originally, most had heard about the viewing experience—tales of people passing out, vomiting in their seats, seeking the advice of priests and ministers immediately upon exiting the theater. Like children waiting for a long-anticipated ghost story, there were some nervous giggles, a low-level anxiety in the class, a few fearless promises among friends to "watch it all."

The result was, shall we say, anticlimactic. There were a few screams and screeches, but far more laughter at what they regarded as hopelessly outdated special effects and a story that is rather difficult to follow if you are not aware of Roman Catholic demonology. Watching some of them even nod off during the film made me wonder what had changed. After all, this was "the most terrifying movie of all time"—at least, that's what the poster said. To mix metaphors for a moment, though, this is the rock video generation, raised on any number of interchangeable Freddy Krueger and Jason Voorhees characters, used to "shock-and-awe" slasher killings in the first minutes of a film, with more following like an inevitable, pounding chorus as the film moves to its utterly predictable conclusion. *The Exorcist*, on the other hand, builds like a symphony, antiphonally almost, growing gradually to the final crashing dénouement in the film's last half-hour. There are, of course, still those who exit the room pale and wide-eyed, but for most of my students, this is just one more in a long list of horror movies—you watch it, perhaps jump at the appropriate moments, then move on to the next one.

Of all the fears exemplified and explored through cinema horror in North America, the fear of supernatural evil internalized and externalized illustrates the principles of sociophobics most clearly and most paradoxically. To reiterate briefly, rather than simply a psychological state or a set of physical reactions to adverse stimuli, sociophobics suggests that what we fear, how we fear, and the ways in which we react to fear are profoundly shaped by the cultures in which we live. In many parts of the world, for example, temporary possession states—whether by harmful or benevolent spiritual entities—are an accepted part of the community's religious worldview, an integral and often fundamental component of the relationship between the seen and the unseen orders (for a variety of perspectives on this, see, for example, Eliade, 1964; Oesterreich, 1966; Olmos and Paravisini-Gebert, 1997). Thus, possession experiences do not necessarily elicit the same degree of horror as they do in other cultures. On the other hand, while the fear of being turned into a zombie may titillate North American audiences, it does not possess the power to horrify that it does among the people of Haiti. However scary we may find mummies and vampires onscreen, few in the audience expect ever to meet one of these creatures outside the theater. All three belong to the sociophobics of other times and other cultures. They speak to unseen orders in which we, by and large, do not believe and do not participate. The fear they generate around the campfire of the movie screen is imaginal—as opposed to imaginary—the thought that something like this might exist rather than the belief that it does (Carroll, 1990, 79–88). Even though nearly 40 percent of Americans believe in ghosts and haunting spirits, as I suggested in my discussion of *Ju-On* and *The Grudge*, the dominant religious tradition in North America—Christianity—makes neither theological nor ritual room for them. Not so for the sociophobics explored in this chapter, all of which lie at or near the heart of certain streams of Christian theology, popular belief, and religious practice, both Protestant and Roman Catholic.

The fear of supernatural evil internalized and externalized emerges in three basic cinema horror themes: possession and exorcism, insemination and naziresis, and incarnation and apocalypse. We will consider these themes principally through the best known examples of each: *The Exorcist*, *Rosemary's Baby*, and *The Omen*. More than any others, these three films brought supernatural horror into the mainstream for North American audiences, legitimizing it with big-name stars, A-level production values, and themes that resonated with millions of potential viewers.

## POSSESSION AND EXORCISM: DIABOLISM AND THE CULTURAL GROUND OF HORROR

Tunisia banned *The Exorcist*, calling it "'unjustified' propaganda in favor of Christianity" (UPI, 1974a), while the Soviet press condemned it as "pornographic and sadistic," simply more evidence of a pervasive American immorality from which the Soviet citizenry must be protected (Reuters, 1974). On this side of the Atlantic, also claiming it was "obscene and immoral," a Boston woman sued a local theater under Massachusetts' blasphemy statute (UPI, 1974b). Nikolas Schreck, on the other hand, the son-in-law of Church of Satan founder Anton LaVey, called it "absurd" and "one of the most laughable presentations of the Devil onscreen" ever, "the kind of spook-house effect trotted out by evangelists to scare their congregations" (2000, 168).

*The Exorcist* was based on the best-selling novel by William Peter Blatty, who also produced the film. For all the hype (hundreds of extras turning up to a casting call, stories of strange phenomena both on the set and off, and tens of thousands of people waiting hours in the rain, wind, and snow to see the film), critical reaction to the film was decidedly mixed. The *Chicago Tribune*'s

Gene Siskel gave it four stars, calling it "brutal in its brilliance" (1973b, sec. 2, A1), though in a sidebar he noted that the priest with whom he saw the film feared "a rash of pseudopossessions" (1973a, sec. 2, A1). In another four-star review, Roger Ebert, Siskel's then-collaborator and rival at the *Chicago Sun-Times*, thought it "an exploitation of the most fearsome resources of the cinema," and "one of the best movies of its type ever made" (1973). At the *New York Times*, however, the often acerbic Vincent Canby, demurred, dubbing it "a chunk of elegant occultist claptrap" (1973, sec. L, 46). Whereas the *Tribune* featured Siskel's review above the fold on the front page of the Friday entertainment section, the *Times* buried Canby's reaction nearly fifty pages in, above an article about a potential strike by off-Broadway Actors Equity members and opposite an ad for Woody Allen's *Sleeper*. Writing for the *Hartford Courant*, John Massaro could not believe anyone would take William Friedkin's film seriously. "It's a childish prank," he wrote (Massaro, 1974, 4), "which pretentiously deals with the struggle over evil in narrow gothic terms." Months after its release, the *Chicago Tribune*'s book reviewer, Clarence Petersen, saw the film with his two teenaged daughters and wrote that *The Exorcist* "was, at best, an entertainment, a folk dance, a ditty, a highly publicized carnival sideshow on film" (1974, 18). On the west coast, *Los Angeles Times* reviewer Charles Champlin called it a "theological Grand Guignol" (1973, H1), while in Canada, the *Globe and Mail*'s Martin Knelman dismissed it as "utterly contemptible" (1973b, 10), a movie "so appallingly crude and so hideously inept that it's really beneath discussing on artistic grounds" (1973a, 10). Locating his review opposite the Contract Bridge column and an advertisement for a televised interview on "The National Crises" with American evangelist Billy Graham, Knelman did allow that "the picture is something of a popular phenomenon—so it can't be ignored" (1973a, 10).

Whatever one may think of Knelman's review, his evaluation is correct. *The Exorcist* cannot be ignored, though its cultural importance is less the film itself than the popular reaction to it and the mythology that has evolved in the generation since its release—both evidence of the rich sociophobic vein into which it tapped. In 1973 it was the most successful motion picture to date. While it has been eclipsed now by any number of films, and even its $12 million budget is paltry by today's standards, it marks something of a watershed in the history of Western cinema horror. As noted, few in the West actually believe in the offscreen reality of zombies, mummies, and vampires, and while millions of people believe in ghosts, relatively few expect to see them on a regular basis. The Devil and his unholy minions, on the other hand, the fallen angels, are an integral component of the central mythology of the dominant religious tradition in North America. This locates *The Exorcist* squarely within the sociophobics of Christianity, three aspects of which reinforce its potential to terrify a North American audience: the history of the Devil in Christian theology; the practical reality of recurring satanic panics in late modern society; and the sociological effect of the "true story."

Theologically, though in many different guises, the Devil has been an integral part of the Christian church since its inception. Christian theologians have carefully interpreted the relationship of the Devil and his angels, priests and ministers have preached his power and the need to seek safety and salvation in the Church, and, occasionally, those believed to be in league with or possessed by the Devil have been the victims of horrific cruelty. As historian Jeffrey Burton Russell, whose magisterial work remains the best set of resources for the history of the concept of the Devil in Christianity, points out, "a central thesis of the New Testament . . . is that the powers of darkness under the generalship of the Devil are at war with the power of light" (1977, 227; see also Carus ([1900] 1996; Garrett, 1989; Pagels, 1995; Russell, 1981, 1984, 1986).

Though relatively rare in the Old Testament, the Devil and his fallen angels make regular appearances in the New Testament as a more complex demonology developed during the early Christian era. Many of the passages in which Jesus heals people are coupled with instances of demonic possession and exorcism. Matthew 8:28-33, for example, tells the story of two demon-possessed men who survived in the tombs on the outskirts of Gadara, a town northeast of Jerusalem. Faced with the power of the Son of God, the demons plead with Jesus to be sent into a herd of swine instead of returning them "to the abyss"—a request Jesus grants, though the pigs immediately ran off a cliff into the sea (cf. Mark 5:1-13; Luke 8:26-33). Believing that epilepsy was the result of demonic possession—a rare instance in the gospels when medical and spiritual afflictions coincide—Jesus exorcizes a young boy who had been constantly throwing himself into fires (cf. Matt 17:14-18; Mark 9:14-27; Luke 9:37-42). In Friedkin's film, epilepsy is one of the first medical diagnoses offered for Regan's condition. Both Mark (16:9) and Luke (8:2) claim that Jesus cast seven demons out of Mary Magdalene, one of his closest disciples, and a number of times detractors accused Jesus of either being possessed by demons himself or relying on the power of demons to perform exorcisms.

Belief in the Devil's power to tempt humankind away from God was so strong that it has also formed an integral part of the liturgical framework for the yearly remembrance and celebration of the Paschal Mystery. For the first Sunday of Lent, for example, the gospel passages recommended for two of the three years in the Common Lectionary (a set of planned readings for use in Christian worship worldwide) prescribe the well-known story of Jesus' temptation in the desert (Matt 4:1-11; Luke 4:1-13). According to Christian scripture, immediately after his baptism by John, Jesus retreats into the wilderness to pray, to fast, and to gather strength for his mission. There, the Devil tempts him in a variety of ways, suggesting that he turn stones into bread to assuage his hunger, throw himself from the top of the temple in Jerusalem to demonstrate his position as the Son of God, and fall down and worship the Devil in return for power over all the kingdoms of the Earth. Of course, while the liturgical use of these passages usually turns on the dialectic between the power of the Devil to tempt and the example of Christ to resist, the important point to note here is that, unlike ghosts, vampires, mummies, or zombies, the diabolic is firmly embedded in Christian scripture, mythistory, and worship.

Throughout Christian tradition, belief in the power of the demonic to invade our world has ebbed and flowed, but it never disappeared entirely. Conflating belief in witchcraft with the Devil and his fallen angels, the Roman Catholic Church developed during the Middle Ages an extensive demonological literature, one of the most notorious examples of which is the *Malleus Maleficarum*, the "Hammer of Witches." Written by two Dominicans friars, Heinrich Kramer and James Sprenger, and published in 1486, the *Malleus* was one of a number of manuals used in "the systematic persecution of witches as devil-worshippers" (Thomas, 1971, 521). As historian Keith Thomas notes, though an English edition did not appear until the late nineteenth century, it went through "thirteen editions on the Continent by 1520" and "was issued sixteen times in Germany before 1700 and eleven times in France" (1971, 523). Among others, the sixteenth century also saw *De Magorum Dæmonomania* (1586) and *De la Demonomanie des sorciers* (1587), both by Jean Bodin, an eminent French jurist and philosopher. One hundred and fifty years after the *Malleus*, an Italian monk named Francesco Maria Guazzo published the *Compendium Maleficarum* ([1608] 1988), a veritable catalogue of demonic cause-and-effect, complete with dozens of woodcuts illustrating various aspects of diabolism and detailed instructions on "How to Distinguish Demoniacs, and Those who are Simply Bewitched" (Guazzo, [1608] 1988, 167–69). In the case of the former, Montague Summers notes in his gloss that rather than more standard treatments, in these cases "the rubrics of 'De Exorcizandis Obsessis a Daemonio' in the 'Rituale Romanum' should be consulted" (Guazzo, [1608] 1988, 167n). That is, the Rite of Exorcism should be performed. Even today, as part of the Rite of Baptism, the Church requires that the parents and godparents of the child renounce the Devil and his works, and during the sacrament itself the priest offers a brief prayer of exorcism on the child's behalf.

Practically, the mythistory of diabolism embedded in Christian tradition has been significantly reinforced by intermittent waves of "satanic panic" offscreen, which include a thriving subculture described by late modern possession and exorcism narratives. For many people, demonic possession or oppression, and either exorcism or deliverance, are predominantly Roman Catholic beliefs, vestiges of the sixteenth-century sociophobic to which Damien Karras felt them safely relegated. For millions of others, however, they are an integral part of an ongoing cosmic battle between the forces of good and evil. Every day, they believe, is spent on the front lines, as Christians and their angelic allies wage spiritual warfare against the Devil and his demonic minions (see, for example, Lewis, 1996; Peretti, 1986, 1989, 1995; Viser, 1994; Weldon and Bjornstad, 1984). Even UFOs have been pressed into service in support of a fundamentalist Christian demonology (see, for example, Larson, 1997; Rhodes, 1998; Weldon and Levitt, 1975; Wimbish, 1990). Though it may be surprising to some, in the same way that the mythology of Vodou and the folklore of zombies permeate Haitian culture, belief in the possibility of demonic possession and oppression is alive and well in late modern North America. In 1991, nearly half the American population believed in the possibility of demonic possession, a figure that must surely increase among regular church-goers (Newport and Strausberg, 2001). Over a decade later, though belief in demonic possession had dropped slightly, 70 percent indicated belief in Hell—92 percent among those who attend church on a weekly basis (Winseman, 2004a). In terms of the sociophobic out of which a film like *The Exorcist* emerges, then, these are hardly insignificant figures.

Shortly after *The Exorcist*'s release in 1973, the *Chicago Tribune* reported on an Anglican priest from London who claimed to have performed more than two thousand exorcisms in five years (Merry, 1974). Pastors across the United States based sermons on the film, some debunking the possibility of demonic possession, others using it to warn their flocks of its dangers and challenge them to deeper Christian commitment. Billy Graham told his audiences that "the true Christian cannot possibly be possessed," and attributed the success of such books and films as *The Exorcist* to "a modern lack of faith" (Satter, 1974, 14). However, the Western fascination with the demonic does not so much indicate a lack of faith as a profound ambivalence about the faith in which that demonology comes embedded. Millions of people, both Protestant and Roman Catholic, believe in these phenomena, and *The Exorcist*, as it were, opened a sociophobic window onto that belief—one that remains open to this day.

Three years after Friedkin's film, an ex-Roman Catholic priest named Malachi Martin released a book called *Hostage to the Devil* (1976), which purports to tell the in-depth stories of five Americans who underwent possession and exorcism experiences. Although his work has been criticized as hyperbolic and inflated—"converting, by literary sleight-of-hand, half-truths and innuendo into immutable facts of history" (Cuneo, 2001, 17)—Martin's book fanned the flames of demonology in late modern society. The *New York Times* ran a quarter-page advertisement, complete with a picture of the book jacket and the headline, "Forget every other book about possession... this is THE BOOK" (1976, 217). Arguing, however, that *Hostage to the Devil* was "Giving Possession a Bad Name," William Peter Blatty responded with a lengthy, peevish review in the *Los Angeles Times* (1976, P1). Filled with "errata and drivel," Blatty concludes that "reading this book—considering the credentials of its author—is like being mugged by a Hare Krishna follower" (1976, 13, 14). Letters to the editor appeared for each of the next four weeks, some praising his candor, others criticizing Blatty for his tone and his obvious chagrin that he had been supplanted as the pop culture expert on the phenomenon. Novelist and critic Francine du Plessix Gray takes a less grumpy approach, though her assessment is no less dismissive. *Hostage to the Devil*, she writes, "is a book that may prove to be profoundly seductive to an unholy alliance of audiences—porn show freaks, fundamentalist church-goers obsessed with the threat of Satan's work, and those back-to-myth academics chicly announcing The Bankruptcy of the Scientific Worldview and their disenchantment with rationalism" (1976, BR3). All of which only improved the chances that it would continue to sell. And sell it did—very well indeed. The Book-of-the-Month Club offered *Hostage* as one of the featured selections in its "4 Books for $1" membership promotions. 1992 saw the release of a new edition, in the preface for which Martin writes that the incidence of demonic possession, as well as popular involvement in Satanism, has steadily increased since the book was first published. Believing the threat even more imminent (though he provides no indication how he came to possess these facts—for which there is no empirical evidence), he writes:

> We know, for example, that throughout all fifty states of the Union, there are now something over 8,000 Satanist covens. We know that in any major city or large town, a Black Mass—almost always organized by covens—is available on a weekly basis at least, and at several locations . . . In at least three major cities, members of the [Roman Catholic] clergy have at their disposal at least one pedophiliac coven peopled and maintained exclusively by and for the clergy . . . we have enormous amounts of anecdotal evidence indicating that some thousands of infants and children are intentionally conceived and born to serve as Victims in Satanist sacrificial rites. (Martin, 1992, xii)

In the late 1970s and early 1980s, a resurgence of fundamentalist Protestantism, coupled with burgeoning fears about new religious movements in general, the rise of such dedicated countermovements as the secular anticult and the Christian countercult, the appearance of groups like Anton LaVey's Church of Satan, allegations of Satanism in heavy metal music and fantasy role-playing games, and elaborate claims of Satanic ritual abuse captured public attention. Often using (now suspect) techniques designed to recover memories supposedly long repressed, psychiatrists, psychologists, and anticult "counselors" encountered patients who related bizarre instances—and in some cases long histories—of ritual abuse at the hands of Satanic worshippers (Mulhern, 1991; Nathan, 1991; Ross, 1995; Sakheim and Devine, 1992). "True life" accounts of Satanic ritual abuse proliferated on bookstore shelves, the most famous of which, *Michelle Remembers* (Smith and Pazder, 1980), is so flawed and so obviously fabricated that sociologist Michael Cuneo contends it "makes *Hostage to the Devil* look like a textbook study in fact-based reporting" (2001, 204). Law enforcement officials began to investigate "ritual crimes," some even producing handbooks on the subject for use by other agencies (Crouch and Damphouse, 1991; Gray et al., 1992; Hicks, 1991; Lanning, 1992). Not surprisingly, like moths to a flame, the media saw another modern panic to which it could hitch its own particular commercial wagon (Ellis, 2000; Rowe and Cavender, 1991; Victor, 1991, 1993). "Ritual Abuse: A Perplexing Pattern of Reports" reads one *Washington Post* article (Gorney, 1988), for example, though a *New York Times* piece six years later suggests "Proof Lacking for Ritual Abuse by Satanists" (Goleman, 1994). Cinema horror, of course, had been playing the ritual abuse card for decades, leading the trick, as it were, for a more profound cultural reaction. Because all of these different narratives purport to be true stories that have happened to men and women who would otherwise not seek publicity, they contributed to the social construction of a satanic panic that was out of all proportion to any actual danger.

For their part, conservative Christians—du Plessix Gray's "fundamentalist church-goers obsessed with the threat of Satan's work"—have developed something of a cottage industry warning each other in often gruesome detail about the dangers of the demonic world. As *The Satan Seller* (1972), for example, comedian and evangelist Mike Warnke claimed to be a Satanist high priest who regularly recruited witting and unwitting victims into his coven. Lauren Stratford wrote of being an unwilling victim of *Satan's Underground* for many years (1988). And Rebecca Brown, the nom de plume of an Indiana woman named Ruth Bailey, told her story of battling demonic forces in two evangelical potboilers, *He Came to Set the Captives Free* (1992a) and *Prepare for War* (1992b). Though all of these have been exposed as frauds (on Warnke, see Hertenstein and Trott, 1993; on Stratford, see Passantino, Passantino, and Trott, 1990, 1999; on Brown, see Fisher and Goedelman, 1996), belief in the reality of spiritual warfare, demonic possession, and the need for exorcism continues, largely promoted in recent years by a fundamentalist radio host, author, and freelance exorcist named Bob Larson.

During a 2007 appearance on the enormously popular *Dr. Phil* show, Larson claimed to have performed more than ten thousand exorcisms over the past thirty years—an average of almost one per day. He has written a number of books promoting his fundamentalist vision of a "demon-haunted world," including *Satanism: The Seduction of America's Youth* (1989), *In the Name of Satan* (1996), *UFOs and the Alien Agenda* (1997), and *Larson's Book of Spiritual Warfare* (1999). Delivered to tens of thousands of contributors monthly, his ministry newsletter is an ongoing compendium of demonic malfeasance, his own selfless evangelical heroism, and the constant need for cash donations to help him carry the battle to satanic strongholds he believes are everywhere. In 1998, for example, in exchange for a $100 donation, Larson offered to send supporters his "Demon Proofing Protection Package," which included "Songs of Spiritual Warfare" ("the praise and worship songs I have found most effective to defeat demons"); "Devil-Proofing Prayers" ("to keep you and your family free from Satan's attacks"); "S.W.A.T. Tapes" (i.e., Spiritual Warfare Action Training; "Six tapes with six hours of the most intense teaching on demons and deliverance you'll ever find anywhere"); and, perhaps most significantly in terms of this chapter's principal sociophobic,

"Exorcism in Action" ("You'll see what thousands have seen live, in person, as I've traveled from city to city across America, doing public exorcisms"; 1998b).

That same year, I attended what Larson advertised as "Calgary's First Public Exorcism." The small hotel conference room was filled that hot summer evening; over a hundred people had come to hear Larson and, presumably, to see an exorcism. Headlining himself as the "World's Most Recognized Authority on the Supernatural and Spiritual Success," he told the audience at the program's beginning that he is "probably the worldwide expert on the occult. No one knows more about spiritualism and demon possession than I do" (Larson, 1998a). During the evening, though, no exorcism took place. There were none of the outrageous theatrics that characterize his advertising videos. No one frothed or writhed or threatened to attack him. A few people repented of various minor transgressions and turned their lives over to Christ (again), but there was no "main event," as it were. The closest was a young female goth whom Larson confronted in a particularly belligerent manner. Alleging that her facial piercings were the Devil's point of entry, he attempted briefly to cast from her the "demon of teen rebellion," but could not because he spot-diagnosed her as "bipolar" (1998a; see Cowan, 2003a, 80–86; cf. Trott, 1993). While this proved something of an anticlimax, and many readers may dismiss Larson at this point as a charlatan, it highlights once again the not-insignificant sociophobic that still thrives in certain religious subcultures in North America. It does not stop there, though, and this is the power of mass media in all its forms. While it may be that, sociologists of religion notwithstanding, only those inclined to Larson's particular brand of fundamentalist Christianity attend his seminars and public exorcisms, a much broader audience is exposed to it through his appearances on such high-profile television shows as *Dr. Phil, Oprah Winfrey, Good Morning America, Inside Edition*, and the literally scores of local news broadcasts that have run feature stories on him. This kind of exposure contributes significantly to the third sociophobic aspect implicated by *The Exorcist*: the sociological power of the "true story."

Long before it hit the theaters, potential moviegoers were aware that *The Exorcist* was based on what Blatty claimed was a real exorcism, according to the *Los Angeles Times*, "the last official, church-verified case of demonic possession in America" (Reed, 1973, U28). From the beginning, it was presented as a true story, the fictionalized elements of which few in the audience would be equipped to discern.

Immediate physical reaction to the film notwithstanding, that people took the ideas seriously is not in doubt. Located beneath a story on an elementary school shooting, for example, the front page of the *Chicago Tribune* reported that a number of people who saw *The Exorcist* were now under psychiatric care, two of them in restraints (Page, 1974, 1). Parish and diocesan offices received hundreds of calls requesting information on possession and exorcism. On the one hand, sales of occult-related books soared in the wake of the movie's popularity, while, on the other, a fundamentalist youth group in Illinois staged a book-burning in protest against the occult's growing power in late modern society. Church members "said they were concerned over publicity about the world of evil spirits, some of it in connection with the showing of 'The Exorcist.' They said they burned [the books, including Blatty's] to repudiate black magic" (AP, 1974, D14). Curious crowds descended on the ordinarily quiet campus of Georgetown University wanting to see the locations where the film was shot, including the chapel that was desecrated in the story, and to discuss with the Jesuits there the phenomena of possession and exorcism (Wolhowe, 1974, C1). So intense was the reaction that *Los Angeles Times* reporters convened a panel of Catholic priests at Loyola Marymount University to discuss the film and its effects (Kilday, 1974). Within a month of the film's opening, Father Richard Woods, a Dominican faculty member at Loyola University in Chicago and the author of two books on the occult (1971, 1973), "received dozens of calls from people who are horribly frightened or so confused that they have begun to lose their grip on reality" (Fiske, 1974, 15). In an admirable description of the ambivalent sociophobic reality into which *The Exorcist* tapped, Woods concluded that "a high percentage of his calls came from persons who were raised as Catholics but no longer practiced their religion. 'It stirs up memories of all those descriptions of hell that you got from nuns,' he said" (Fiske, 1974, 15).

Both ecclesiastical tradition and popular mythology, reinforced by the sociological power of the "true story" and the supernatural "buzz" that built up around the film before its release, contributed to an urban legend that almost immediately possessed the film once it hit the theaters, and demonstrated among its audiences an arguably unsophisticated yet tremendously powerful connection to the unseen order *The Exorcist* purports to represent. The message, it seems, is clear: Satan is real, and he has a plan for your life.

## DEMON SEED: INSEMINATION AND THE NAZIRESIS OF EVIL

> ROSEMARY
>
> Dr. Hill, there's a plot. I know that sounds crazy, and you're probably thinking, 'My God, this poor girl's really flipped,' but I haven't flipped, Dr. Hill. I swear by all the saints, I haven't. There are plots against people, aren't there?

Convinced that her husband has made a deal with the Devil and offered their unborn child in return for professional success, Rosemary Woodhouse (Mia Farrow) tries desperately to convince her erstwhile obstetrician, Dr. Hill (Charles Grodin), that a coven of Satanists is after her. Nine months pregnant though still waif-thin, standing in a corner telephone booth on a sweltering New York day, she pleads with him to see her, to believe her story, to assure her that she hasn't flipped. Believing, however, that she is suffering from some kind of prepartum paranoia, Dr. Hill returns her to the dubious care of her husband, her doctor, and, ultimately, the Devil worshippers next door. Her baby is delivered and the coven celebrates the advent of their dark prince. There are plots against people, aren't there?

Though neither as hotly debated nor as fraught with social upheaval as *The Exorcist*, *Rosemary's Baby* is just as effective a mirror of cultural concerns. Like the largely unadorned white walls of the apartment Rosemary and Guy (John Cassavetes) rent in New York's historic "Brampton Building"—in reality, the famous Dakota on 72nd and Central Park West—the film itself is something of a blank canvas. Partly because Polanski gives us so few clues about what, if anything, is actually happening, a tactic that leaves the range of interpretation uncomfortably wide. Are the elderly couple next door really Satanists, or merely nosey and overbearing? Are they responsible for Guy's sudden success as an actor, or is that a coincidence? Has Rosemary become caught up in the supernatural history of the Brampton, or is it her own neurotic reaction to a pregnancy for which she seems distinctly unready? As much as any other example from the vaults of cinema horror, *Rosemary's Baby* highlights one of the principal realities disclosed by sociophobics: what we see in a film is informed at least as much by what we bring to the theater as by what the director offers us onscreen.

Clifford Terry's *Chicago Tribune* review called it "a masterful mixture of obstetrics and the occult" (1968, F7), while the *Los Angeles Times*' Charles Champlin felt it "a most desperately sick and obscene motion picture whose ultimate horror—in my very private opinion—was that it was made at all" (1968, H11). Although Renata Adler hyped it as "a highly serious lapsed-Catholic fable" (1968, 57), Robert Chappetta dismissed it as "a piece of pulp-fiction," in which "the extravagance of the coincidences act as a guarantor of the reality of the supernatural and the extraterrestrial" (1969, 37).

Film scholars, on the other hand, for the most part cleave to a rather singular interpretation: whatever it is, it is about something else. That is, not the supernatural, not the extraterrestrial (whatever Chappetta means by that), and certainly not elderly Satanic covens in uptown Manhattan. David Hogan regards it as "a wicked parody of middle-class domesticity and sexual role-playing" (1986, 80), while Vivian Sobchak sees in it "the radical beginning of patriarchal failure: of paternity refused, denied, abandoned, hated" (1987a, 184–85). Citing the *New Yorker*'s review of the film, Lucy Fisher labels it a "gynecological gothic," "an odious fable of parturition," "a skewed 'documentary' of the societal and personal turmoil that has regularly attended female reproduction" (1992, 4). For Virginia Wexman, Rosemary represents the helpless child in all of us; she is a celluloid vision of those "disturbing intimations of infantile psychological states" (1987, 41) to which all good Freudians feel human beings are somewhat inevitably bound.

*Rosemary's Baby* can certainly be seen as all these things. Many women regard the presence of a fetus—especially during a first pregnancy—as an intruder, an alien, something over which they have no control and that slowly but surely takes over their lives. The film can be explained away as a psychosexual melodrama about a naïve, almost child-bride; an overbearing, detached father-husband; and the baby neither of them seems to know what to do with. John Cassavetes was, after all, sixteen years older than Mia Farrow and looks every minute of it in the film, and we never actually see the infant. Indeed, for all we know, the black-draped bassinet in the film's final sequence is nothing more than the central fixture in some bizarre wake for a stillborn child and the moment when Rosemary completely loses touch with reality. Whereas *The Exorcist* is presented from multiple points of view, thereby minimizing the potential for a purely psychological reading of the story, Polanski shot his film entirely from Rosemary's perspective. As events unfold and the alleged plot thickens, the audience is often placed in the position of the unfortunate Dr. Hill, watching and wondering whether the poor young thing has, in fact, flipped. How much of what happens occurs solely in Rosemary's imagination? During the ritual rape that takes place in the context of a drug-induced nightmare, Rosemary suddenly opens her eyes wide and cries, "This is no dream. This is really happening!" But, is it? As far as we can tell, it really happened onscreen, but in Rosemary's befuddled, increasingly paranoid state, is it meant to serve as an allegory for more serious social problems offscreen?

Though all of the critics noted above advert in some way to the supernatural aspect of the film—the story, after all, is that Rosemary's baby has been sired by Satan himself—each finds another way to explain the film's events. Each rejects the principal sociophobic around which the film is based: the belief in a satanic conspiracy that, in this case, involves the birth of the Devil's child. Recall that Wexman contends the film presents the audience with nothing so much as "the ludicrous nature of all religious beliefs" (1987, 39), regardless of whether one is a lapsed Catholic or a practicing Satanist. As with all interpretations, though, these say as least as much about the interpreters (myself included) as they do the film. Rejecting the supernatural elements in favor of naturalistic or psychological explanations does not relieve one of the burden of sociophobics—it simply locates that burden elsewhere. The cultural fear surfaced by the film is different, but that's all. What is unfortunate—and short-sighted—about these interpretations is that they present themselves either implicitly or explicitly as the film's only logical, rational explanation, and in so doing ignore the more deeply embedded cultural fears into which the film taps. Indeed, as Norma Lee Browning wrote in her *Chicago Tribune* review, "Audiences probably will look at the movie in different ways depending on their religion—or lack of it" (1968, B2).

This is exactly the point.

Setting aside the vast historical and theological differences between Satanism and modern Pagan witchcraft, but recognizing the surprisingly resilient pop cultural equation of the two,

*Rosemary's Baby* draws on centuries of suspicion, propaganda, and Christian persecution of those the church has chosen to label "witches" (see Barner-Barry, 2005; Cowan and Bromley, 2008, 193). From this perspective, *Rosemary's Baby* is arguably the leading example of cinema horror that bridges the sociophobics of possession and exorcism, and incarnation and apocalypse. It presents us with the naziresis of evil, the fear of a child dedicated in some way to Satan.

In ancient Hebrew tradition, a Nazirite was someone consecrated to God through a series of ritual actions and prohibitions (Num 6:1-21). A well-known biblical example is Samson, who was born to a barren mother and whose parents were instructed never to cut his hair, "for the boy shall be a Nazirite to God from birth. It is he who shall begin to deliver Israel from the hand of the Philistines" (Judg 13:5). In the cinema horror inversion of naziresis, a variety of ritual preparations seek to ensure the birth of a satanic savior who will deliver the world *from* the power of God. "Year One!" the Satanists proclaim jubilantly at a New Year's Eve party at the end of Rosemary's first trimester. "They had their two thousand years," says Father James to his followers in *Lost Souls*. "Now it's our turn"—a theme that has been taken up in a number of different films.

In 1972, for example, a made-for-TV imitation of *Rosemary's Baby* brought Belinda Montgomery to the small screen as *The Devil's Daughter*. Four years later, Hammer Studios released its last, and some say its finest, horror film, *To the Devil... a Daughter*. Based on Dennis Wheatley's best-selling novel of the same name—which was published in 1953, fifteen years before the release of *Rosemary's Baby*—*To the Devil... a Daughter* makes the claim to a satanic naziresis most explicit. Inverting both the cosmological order and his ecclesiastical calling, an excommunicated priest (Christopher Lee) vows to use an impressionable, teenage nun (Nastassia Kinski) as the vehicle for Satan's child and the end of the Christian era. In Carl Schultz' *The Seventh Sign*, Demi Moore plays a woman whose child will be the first in history born without a soul—and easy prey to satanic forces as the apocalypse looms. On the eve of the third millennium, as Jericho Cane, Arnold Schwarzenegger struggles to protect Christine York (*The Craft*'s Robin Tunney), who has been prepared from birth to bear Satan's child and usher in a new era of darkness at the *End of Days*. In most cases, the naziresis of evil is defeated. In others, however, the question of whether God triumphs in the end is left open—as it is in *Rosemary's Baby*.

Film studies scholar Vivian Sobchak distinguishes horror from science fiction on the basis of—or at least according to the site of—the disruption each narrates. "The horror film deals with moral chaos," she writes, "the disruption of natural order," while science fiction "is concerned with social chaos, and the disruption of social order" (1987b, 30). Although one could question in the first instance whether "moral" should be equated with "natural," cinema horror that posits the naziresis of evil explicitly challenges Sobchak's notion that the potential for social upheaval is limited to science fiction. Implicit in each of these films, and in each of the many "demon seed" movies to which *Rosemary's Baby* gave birth, is the potential for social chaos at the most profound level—God's order traded for Satan's, another fundamental fear that has animated Christian imagination, theology, and practice for centuries. On the other hand, Sobchak's distinction explicitly ignores the kind of eschatological cinema that is most commonly recognized in such films as *The Omen*, and which is rooted in deeply held, devoutly believed, and fervently defended perceptions of the end of days. While films like *Rosemary's Baby* and *To the Devil... a Daughter* present the possibility of a Satanic heir, they rarely identify the child as the Antichrist. This identification falls to the cinema of incarnation and apocalypse.

## INCARNATION AND APOCALYPSE: SCREENING THE END OF THE WORLD

Stretching back to the New Testament Letters of John and the Book of Revelation, for two millennia the Antichrist has symbolized for Christians the ultimate in human evil, the one who, at the end of time, challenges God for the throne in the same way Lucifer did before the beginning of time (for some of the best scholarly treatments on the obsession with the Antichrist and the end times, see Boyer, 1992; Fuller, 1995; McGinn, 1994; O'Leary, 1994; Wojcik, 1997). According to these beliefs, the Antichrist will usher in a period of global devastation such as the world has never known, a brutal totalitarianism that will be halted only by the return of Christ.

Who, though, is the Antichrist, and when will he appear? While many Bible scholars insist that the term was meant as a code for Nero during his persecutions of the early Christians, nearly sixteen centuries later, both Martin Luther and John Calvin identified him as the Pope. About the same time, as Paul Boyer points out, "Puritan pamphleteers identified Antichrist with Church of England bishops" (1992, 63). In *War and Peace*, Tolstoy argues for Napoleon, and in the twentieth century numerous political, military, and religious leaders have been suggested. Adolf Hitler, Benito Mussolini, and Josef Stalin; Henry Kissinger, Moshe Dayan, and John F. Kennedy; Saddam Hussein and Ronald Reagan—all have been proposed, often based on a tortured numerology by which their names are supposed to reveal the dreaded "666," the mysterious number from Revelation 13:18 that the dispensationalist faithful believe encodes the Antichrist's identity.

For some of these believers, the Antichrist must be a Jew. In a widely reported 1999 statement, Jerry Falwell declared, "Of course, he'll be Jewish. Of course he'll pretend to be Christ. And if in fact the Lord is coming soon, [then] . . . he [i.e., the Antichrist] must be alive somewhere today" (AP, 1999, A8). On the other hand, in *When Your Money Fails*, an enormously popular

Christian prophecy book published in 1981, Mary Stewart Relfe predicted that the Antichrist would have to be a Muslim. Based on the peace he brokered with Israel (and her claim that an Egyptian Navy vessel in the Suez Canal bore the registration number "666"), Relfe identified Egyptian president Anwar el-Sadat as the most likely candidate. Sadat was assassinated only a few months after her book appeared. For still others, the Antichrist is irretrievably allied with new religious forces. Claiming to be the first to have warned Christians of the alleged threat represented by the New Age movement, lawyer Constance Cumbey has for years been building a case against King Juan Carlos II of Spain, though she has also suggested that, no matter what system of numerology one employs, the name of theologian and former Roman Catholic priest "Matthew Fox adds up to a perfect 666" (1985, 145). While, for many readers, these may seem little more than the mutterings of a fringe fundamentalist few, that assumption would be a mistake. As Bernard McGinn points out, "too many people still believe in a literal and imminent Antichrist for skeptics to pronounce his epitaph with easy security" (1994, 1). Indeed, less than a year after McGinn published those words, arguably the most remarkable event in the late modern search for the Antichrist occurred: the appearance of Tim LaHaye and Jerry Jenkins' *Left Behind*, the latest in a century-long genre of evangelical apocalyptic fiction, and the first in a thirteen volume series that has gone on to sell more than 70 million copies and spawned a number of spin-off book series, a videogame, three feature films, and significant debate about the place of eschatology in Christian evangelicalism (cf. Forbes and Kilde, 2004; Frykholm, 2004; Shuck, 2005). Not insignificantly, Amazon.com lists the many *Left Behind* titles as both fiction and nonfiction.

Over the years, a number of films have tried to impress audiences with their visions of the end of days and the rise of the Antichrist, but none has so epitomized that attempt as Richard Donner's *The Omen*. Written by David Seltzer and originally titled *The Anti-Christ* and *The Birthmark*, the script languished at Warner

Bros. until Donner brought it to Twentieth Century-Fox when the other studio's option expired. It could easily have been just another low-budget horror film, but Donner was able to attract Gregory Peck and Lee Remick for the lead roles, a casting coup that guaranteed media and public interest in the film.

The story itself is unremarkable and predictable. Indeed, with a few cinema horror exceptions, it replicates in many ways the Antichrist's mysterious rise to power that Christian dispensationalists have been predicting since British writer Sydney Watson wrote *In the Twinkling of an Eye* and *The Mark of the Beast* in 1910 and 1918, respectively. When his child is allegedly stillborn, U. S. diplomat Richard Thorn (Peck) accepts an offer from a mysterious priest to take a baby born that same night, but whose own mother died during childbirth. He does not tell his wife (Remick), and they raise the boy as their own. Everything seems fine until Thorn moves up the diplomatic ladder, and strange events begin to surround young Damien (Harvey Stephens). Shouting "It's all for you, Damien," a young nanny hangs herself in full view of an elaborate birthday party the Thorns have thrown for their son. A new nanny mysteriously appears and, with the aid of a demonic Rottweiler, promises that no harm will come to the boy. A priest dies, impaled, after trying to warn Thorn of the threat represented by the boy. Damien throws a violent fit when his parents try to take him into a church. Gradually, the Thorns realize that all is just not right with their son. When his wife is mortally injured in a fall Damien causes, Thorn sets out to learn the truth—which includes a set of ritual daggers said to be the only weapons capable of destroying the Antichrist.

The line-ups were not as long for *The Omen*, and its budget was not a quarter that of the money spent making *The Exorcist*. Even with bankable, A-list stars like Peck and Remick, compared to the ink spilled on Friedkin's film, the press all but ignored Donner's effort. Perhaps peripherally aware of such massive best-sellers as Hal Lindsey's *The Late Great Planet Earth*, Malcolm Johnson's otherwise lukewarm review found "especially provocative" the film's "linking of the prophesies of the Book of Revelation with modern political phenomena" (1976, 18F), while the *Washington Post*'s Tom Shales dismissed as "over-rationalized mumbo-jumbo fantasy" Seltzer's "arduously over-stated gimmick" of the Antichrist (1976, C1, C4). Calling it "the latest 'Exorcist' imitator," Gene Siskel panned the film, reserving his praise only for Jerry Goldsmith's original soundtrack (1976, sec. 3, B5). Unlike the pride of place the *Chicago Tribune* gave his review of *The Exorcist* three years before, this one received barely a notice beside theater ads for such competitors as the sentimental *Ode to Billy Joe* and the science fiction thriller *Logan's Run*. Criticizing "the story's basic idiocy," in a passage worth quoting at length for the significant sociophobic Siskel either misses or ignores, he writes:

> Actually, the story is goofy. It claims inspiration from a Book of Revelation passage that says an anti-Christ child will be born when "the Jews return to Zion, a comet rips the sky, and the Holy Roman Empire rises." Well, the Jews have returned to Zion, and comets always are zipping across the sky (even though Kahoutek fizzled), but what about the Holy Roman Empire? Well, explains Peck in the movie, the growth of the European Common Market can be interpreted to be just that. Oh, come off it, Greg. (Siskel, 1976, B5)

A couple of points are worth noting here, both of which speak to the underlying sociophobic represented by the ongoing search for the Antichrist. Among the dozens of examples of Christian eschatological fiction, of which the *Left Behind* series is only the most recent and prolific, one of the most common characters is the skeptical journalist. The cultural icon of objectivity, rationalism, and often disdain, they are the ones left behind following the rapture—the disappearance of all "true" Christians either before or during the rise of the Antichrist—and their skepticism becomes the metonymic lens through which the real import of events is explained. If a hard-nosed journalist can be convinced of the truth of fundamentalist Christianity, then can the rest of the world be far behind? Disdain like Siskel's, though, often masks an inability or unwillingness to acknowledge the unseen order as it is understood by millions of Christians around the world. Indeed, at precisely the time Siskel was chiding Peck for his allegedly strained interpretation of political events—and by implication Seltzer's credulity for expecting audiences to accept their connection to cosmic battles between good and evil—in both fiction and nonfiction a number of popular Christian writers were making exactly the argument Siskel scorns.

In her novel *The Undelivered*, for example, which was published in 1969, Olive Pattison makes it clear that the budding European Common Market is precisely the organization those left behind when the Antichrist comes must face. Gary Cohen's 1974 effort, *Civilization's Last Hurrah*, makes a similar case. In a thinly veiled reference to the ECM, the Antichrist reveals his plans to lead a united Europe, otherwise known as "the Republic of Mediterranean Europe. Please note that the new initials of our nation are R-O-M-E!" (Cohen, 1974, 118). These echo nonfiction dispensationalist writings from the same era. In *Countdown to Rapture*, Salem Kirban made a similar prediction, one that he has repeated through several later books. "The power of the Common Market nations is growing at a very rapid rate," he writes, and "out of this coalition of nations will come Antichrist" (Kirban, [1977] 1998, 127). In *The Late Great Planet Earth*, Lindsey is just as blunt: "We believe that the Common Market and the trend toward unification of Europe may well be the beginning of the ten-nation confederacy"—the revived Roman empire—"predicted by Daniel and the Book of Revelation" (Lindsey and Carlson, 1970, 94).

Siskel may have scoffed at this as well, but enough people were either intrigued or persuaded by Lindsey's straightforward presentation of Christian apocalypticism that, according to the *New York Times*, *The Late Great Planet Earth* was the best-selling nonfiction book of the 1970s. Nearly four decades after its publication, and especially with the release of the *Left Behind* series, Christian fundamentalists continue to look to a united Europe as the most likely breeding ground for the Antichrist (see, for example, Hindson, 1998; Showers, 1999).

Contrary to Siskel's criticism, Seltzer insists that he did more than just "claim inspiration" from Revelation when he wrote the screenplay for *The Omen*. In *The Omen Legacy*, a promotional DVD that treats the film almost as a fictionalized version of events that are certain to take place and that was released to coincide with a boxed set of *Omen* films, Seltzer is adamant that "everything in the picture is steeped in the scriptures. I mean, even 'Mrs. Baylock' [the demonic nanny], even that name is taken from the Devil's handmaidens, who are called 'Balock' and 'Balaam.'" Neither of these, however, is mentioned in the Bible, which has nothing whatever to say on the subject of diabolical handmaids, and which Seltzer admits he had not read before attempting the screenplay. Yet, the promotional chorus continues. According to *Legacy*'s narration, *The Omen* is "ripped from the pages of the Bible," it has "struck fear in the hearts of the faithful," and it has "forced skeptics to question their beliefs." When Thorn is appointed ambassador to England, this is "a plot twist taken right out of the Book of Revelation." In rewriting the script prior to the beginning of principal photography, Seltzer was told by Donner that "there must be nothing in this movie that you can't believe is actual." Thus, it not only has the power of the "true story," but the added weight of a sociophobic that is deeply embedded in the belief system of millions of Christians and that connects them to a more meaningful conception of reality than that offered by the mundane world.

## MAINSTREAMING SATAN:
## THE MYTHOLOGY OF THE CURSED MOVIE

In *Cosmos and History: The Myth of the Eternal Return*, historian of religions Mircea Eliade points out how even the most prosaic events—events that take place within living memory—are often stripped of their mundane qualities and invested with mythic import. This is true not only for the "wars and rumors of wars" that many Christian believers interpret as signs of an imminent apocalypse, the soon return of Christ, and the end of the world as we know it, but also for the more pedestrian aspects of daily living. No longer the ordinary tales and tragedies of everyday life, events are suddenly connected to a much larger, more meaningful ontology. They relate to a more significant unseen order in a more significant way (see Eliade, 1954, 34–48). This unwillingness to let misfortune be misfortune, accidents be accidents, and human error be simple human error also marks the three films we have discussed in this chapter, contributing self-consciously, to the promotion of any sequels and to the mystery that continues to surround the originals. Each in its own way has been mythologized; they have come to be seen as "cursed," as though dark forces hovered over their production.

In addition to his lengthy description of the original possession case, Rex Reed's *Los Angeles Times* article on *The Exorcist* also detailed what would become the mythology of making the film: props and film stock mysteriously lost, inexplicable fires on the set, sudden deaths and injuries among the families of cast members. Even the shooting itself was troubled. "There are strange images and visions that showed up on film that were never planned," Friedkin told Reed. "There are double exposures in [Regan's] face at the end of one reel that are unbelievable" (1973, U28). Repeated throughout the early media coverage, one reviewer opined that "it may be the most controversial picture ever made" (Scott, 1974, 13F), all of which has earned *The Exorcist* a solid place in the history of "cursed cinema"—something that does little to mitigate the sociophobic effect of the "true story" (see Brottman, 1998; McCabe, 1999).

Like *The Exorcist*, urban legends about Satanism have grown up with *Rosemary's Baby*. Two of the most frequent are the alleged presence of Church of Satan founder Anton LaVey as a technical advisor for the film, and comparisons between events in the story and the brutal murder of Polanski's wife, Sharon Tate, in

1969. Though mainstream media generally avoided suggesting any direct link between *Rosemary's Baby* and the Tate-LaBianca murders—beyond noting their "ritualistic" character—conspiracist film commentators have seen (and continue to see) in the film portents of the real life horror that occurred a little more than a year after the movie's release. In *Hollywood Hex*, for example, Mikita Brottman draws a series of dubious associations between Rosemary Woodhouse and Sharon Tate, concluding somewhat speciously that "those who study the Tate murders soon manage to establish a number of links between Polanski's circle and that of members of the Manson family" (1998, 46). Brottman declines to elaborate on these connections, content to intimate darkly that they are there. He also perpetuates what is arguably the most common urban legend associated with the film, and one that contributed to the fear that there might be more truth than fiction onscreen: that Polanski hired Anton LaVey as a technical advisor, and that LaVey played the role of Satan in the ritual rape scene (Brottman, 1998, 43). Although this claim is repeated on innumerable Web sites, in popular studies, and even in some of the scholarly literature (e.g., Ellis, 2000; Fishwick, 2005; Lewis, 2002), it is not true. In an unfortunately uncredited role (though one that is now acknowledged on the Internet Movie Database), Satan was played by an actor named Clay Tanner, though for the rest of his life LaVey traded on rumors of his participation in the film. Based on this persistent mistake, though, Schreck argues that *"Rosemary's Baby* became a kind of blueprint for the occult renaissance of the late 1960s," and despite an "abundance of evidence to the contrary, LaVey's putative cameo became an article of faith among the Church of Satan's true believers" (2000, 137, 138). And among more than a few who viewed the rise of Satanism in the 1960s and 1970s with alarm.

Finally, *The Omen*. "I really firmly believe," says producer Harvey Bernhard in *The Omen Legacy*, "that the Devil didn't want us to make the film." Though Donner is content to let the ordinary problems and coincidences—both good and bad—involved in making a feature film be precisely those, the myth of an "*Omen curse*" continues both to serve the advertising needs of the studio and to reinforce the sociophobic of those for whom the Devil is very, very real. According to the mythology constructed by *The Omen Legacy*—a mythology fully supported by the original film's publicity unit—Seltzer's first draft was turned down by every studio in Hollywood as being "too frightening." Or, perhaps, because it was not very good, and, filled as it was with "cloven hooves, devil gods, and covens," it too closely resembled any number of other B-grade horror films that had been around for more than two decades. Gregory Peck almost did not receive the script. His son had recently committed suicide, and the producers thought it in bad taste to intrude on his grief with a script of this sort. They did anyway, and Peck was eager to do the film. From the first day of shooting, recalls one of the cast, there was a "strange atmosphere on the set." Indeed, Martin Benson, who played the mysterious priest who gave the Antichrist child to Thorn, remarked that there was "a positive sense of evil" present during shooting. Avoiding his favorite restaurant one evening while filming in London, Peck narrowly escapes an IRA bomb. A producer's plane is struck by lightning. Stunts and scenes take longer to film than predicted; animals on the set are uncooperative—all easily explainable, but all much more useful in the service of an ominous mythology.

 Each of these films brought the spectre of the cinema satanic into the mainstream. Big budgets, big-name stars, and a growing fear of new religious movements of all kinds combined to make them commercial successes. By mythologizing the problems associated with making them, by introducing the concept of a curse or demonic interference, the films become meaningfully connected to the unseen order offscreen that they purport to portray onscreen. The emergent mythology reinforces the very sociophobic from which the films emerged. The demonic is not just a part of Regan; it affects those who seek to tell her story, and, by implication, those to whom the story is told. The supernatural curse of the Brampton not only takes over Rosemary Woodhouse, but those who seek to deliver *Rosemary's Baby* to the screen. *The Omen* is not just the title of the film, but a metonym for the real life horror it purports to represent. And, in each of these cases is the implication that the curse can (and does) extend beyond the theater—a theme taken up explicitly in films like *The Ring* and *Fear dot Com*. This penchant for mythologization, as Eliade points out, is hardly new. Indeed, in his view, it is among the oldest of human religious impulses—the need to be connected to something greater than ourselves, even if that something scares the hell out of us.

# 7

## THE UNHOLY HUMAN
### Fear of Fanaticism and Fear of the Flesh

*You are the devil's gateway: you are the unsealer of that (forbidden) tree: you are the first deserter of the divine law: you are she who persuaded him whom the devil was not valiant enough to attack. You destroyed so easily God's image, man.*
(Tertullian, "On the Apparel of Women")

*Then began the flesh to lust against the Spirit, in which strife we are born, deriving from the first transgression a seed of death, and bearing in our members, and in our vitiated nature, the contest or even victory of the flesh.*
(Augustine of Hippo, *The City of God*)

```
           PINHEAD
    There is no good, Monroe, there is no
    evil. There is only flesh.
```
(*Hellraiser III: Hell on Earth*)

### OUTTAKES: *CULT OF FURY* AND *THE DEVIL'S NIGHTMARE*

A slow helicopter shot follows a remote mountain stream as the gentle sound of the well-known Christmas carol "While Shepherds Watched Their Flock" floats in the background. Peaceful, even idyllic, is the message. Suddenly, incongruously, the film title zooms in—*Cult of Fury*—the metallic rasp of a knife blade slicing through the words of the hymn. Like many low-budget examples of cinema horror, in an attempt to overcome inherent weaknesses in plot, screenwriting, and direction, Yossi Wein's *Cult of Fury* (2001) depends on the intertextual collision of obvious opposites to set the initial mood. As we pan past suddenly barren cliffs, the shot lap-dissolves to the interior of a small cave, the entire scene softly candlelit. Leaving the outside world behind, we have gathered in hiding, as did many early Christians who feared persecution at the hands of Roman authorities. The hymn continues and we are shown the choir—a group of young people, holding candles and singing, standing around an altar, on which is emblazoned a stylized cross-and-swastika. But for the jarring motif on the altar and the stark rock of the cave it could be a Christmas Eve candlelight service in a Christian church almost anywhere in the world. Indeed, their voices beatific, those gathered repeat the refrain and Nahum Tate's famous lyrics fill the space: "The angel of the Lord came down, and glory shone around."

The shot, now shadowy and backlit, shifts to a tunnel entrance as the group's leader, Maxwell (Sonny Suroweic), enters on cue. Tall and broad-shouldered, his Nordic good looks are set off against his long black coat. A cutaway shot shows us a silver altar tray on which lie a medallion of the group's symbol and a dagger—neither of which play any further part in the narrative, but both of which serve to increase the incongruity and the tension. Toying idly with the weapon, Maxwell addresses his followers:

```
            MAXWELL
   Don't let all this good fortune
   distract you. Our work is not done,
   not by a long shot. Where are we
   today? Kids are killing each other in
   school playgrounds. Half-nude women
   are displayed on every billboard and
   magazine cover. In songs, there are
```

> more dirty words than clean. And, yet,
> I'm the one they call 'crazy.'

From a single point of view, as though we too are gathered in the cavern, as though anyone in the audience could potentially be part of the group, the camera moves back and forth between the followers and their leader.

> MAXWELL
>
> Let me remind you, children, that God burned Sodom. He burned Gomorrah. And if the world doesn't want to listen to what I have to say, then they're headed straight back into the fire. All of them! But so long as you all follow me, not us.

Later that night, as an "engagement present" for his disciple and fiancée, Tracy (Marnie Alton), Maxwell blows up a cruise ship in San Pedro, raining down fire on what he considers a floating Sodom or Gomorrah. Tracy runs from him in horror, realizing (finally) the depths of his messianic psychosis.

Two years later, Tracy is working as a cabaret singer in a Las Vegas resort hotel. When one of Maxwell's followers discovers her there, the ominous tagline for the film—"Once in, never out"—becomes clear. In a dual effort to initiate his vision of the apocalypse and recover his apostate lover, Maxwell takes over the hotel. Tracy and two undercover police officers spend the rest of the film running though a maze of theme tunnels in the sprawling complex, explosions going off all around them, the two cops trading barbs over the radio with Maxwell. Catching a breath between blasts, Tracy finally drops the didactic dime. "They're not robbers," she says. "They're not even terrorists. They're his personal army, sworn to his holy war, convinced that they're the saviors of the modern world. They'll do anything that he says. They'll die for him." "Who does he think he is?" asks one officer. "Moses?" "And Jesus," she replies, "and Manson, and Hitler, and the Kennedys, all rolled into one."

Like *Cult of Fury*, Belgian director Jean Brismée's 1971 film, *The Devil's Nightmare*, works entirely too hard to make its all-too-obvious point but is in many ways altogether more enjoyable. Somewhat convoluted and released in different markets under a number of titles—including *La plus longue nuit du diable* and *Au service du diable, La terrificante notte del demonio*, and, in the U.S., *The Devil Walks at Midnight, Succubus*, and, oddly, *Vampire Playgirls*—it features traditional gothic fare: thunder and lightning, a grim castle harboring a centuries-old secret, doors that open by themselves and masonry that detaches from the battlements at singularly inappropriate moments, an alchemist's laboratory hidden in the crypt, and an aloof servant whose sole function seems to be disclosing the terrible things that happened in various rooms in the castle. Throughout all this, Alessandro Allesandroni's faux-gothic harmonium music floats ominously in the background.

Forced to take shelter in a local castle, a motley group of tourists find themselves guests of a former Nazi general, the Baron von Rumberg (Jean Servais). Drawing on a well-established trope of Nazi involvement in the occult (see, e.g., Goodrick-Clarke, 1992, 2002; Ravenscroft, 1973), we quickly learn that seven hundred years ago one of the baron's ancestors made a Faustian bargain with the Devil in exchange for power and wealth. As it happens, the tourists have arrived on the anniversary of the original pact. Explaining the family curse over dinner, the baron reveals the film's central theme:

BARON

In exchange for his services, besides Siegfried's soul, Satan demanded that the eldest daughter of each generation of our family be in his service--that she become a succubus.

> MRS. FOSTER
> What's a succubus?
>
> MR. MASON
> Oh, a kind of vampire, I think.
>
> SORRELL
> You're mistaken, Mr. Mason. They give the name of 'succubus' to demons who adopt feminine appearance in order to seduce man and lead him to perdition.
>
> CORINNE
> It's not at all necessary to be a succubus. Everyone knows women do that quite naturally.

Not unlike the traveling morality plays of the late Middle Ages, each guest represents in some way one of the seven deadly sins, and each is eventually doomed by his or her own particular passion. As Gluttony, for example, the tour bus driver dies gorging himself on greasy chicken, while, as Avarice, the rich wife of an adulterous husband suffocates in a pile of gold dust as she searches for the fabled castle treasure. Her husband's lust for another woman, on the other hand, leads to his own demise: he is beheaded, while his latest object of conquest, Corinne, dies impaled in an iron maiden. In symbolic castration and penetration, sex and death are joined (on this, see Bataille, 1962). These serve to frame the central conflict between a young Catholic seminarian, Albert Sorrell (Jacques Monseau), and a beautiful succubus, Lisa Müller (Erika Blanc), who has arrived innocently enough as another refugee from the storm. While her relationship to the von Rumbergs is implied, but never made clear, she is instrumental in the temptation and death of each of the other guests. As a demon of lust, though, Lisa's principal interest remains Sorrell, aloof and prideful in his calling to a celibate priesthood, but a potentially significant victory in the battle between good and evil.

After dinner, while Sorrell is alone in his room reading, Lisa appears first in four short visions. In each succeeding apparition she wears less and less clothing, finally standing behind him naked, caressing his neck. While Brismée leaves it unclear whether these are the product of Sorrell's own carnal desires or the seductive actions of the demoness, the would-be priest quickly puts Satan behind him, as it were, and retires to the library. A book about the von Rumberg curse conveniently (read: supernaturally) falls into his hands, and as he begins to read, Lisa confronts him, slithering into a chair and toying with her already less-than-expansive blouse.:

>     LISA (reading)
> 'Succubesses manifest themselves
> principally at night. They use all their
> lascivious charms to seduce hermits by
> the vision of their shameless nudity.'
> [Laughing, she undoes her top.] Do you
> think I'm lascivious? Shameless? What
> if I got completely undressed in front
> of you? Do you think I could be. . . a
> succubus?

True, *Cult of Fury* quickly devolves into a predictable "bad cop-alcoholic cop" genre piece, complete with the standard repertoire of unrealistic car chases, interminable "action" sequences, and Wein's clear reliance on films such as *Die Hard*. True, *The Devil's Nightmare* is adequately described online as "a rather captivating piece of vintage gothic Belgian/Italian horror-sleaze" (rottentomatoes.com). But their sublimity, to use Adonis Kyrou's words, lies in their intertextuality, their reliance on well-known offscreen references to tell potentially complex stories in easily understood cultural shorthand. On the one hand, *Cult of Fury* depends for narrative coherence on vastly inaccurate but deeply embedded cultural stereotypes about new religions, megalomaniacal leaders and drone followers, apocalyptic plans, and religious fundamentalism. *The Devil's Nightmare*, on the other hand, looks back fourteen centuries to the seven deadly sins first enumerated by Pope Gregory the Great, the eternal battle that millions of Christians worldwide believe is eternally fought on the plains of the flesh. Each of these films offers a glimpse of one side of the same coin: the power—or the powerlessness—of religious belief; the fear of fanaticism, and the fear of the flesh.

## FEAR OF FANATICISM AND THE POWER OF RELIGION

Consider the word, *cult*. In late modern society, few labels function so effectively as a lightning rod for the fear of fanaticism and the often terrifying power of religion (see Bromley and Shupe, 1981; Cowan and Bromley, 2008; Dawson, 2006). Though there are thousands of new, alternative, and nontraditional religious groups and movements in North America, Europe, and Asia, two comparatively isolated themes have come to dominate popular discourse about them: control and violence. The former is lodged in concerns about "brainwashing" and "cult mind control," while the latter lives in recurring fears over the possibility of religiously motivated mass suicides, ritual murder, violent confrontation with civil authority, or even the potential for attacks on civilian populations—all represented iconographically through groups such as Peoples Temple, the Branch Davidians, the Order of the Solar Temple, Aum Shinrikyo, and Heaven's Gate. Though the now voluminous social scientific literature on new religions demonstrates that there is little if any credible evidence for "brainwashing" (cf. Barker, 1984; Bromley and Richardson, 1983; Zablocki and Robbins, 2001), and that, when we consider the sheer number of new religious movements involved, instances of violence are extremely rare (cf. Bromley and Melton, 2002), panic over the power of religion to motivate antisocial behavior thrives just below the cultural surface, continually reinforced by a wide range of media products.

Written to accompany front-page coverage of the Peoples Temple murder-suicides in Jonestown, Guyana, for example, the lead for a 1978 *Newsweek* sidebar on "The World of Cults" read: "They crouch in dark basements in New York and San Francisco, worshiping the Devil. They wait patiently for the Second Coming or scan the skies for the spaceship that will bring the New Age. A few practice polygamy in isolated mountain communes. Tens of thousands have abandoned their families, friends, educations, and careers to follow the teaching of a leader they will never meet" (Beck and Frakar, 1978, 78). Two decades later, even after the most significant waves of the "great American cult scare" had passed, popular media remained committed to the trope of the dangerous cult. Quoting prominent anticult activist Margaret Singer, in 1998 the otherwise relentlessly upbeat *Homemaker's Magazine* warned readers solemnly that everyone was at risk, and "anyone could be in a cult without knowing it" (Hoshowsky 1998, 55).

From cinema horror to prime-time television, popular entertainment has contributed to reinforcing the sociophobic of religious fanaticism and the power of the dangerous religious Other. As we have seen, a number of films either implicate or rely on the concept of a secretive group working in society's background to ensure one religion's continued dominance or downfall. That these groups form a staple of cinema horror is not at issue. How they are presented, though, how they refract—and, in some cases, reinforce—off-screen experience, expectation, and prejudice, is.

There are, of course, a number of ways to arrange the different frames within which cinema horror re-presents the dangerous religious Other. Here, we will consider the fear of fanaticism in terms of the obvious religious Other, the people next door, the least obvious of those among us, and what I am calling here the "coven cinema"—the horror movie depiction of witchcraft and modern Paganism. It is worth reiterating, though, that these are neither discrete nor comprehensive categories, neither hermetically sealed one from the other nor exhausting the interpretive possibilities of each. Indeed, it is often in their interpenetration, their reliance upon and refinement of the others, that the real horror is disclosed.

## Media Products and the Obvious Religious Other

To this point, we have met the obvious religious Other in a number of guises, from the *Dagon*-worshippers of Imboca and the cult of the Old Ones that constitutes *The Dunwich Horror* to a wide variety of Egyptian priesthoods dedicated to guarding the secret of *The Mummy* throughout both the millennia and his many cinema appearances. In chapter 4, we discussed the North American representation of Vodou, and the titillating sense of danger it provides for audiences all but completely removed from the cultural context in which the real religious practice thrives. In each of these, there is the paradox of connection and disconnection. We are disconnected from the films because in most cases we do not participate in the unseen orders they expose, but we are connected through the characters with whom we are encouraged to identify—Paul Marsh, for example, Nancy Wagner, Helen Grosvenor, and Madeleine Short—our cinematic guides, as it were, into these unseen orders. Other films, though, purport to explore a variety of unseen orders that flourish just beneath the surface of late modern North American society and that, in some cases, bridge the gap between the dangerous religious Other and the people next door. In these films the sociophobic at work hits closer to home, and draws on popular fears of groups that, while already part of the multireligious landscape of North America, remain a mystery to most.

"I don't call cuttin' up chickens a religion!" growls police detective Sean McTaggart (Robert Loggia) in John Schlesinger's *The Believers*. Investigating two gruesome ritual homicides, McTaggart has enlisted the help of Cal Jamison (Martin Sheen), a therapist attached to the member services division of the police department. Ritual implements found at the murder sites lead Jamison to investigate the Afro-Caribbean religion of Santería, the narrative red herring used by the filmmakers to deflect initial attention from the real perpetrators of the crimes—upper-class Americans who believe that the sacrifice of their firstborns will secure them power and wealth. They have made their own deal with the Devil, as it were, but this time the film uses aspects of a real new religion—in the sense that it is relatively new to North American consciousness—and the often-less-than-latent racism of American audiences to mask the rather predictable Faustian plot. Because the concept of dangerous cults involved in hideous ritual practices has deep roots in American popular consciousness, though, and audiences for decades have proven more than willing to believe the worst about those they regard as "primitive," how many moviegoers would be able to distinguish fact from fiction in Schlesinger's presentation? Indeed, *Washington Post* critic Desson Howe quite blithely repeats the film's narrative ploy that the murderers "believe in Santeria, an ancient dark religion with African/Caribbean roots that—among other things—apparently involves child sacrifice" (Howe, 1987, A1). It doesn't—and followers of Santería would be horrified at the thought—but that revelation escapes Howe and, by implication his hundreds of thousands of readers. Though another *Post* reviewer was considerably kinder to the film, his description of the alleged culprits is no less problematic. "The religion of the voodoo murderers," writes Hal Hinson, "is a scrambled up mixture of Catholicism and African mythology called Santeria" (1987, C3). It is as though they could read the mind of the film's central didactic character, Oscar Sezine (Raúl Dávila), a *sentero*, or Santería priest, who explains to Jamison the real significance of events. Confronted by McTaggart and desperate to separate his faith—which is also known as "the way of the saints"—from what he calls *brujería*, or "bad magic," he asks Jamison pointedly:

SEZINE

Name one religion where atrocities have not been committed in the name of a god. Santería is a force for good. It is not a blood cult trading on innocent lives.

JAMISON

Then what are you people afraid of?

SEZINE

Of your ignorance, of your prejudice, because you use it as a weapon against us.

Given the popular sociophobic of the dangerous religious Other, as well as the general ignorance and prejudice that pervades North American culture when it comes to nondominant religions, is Sezine's fear so unrealistic? Is the fear he represents for many new and alternative religious movements—often nonchalantly and inaccurately labeled "cults"—so hard to understand?

Not really.

"62 Animals Rescued From Cult Rites," read the headline for one 1980 *Los Angeles Times* article (AP, 1980), while another reported, "Two Refugees Shot After Cult Mass" (UPI, 1980b), and a third warned that "Cult Mixing Voodoo and Christianity Believed Flourishing in Miami Area" (UPI, 1980a). All were ostensibly reporting on Santería, and all did so in pejorative terms: it is never referred to as a religion, always a "cult," its followers always "cultists," never believers. Coming less than two years after the Peoples Temple deaths in Jonestown, Guyana, "cult" was the watchword for all things religiously dangerous, and popular hysteria was growing. About the same time *The Believers* was released, a group just outside Miami applied to establish the first formal Santería church but was met with stiff resistance from local residents. The lawyer who represented those opposed stated unequivocally that "Santeria is not a religion. It is a throwback to the dark ages. It is a cannibalistic, voodoo-like sect which attracts the worst elements of society" (Volsky, 1987, A15). A year later, in *America: The Sorcerer's New Apprentice*, fundamentalist Christians Dave Hunt and T. A. McMahon describe Santería as "one of the fastest growing witchcraft cults in America, with an estimated 100 million adherents worldwide" (1988, 90). Though this would make Santería nearly ten times the size of the Mormon church and a major world religion in its own right, Hunt and McMahon offer no support for their claim. They do continue, however, that "while most of its practitioners would deny any involvement in human sacrifices, that side of Santería was depicted in *The Believers*, one of the most horrifying feature films to come out of Hollywood in 1987" (Hunt and McMahon, 1988, 90). Part of the Christian countercult movement, a broad network of conservative Protestants who see their mission as combating the rise of new religions in late modern society, Hunt and McMahon are sought-after conference speakers, prolific authors whose many books are featured in thousands of Christian bookstores and have sold hundreds of thousands of copies, and whose monthly newsletter has tens of thousands of subscribers. Their popularity, combined with the rampant misunderstanding of religious traditions such as Vodou and Santería, means that for the hundreds of thousands of people relying on Hunt and McMahon's work for spiritual guidance and religious information their misrepresentation becomes the reality of these practices. In 1989, a series of newspaper articles linked Santería to a grisly series of ritual killings on the Gulf coast between Texas and Mexico—the infamous, drug-related Matamoros murders. Citing a single U.S. Customs agent, newspapers across the country repeated the now-common refrain: the murders "had overtones of a religious cult from Cuba and Haiti known as 'Santeria'" (Hudson, 1989, A3), and some reports even linked them to repeated viewings of Schlesinger's film (AP, 1989). Indeed, two decades after the film's release, even the *Oxford American Dictionary* defines Santería as a "pantheistic Afro-Cuban religious cult," not as the traditional religion it is.

It is important to point out that none of these depictions is accurate—Santería is not "cannibalistic," it is not a "blood cult trading on innocent lives," and human sacrifice plays no part in its rites (Brandon, 1993; Brown, 2003). Together, however, whether cinematic or journalistic, depictions such as these demonstrate clearly the intertextual power of media products both to mine and to reinforce cultural fears and prejudices about religious traditions other than our own. The dangerous religious Other, the threatening unseen order, continues to lurk just beyond the glow of our city lights. Indeed, sometimes it lurks just down the hall.

*Power and the People Next Door*

Like the obvious religious Other, we have also met the people next door, most notably Minnie and Roman Castavet, the neighbors who take such inordinate interest in *Rosemary's Baby*. Because, in *The Believers*, most of those following the evil *brujo* are also upper-class Manhattanites, that film nicely bridges the two categories. Abandoning society's dominant faith, which is presented as either implicitly or explicitly ineffectual, we are presented with people who follow very different gods, all the while maintaining the appearance of cultured normality. Indeed, the lore of satanic panics is filled with conspiracy theories that the only way such groups can operate is through the active collusion of those in positions of social prominence. Updated and often overdecorated versions of Faust's famous bargain, these films raise the question of how riches and power come to some and not others, and why we so often associate the wealthy with the satanic.

Regarded by some commentators as the cinematic version of a "medieval morality play" (Hunter, 1994, 137), Terence Fisher's adaptation of Dennis Wheatley's *The Devil Rides Out*, for example, pits icons of good (Christopher Lee) against evil (Charles Gray) as well-heeled Britons dance around the Goat of Mendes seeking Satan's favor. Though the Devil has a lengthy iconic history—indeed the film's representation draws explicitly on such works as Jacques Callot's "The Goat of the Demon" (1627) and "Adoration of the Great He-Goat" by Francisco de Goya (1798)—as Hunter points out, actually showing Satan onscreen, however briefly, was a daring move in 1968. When we first meet them, though, the Devil's gowned and tuxedoed followers are introduced as an innocent "astronomical society" meeting at a large and opulent country house. Reminiscent of a nineteenth-century salon, it's eccentric, perhaps, but hardly dangerous. Three decades later, Roman Polanski returned to satanic cinema with *The Ninth Gate*, a supernatural thriller about the hunt for the one remaining copy of a book reputedly coauthored by Satan himself—*The Nine Gates of the Kingdom of Shadows*. Like *The Devil Rides Out*, the film is played against the backdrop of international socialites seeking to raise the Prince of Darkness for their own selfish purposes. A twist added by Polanski and his screenwriters, there is no such satanic cabal in the novel on which the film is loosely based—Arturo Pérez-Reverte's *The Club Dumas* (1993). Polanski's experience with *Rosemary's Baby* clearly taught him how little audiences actually have to suspend their disbelief in a diabolical conspiracy. This motif, however, has a much longer pedigree than these films alone would indicate. Consider, for example, Mark Robson's *The Seventh Victim*, released in 1943.

More a film noir thriller than a true horror movie—that is, terrifying in its implication rather than horrifying in its exposition—*The Seventh Victim* is regarded by many critics as among the finest of the horror films released by RKO during the understandably lean 1940s. Produced by the legendary Val Lewton—whose other horror classics include *Cat People*, *I Walked with a Zombie*, and *Isle of the Dead*—it sets the stage for any number of similar cinematic ventures. Though no actual "Satanic" activity is shown onscreen—unlike the Hammer films two decades later, there are no naked revelers, no presiding Goat of Mendes, no nubile sacrifice—what is implied, what relies on audience sociophobics to fill in the blanks, led film critic and first editor of *Fangoria* magazine Ed Naha to opine that "some of the Satanic elements" made "later films like *Rosemary's Baby* look like *Bambi*" (1975, 252).

The story itself is simple enough. Mary Gibson (Kim Hunter) has not heard from her sister, Jacqueline (Jean Brooks), a wealthy New York cosmetics entrepreneur, in some time, and sets out to find her, leaving the almost cloistered environment of her all-girls school for the varied dangers of the big city. After a series of film noir set pieces, Mary finally learns that Jacqueline has become involved with a shadowy group called the Palladists, the significance of which is disclosed by Jason (Erford Gage), a local poet, who in his unrequited love for Mary has vowed to help her in her search. When Jason tells her that "the Palladists are a society of devil worshippers," she reacts with amused disbelief. "Look, I'm serious," he insists, "it's a very real and earnest society, a dangerous society." As the plot unreels, we learn that Jacqueline is not so much a victim of the group as an apostate; she wants to leave, but the maxim "once in, never out" holds true in this world as well. Six others tried to leave, and, though the group insists that it is committed to nonviolence, the remaining members did encourage their recalcitrant coreligionists to take their own lives. Pouring tea in an upscale apartment, calmly discussing the impending death of their erstwhile friend, it is the utterly ordinary tone of their conversation that is so frightening. Essentially, they are discussing murder-by-suicide in the same way they might decide whether to fix the church roof or order new sofa cushions. When finally confronted by Jacqueline's friends, even the Palladist leader's rationale for belief seems frightening in its banality:

JASON

```
You're a poor, wretched group of people
who have taken the wrong turning.
```

MR. BRUN
Wrong? Who knows what is wrong or right? If I prefer to believe in Satanic majesty and power who can deny me? What proof can you bring that good is superior to evil?

Though here, Mr. Brun (Ben Bard) offers a clear challenge to the "good, moral, and decent fallacy," Jason and Dr. Judd (Tom Conway), Jacqueline's psychiatrist, fall back on dominant North American Protestant values, citing the Lord's Prayer as proof refuting the Palladist claims and insisting on its power as an unparalleled "rule for human relationships." One could interpret the reaction of the Palladists as mild chagrin—some look at the floor, others look away—but the resolution of the argument is left suitably ambiguous. In the final shot, though we do not actually see it, we hear Jacqueline commit suicide.

Once in, never out.

*"And a little child shall lead them . . ."*

Cinema horror that revolves around children accesses an entirely different part of our sociophobic register. These movies scare us, but for different reasons, often exploiting the stereotype of the youthful, naïve, "cult recruit" that has been a staple of anticult ideology for decades, while challenging the mythology of innocence with which North American culture tends to surround children. William Golding's classic novel *Lord of the Flies* is as disturbing as it is precisely because it concerns children, not adults. We react viscerally to Regan's possession in *The Exorcist* because she is a perky twelve-year-old girl, not a jaded thirty-something. *The Omen*'s Damien is at least as frightening because he is a small child—and, therefore, culturally coded as innocent—as because he is the Antichrist. Indeed, it could be argued that neither of the two *Omen* sequels succeed precisely because they lack this crucial element. Similarly, were *Village of the Damned* and *Children of the Damned* about adults, they could safely be shelved alongside any number of other alien-puppetmaster movies: *Invaders from Mars*, *Invasion of the Body Snatchers*, or *Strange Invaders*, to name but a few. Because of the mythology of innocence with which they have been invested, however, children are normally portrayed as the victims of an horrific Other. They are the ones taken in *Poltergeist* and threatened in such films as *The Amityville Horror* and *Bless the Child*. Only rarely are they themselves the agents of a dangerous unseen order.

One film franchise that has proven particularly durable in this small, dark corner of the genre, though, is *Children of the Corn*, the first of which was loosely based on an eponymous Stephen King short story and that from 1984 to 2001 generated seven installments. The quality within the series varies widely—as does fan response to the individual films—but they all turn on a similar sociophobic: the power of religious belief to turn children against their parents. Though the biblical tagline for the original is "a little child shall lead them" (Isa 11:6)—which many Christians believe is a prophecy of the millennial kingdom—it could as easily be Luke 14:26: "If anyone comes to me and does not hate his father or mother . . . he cannot be my disciple."

*Children of the Corn* opens on a late summer Sunday in the drought-ridden farming community of Gatlin, Nebraska. The local minister greets his parishioners after services at Grace Baptist Church, his sermon that day on "Corn Drought and the Lord." Families stop at the local soda fountain for their regular after-church lunch. Coffee is poured, gossip exchanged, life carries on. That is, until the children in town lock the doors, turn on their elders, and slaughter them in various and sundry gruesome ways. Once the frenzy of killing is over, though, most of the children become suddenly vacant, plodding slowly out of the frame like zombies, seemingly controlled by a mysterious boy-preacher named Isaac (John Franklin). And all this before the credits have even rolled.

218 / *The Unholy Human*

While each installment takes its own approach to the central mythology—a supernatural force known only as "He Who Walks Behind the Rows" demands worship, tribute, and blood sacrifice as part of the group's harmonious adjustment to his particular unseen order—the films specifically deploy a set of common stereotypes about rural, fundamentalist Christianity to lay the foundation for the principal narrative. When we pick up the story three years after the massacre, for example, newly minted M.D. Burt Stanton (Peter Horton) and his girlfriend Vicky Baxter (Linda Hamilton) are driving through Nebraska near Gatlin. Searching for music on the radio, all they can pick up is the blatant moralizing of radio preachers. "Hallelujah," shouts one, "for there are many mansions in his house, but there is no room for the fornicators! No room for the homosexuals! No room for [those who play] rock-n-roll music!" Representing the rational, the enlightened urban as opposed to the benighted rural—and inviting the audience to participate for the moment in the dichotomy—Burt and Vicky begin to mock what they consider the retrograde beliefs of the "hicks." "Amen!" she laughs, caught up in the game. "There's no room for the college graduate!" he hoots in reply. "No room for people who watch public television!" Since the so-called Scopes "monkey" trial in 1925, fundamentalist Christians have regularly been depicted in the media as uneducated and irrational in their devotion—both of which are reinforced early in the film.

This devotion is mirrored later when Isaac preaches to his young flock about the outsiders who have come into their midst. As the children sit on the ground in the cornfield, Isaac moves among them, holding aloft a corn-husk cross and dressed in the drab, dark suit often cinematically associated with rural ministers and church-goers.

                    ISAAC

Behold! A dream did come to me in the
night. And the Lord did show all this
to me.

> CHILDREN
>
> Praise God! Praise the Lord!
>
> ISAAC
>
> A time of tribulation has come, a test is at hand. The final test . . . In the dream, the Lord did come to me, and he was a shape. It was He Who Walks Behind the Rows. And I did fall on my knees in terror and hide my eyes, lest the fierceness of his face strike me dead. And he told me all that has since happened.

Like other religious *virtuosi* before him, including not a few from the Christian Bible, Isaac claims unique insight into the mind of the divine, weaving current events in Gatlin—the apostasy of one of their own and the arrival of the two "unbelievers," Vicky and Burt—into the vision he claims to have been given by He Who Walks Behind the Rows. Isaac assures his followers that their god will punish all who oppose them—just like the "blue man," pointing to the decayed corpse of a police officer crucified on a large corn-stalk cross. At this point, in an angle used rarely in cinema horror, Isaac crosses through the seated crowd of children and addresses his final words directly to the camera. Once again, as in *Cult of Fury*, we have become members of the group. Once again, the onscreen representation reinforces the cultural fear that "anyone could be in a cult without knowing it":

> ISAAC
>
> And just as the Blue Man was offered up unto Him, so shall be the unbelievers!

MALACHI

Make sacrifice unto Him! Bring him the blood of the outlanders!

CHILDREN

(chanting, while waving machetes and scythes) Praise God! Praise the Lord! Praise God! Praise the Lord! Praise God! Praise the Lord!

This is precisely the kind of fervor people often fear in those they regard as fundamentalists, something that is even more disturbing when children are involved. While this is also the kind of cinematic representation to which critics such as Bryan Stone might object, it is worth remembering that, though the instructions to the faithful obviously differ, the sawdust trail of tent revivalism on which this scene explicitly draws is fraught with similar emotion—and no less emphasis on the salvation of the young. And that is precisely the point of intertextual sociophobics: they work because they resonate with the target audience, they don't need to be explained in great detail, and there are occasionally aspects that are not that far from reality. Listen to religious radio in the southern United States, often called "the Bible belt," and the rantings of the radio preacher in *Children of the Corn* don't seem quite so bizarre. In the 1980s, as televangelism was reaching the height of its power in the late twentieth century, many commentators saw such groups as the Moral Majority and the Christian Coalition as explicitly dangerous (see, for example, Diamond, 1989; Fackre, 1982; Haiven, 1984; Spong, 1991). More than a few televangelists claimed (and still claim) extraordinary access to the mind of God. Oral Roberts, for example, who started his career as a tent revivalist, is arguably best remembered for his 1980 vision of a 900-foot-tall Jesus directing him to build a multimillion dollar medical center in Tulsa, Oklahoma, and for his fundraising claim seven years later that God would "call him

home" (that is, kill him) if ministry supporters did
eight million dollars within three months. While there
cant range of belief and practice within conservative C.
the nuances are often lost on cinema audiences. Roberts' antics may have outraged fellow fundamentalists as well as less conservative Christians, but these remain potent images, images audiences easily retain, and images filmmakers both exploit and reinforce.

## *Coven Cinema*

Few religious groups have figured so prominently in cinema horror history as the witch's coven—though it does not always go by that name. Although audiences have been offered altogether more positive treatments—in theaters, we have seen films such as Richard Quine's delightful *Bell, Book and Candle* and, more recently, *The Witches of Eastwick*, *Practical Magic*, and a cinema version of the enormously popular 1960s sitcom, *Bewitched*, while the small screen has provided such fare as *The Mists of Avalon*; *Charmed*; *Sabrina, the Teenage Witch*; and *Buffy the Vampire Slayer*—cinema horror portrayals of the evil witch and her (or his) malevolent coven remain far more common. Since we have already discussed to some extent the salient differences between cinematic presentation of witches and modern Pagan belief and practice offscreen, in this section I would like to concentrate on the trajectory of presentation that has occurred over the past fifty years. To that end, let us consider three films: *Horror Hotel*, *The Wicker Man*, and *The Craft*.

Released in 1960 and produced by one of Hammer Studio's principal competitors, Vulcan Productions, *Horror Hotel* (also known as *The City of the Dead*) is set in the gloomy backwoods of Massachusetts during what was an historical epidemic of witch-hunting and accusations (see Godbeer, 1992, 179–222). Dragged from her home by frightened and vengeful Puritans, Elizabeth Selwyn (Patricia Jessel) is condemned as a witch and burned at the stake in the late seventeenth century. Calling on Lucifer with her dying breath, she curses the village and all who dwell within it. Nearly three centuries later, it appears, she and her coven are still around, haunting the tiny hamlet of Whitewood, driving out the regular "God-fearing folk," and sacrificing two young women per year in order to maintain their shadowy existence.

On the advice of her professor (Christopher Lee), a young history student named Nan Barlow (Venetia Stevenson) comes to Whitewood to research witchcraft for her term paper. Functioning as our chorus, she reads to the innkeeper, Mrs. Newliss (also Patricia Jessel), from an old *Treatise on Devil Worship in New England*:

>       NAN (reading)
> 'On Candlemas Eve, February 1, in the
> year 1692, a coven of witches'--a
> coven, that's thirteen, some men, some
> women--'whose power came from the
> devil, gathered beneath the Raven's Inn
> to perform a black mass in the honor of
> Lucifer. The witch, Elizabeth Selwyn,
> later to be burnt at the stake, marked
> a young girl for sacrifice . . . the
> witches sacrificed her on the altar,
> and drank her blood at the hour of
> thirteen.'

Not surprisingly, Nan is the one marked next for sacrifice, which takes place that very night. In a scene that recalls many of the pulp cover illustrations of female sacrifice that we discussed in chapter 3, she is thrown on the altar, her blouse torn open to reveal a black-lace merry widow (a point to which we will return below), and she perishes under the ritual blade of Elizabeth Selwyn/Mrs. Newliss.

Though set in Massachusetts among the cultural memories of the Salem witch trials, *Horror Hotel* was made in Britain only a few years after the repeal of the last of the British Witchcraft Acts in 1951—the most draconian of which was instituted under Elizabeth I in 1563. Old stereotypes and well-entrenched sociophobics die extremely hard, and though the publication of Gerald Gardner's groundbreaking *Witchcraft Today* in 1954 and *The Meaning of Witchcraft* five years later stirred public interest in what has become modern Wicca, they did little to alleviate hundreds of years of popular fear and superstition. All of which John Llewellyn Moxey exploited to the fullest in *Horror Hotel*. In many ways the film is little more than a framework for a variety of gothic set pieces—fog-enshrouded graveyards and shadowy crypts with secret passages, moldering buildings that are almost Lovecraftian in their menace, hooded acolytes offering nubile sacrifices in the service of a centuries-old curse, and a thrilling last-minute rescue that restores order and balance to the world.

Searching for his sister in Whitewood, Dick Barlow (Dennis Lotis), a scientist who believes only in what he can see and touch and for whom witchcraft is nothing more than "fairy tale mumbo-jumbo," learns the truth from the old pastor (Norman Macowan) who has remained in the village and whose speech sounds remarkably similar to that of Malachi Martin nearly thirty years later:

BARLOW

You mean they worship Satan here?

REV. RUSSELL

Satanism was never stronger than at the present time. For two hundred years, the people of Whitewood have carried out rituals that mock the Church's teaching . . . I know these people have a pact with the Devil, to worship him and do his works. In return, he gives them eternal life . . . and to seal the

> bargain, they must sacrifice a young
> girl two nights of the year.

Russell's own granddaughter, Pat (Betta St. John), is the sacrifice of the day this time, and he tells Barlow the only way to destroy the witches is with the shadow of the cross. "Use the cross," he urges, though one wonders why none of the villagers has done this before. As Barlow struggles to free Pat, Nan's erstwhile boyfriend, Bill Maitland (Tom Naylor), uproots a huge cross from the cemetery and wades into the coven, shouting, "I abjure thee by the living God!" Sure enough, as the moonlit shadow of the cross touches them, the satanic acolytes burst into flame. The curse is ended, the dominant order is restored, and the conflict is reduced to a black-and-white dichotomy between culturally bound understandings of the sacred and the profane, between socially approved and socially proscribed versions of magic. Declaring, however, that *Horror Hotel* "is as accurate in its portrayal of Witches as 'The Birth of a Nation' was in its portrayal of blacks," modern Pagan Tom Canfield suggests that "perhaps what is more frightening than [the film itself] is that there are people who consider it to be a documentary" (1999).

If we are content to include the witches of Whitewood under the broad rubric of Paganism—and some, like Canfield, are clearly not—Robin Hardy's cult classic *The Wicker Man* presents a very different portrait. Called by *Cinefantastique* magazine "the 'Citizen Kane' of horror films" and winner of the 1974 Grand Prix of the International Festival of Fantasy and Science Fiction Films, it presents revived Paganism as a society complete with its own culture, language, art, and religion, a community that is not reducible to such simplistic dichotomies as sacred and profane, and one that, for most of the film at least, offers a reasonably attractive alternative to Christianity. Indeed, the producers deliberately introduced a "true-to-life" element in the form of an epigraph at the beginning of the film in which they thank "the Lord Summerisle and the people of his island . . . for this privileged insight into their religious practices and for their generous co-operation in the making of this film." All this is, however, entirely fictitious and intended for no greater purpose than to generate buzz about the film. There is, in fact, no "Summerisle" as portrayed in the movie, and the film was not shot in the Hebrides, but mostly at Dumfries and Galloway on the southwest coast of Scotland. Judging by a good deal of the Internet chatter about the film, though, especially in light of the dismal 2006 remake, Canfield's concerns resurface: many fans regard *The Wicker Man* as almost a documentary.

Though regularly listed as a horror movie, there is actually very little traditional horror—either in terms of atmosphere or onscreen action—until the film's final six minutes. Indeed, without those final scenes, it would find no place in the vaults of cinema horror at all. Instead, making explicit the clash between dominant and nondominant religious traditions, the first hour is an extended theological debate about religious power, devotion, contest, and survival. While the main character certainly considers what he finds on a remote Hebridean island horrifying, the vast majority of the narrative presents an idyllic, agrarian existence far from the concerns of the late modern world and seemingly unaffected by the inhibitions that mark so many other religious traditions.

Neil Howie (Edward Woodward) is a West Highland police sergeant investigating the alleged disappearance of a young girl on a small island inhabited by a community dedicated to the religion of the old gods, the pre-Christian deities that framed the unseen order in the British isles long before (and, arguably, long after) the arrival of Christianity. A deeply devout Christian—in one extended scene we see him on his knees praying, while memories of reading the gospel lesson and taking communion in his local church flash back before us—Howie is alternately incredulous and outraged at what he finds as he searches for the girl. Patrons at the local pub, the Green Man, burst into a ribald song called "The Landlord's Daughter" when the real landlord's daughter, Willow (Britt Ekland), leads Howie to his room. Out walking that evening, he comes upon a number of couples making love openly in the fields. In a cemetery, a family waters a fresh grave, while a naked woman clings to another gravestone, weeping. When he is safe in his room, or so he thinks, Willow attempts to seduce him in none-too-subtle fashion. As Howie bursts out later in the film, the people of Summerisle seem to him nothing more than "Heathens! Bloody heathens!"

The more he learns about the island, the more Howie feels he has gone completely down the rabbit hole, for here is a world that seems to function perfectly well, yet does so outside all the conventions he knows and trusts. Indeed, throughout the film, director Robin Hardy makes the most of this disjunction, juxtaposing Summerisle's seemingly edenic community with Howie's sanctimonious indignation. Watching a class of schoolgirls, for example, which to the audience looks no different than a class in any other small schoolhouse, he is astonished to hear their response to the simple question, "What does the Maypole represent?"

      SCHOOLGIRLS

Phallic symbol!

      MISS ROSE

The phallic symbol, that is correct.
It is the image of the penis, which is
venerated in religions such as ours as
symbolizing the generative force in
nature.

Confronting Miss Rose (Diane Cilento) outside, Howie accuses her of teaching "degeneracy," of promoting "corruption of the young," and is appalled when she tells him that the children learn about Christianity "only as a comparative religion."

When he finally meets the Lord Summerisle (Christopher Lee, in a role for which he took no payment and that he considers among the finest in his long career), the lines between the worlds are even more clearly drawn. On his way to the manor house,

Howie passes a stone circle—meant clearly to emulate Stonehenge—within which a number of young women are dancing and leaping the Beltaine fire, naked. In an exchange that defines the central conflict in the film, and one worth quoting at some length, the policeman reveals his suspicions to "his Lordship":

> SUMMERISLE
>
> We don't commit murder up here, Sergeant, we're a deeply religious people.
>
> HOWIE
>
> Religious!? With ruined churches, no ministers, no priests, and children dancing naked?
>
> SUMMERISLE
>
> (smiling) They do love their divinity lessons.
>
> HOWIE
>
> But they are-- are naked!
>
> SUMMERISLE
>
> Naturally, it's much too dangerous to jump through fire with your clothes on.
>
> HOWIE
>
> What-- what religion can they possibly be learning jumping over bonfires? . . . Och, what is all this? I mean you-- you've got fake-- fake-- fake biology, fake religion. Sir, have these children never heard of Jesus?

Once the battle is joined, as it were, the film becomes an extended exercise in dueling theologies.

> SUMMERISLE
> It's most important that each new generation born on Summerisle be made aware that here the old gods aren't dead.

> HOWIE
> And what of the true God, to whose glory churches and monasteries have been built on these islands for generations past? Now, sir, what of him?

> SUMMERISLE
> Well, he's dead. He can't complain. He had his chance and, in the modern parlance, he blew it.

What is for the most part an intellectual contest of viewpoints becomes terrifyingly real—at least from Howie's perspective—in the final few minutes of the film. Rather than the young girl who he believes was "murdered under circumstances of Pagan barbarity," he discovers to his horror that *he is* the intended sacrifice. The Wicker Man has been built for him. Recalling explicitly any number of Christian martyrdoms throughout history, Howie goes to his death praying—though still uncertain of his salvation—while the Summerisle community offer their prayers to the god of the sun and the goddess of the orchards. As the flames rise in the Wicker Man, he sings Psalm 23 as the islanders link arms and offer a happy tune in hopes of a better harvest in the coming year.

Though there are more mundane and, indeed, insidious explanations offered for the Paganism that has taken root on

Summerisle—in a quasi-Marxist manner, Lord Summerisle's grandfather used the old religion to rouse the islanders from apathy when he took over the island in the mid-eighteenth century—we are left at the end ambivalent about the nature of religion and the power it wields over its followers. The theological conflict remains unresolved, allowing viewers to map onto the story their own experiences and expectation of religious belief and practice. When Summerisle tells Howie, for example, "We don't commit murder up here, Sergeant, we're a deeply religious people," he is being entirely truthful. In his mind, and in the minds of the islanders, the Wicker Man sacrifice is not murder; it is, in fact, an honor for the victim. While Howie dies hoping for the life everlasting his religion has promised him, the Summerisle pagans continue hoping that their propitiatory sacrifice will bring back a bountiful harvest. Both, though, are caught between faith and fear: with his dying breath, Howie entreats his god, "Let me not undergo the real pains of hell because I die unshriven," while the final shot of the film shows the sun setting in the Atlantic, as the Wicker Man's head falls, burning, out of the frame. Is Howie right, then, that the bounty will not return because apples were never meant to grow in the Hebrides, and the sun has indeed set on their Pagan beliefs?

From the gloomy Massachusetts backwoods to a remote Hebridean island to the epicenter of American entertainment culture, in the decade since its release, Andrew Fleming's *The Craft* has been called a modern Pagan version of *Mean Girls* (or the vastly superior *Heathers*), a cinematic invitation into Wicca and Witchcraft for any number of impressionable adolescents and, according to one tagline for the film, "*Carrie* meets *Clueless*." Though the trend toward Paganism appears to be slowing as the pop cultural fad passes, *The Craft* does reflect extremely well the entrée many young women (and men) made into Paganism in the 1990s and early 2000s. That is, for the main characters, it is an experimental religious path; they are self-taught and self-initiated, learning everything they know from books purchased (or stolen) from a local Pagan shop. During production and distribution, much was made of the fact that a practicing Pagan, Pat Devin, had served as the film's technical advisor, and many of the rituals—both small and large—do accurately portray practices within Wicca and modern Witchcraft. Indeed, the words of the self-initiation rite the young women perform when they constitute their group—which they do not call a coven, but a circle—are taken directly from the First Degree Initiation liturgy in Gardnerian Wicca (see Farrar and Farrar, 1984, 9–20). Similarly, the warning given them about the karmic "Law of Threefold Return" is an integral part of many Pagan ethical systems. However, like many modern Pagans who profess an authoritative personal gnosticism as the ground of their faith—the belief that what feels right must be right (Cowan, 2005, 35–37, 75–78)—what the young Witches learn from books is modified by what they imagine and invent among themselves.

A classic story of social outcasts who find strength facing the world together, each of the main characters is an outsider in one way or another. Sarah (Robin Tunney) is the new kid in school, while Bonnie (Neve Campbell) lives with the physical and psychic pain of serious burn scars, and Rochelle (Rachel True) is an African-American facing the overt racism of her schoolmates. The strongest character, Nancy, played by Fairuza Balk (and whose performance dwarfs that of the others), is poor, "white trash" condemned to live in a trailer with her alcoholic mother (Helen Shaver) and her mother's boyfriend du jour. Each powerless in her own way, they seek to take control of their lives through their shared bond and their collective exploration of Witchcraft. They find themselves alternately thrilled and frightened by what they believe are their growing powers. The bookshop owner, Lirio (Assumpta Serna), provides the story's cautionary linchpin:

```
                       LIRIO
         True magic is neither black nor white.
         It's both because nature is both.
         Loving and cruel, all at the same time.
         The only good or bad is in the heart of
```

the witch. Life keeps a balance on its
own, you understand?

                        NANCY
Not really.

Exactly. Lirio repeats an epistemology one finds in any number of modern Pagan texts, while Nancy reiterates the lived inexperience of so many who think that magic is only about making things happen.

Though set within the cinematic domain of the supernatural and clearly meant to exploit the growing interest in modern Paganism, on the surface this is a fairly predictable teen coming-of-age film, with all the angst, the right and wrong choices, and the moralistic resolutions we have come to expect from Hollywood. Two less-obvious aspects, however, are worth closer attention: the dueling theologies that underpin the narrative, and the nature of the interpretive act—both by the characters within the film, and by those who have seen it and found within it something of religious value.

First, on a less-obvious level than simply the undisguised cruelty of high school, Fleming offers a sophisticated intertextual layer that passes almost unnoticed unless the viewer pays particular attention. Though not nearly as explicit as in *The Wicker Man*, the dueling theologies of modern Paganism and Christianity are no less present in *The Craft*. The girls, for example, form their circle initially within the educational confines of a Roman Catholic prep school, St. Benedict's Academy. Although they are in little danger of being burned at the stake, their story is clearly located in the Catholic fear of Witchcraft extending back more than a thousand years. Even this is ambiguous. As Sarah enters the campus for the first time, she passes under a life-size crucifix, the left hand of which has its middle finger extended. To whom is this directed—the wannabe Witches or the religious institution that frames their alienation? Later that morning, as the three other "bitches of Eastwick" watch Sarah from across the courtyard, they are shown seated under a large mural of the Madonna, her head inclined toward them and her hands folded in prayer. Prayer for them? For those they will encounter? A similar image is placed behind Lirio in the Pagan bookshop. Later in the film, at daily mass in the school chapel, while Nancy reads a book on *The Qabalah* and Sarah flirts with her now spell-smitten love interest, Chris (Skeet Ulrich), the priest's homily floats in the background. On the one hand, it is hard to imagine a more ordinary scene in a Roman Catholic school's daily chapel service: scores of hormonal adolescents shifting and fidgeting while the priest tries to convey something meaningful. On the other hand, what the priest says relates directly to the power the four girls have begun to taste. Paraphrasing the Fall narrative from the book of Genesis, he warns his youthful congregation, "Do not eat from the Tree of Knowledge," and, further, "Do not compare thyself to the heavenly Father. Do not even try to know what only God can know." Of course, we know by this point that that particular apple has already fallen from the tree and been consumed in full.

Second, as in *Rosemary's Baby*, there is the issue of interpretation. How are events in the film understood by the characters onscreen, and how are they meant to be understood by those who see the film as an attractive invitation into the Pagan world or as a cautionary tale to avoid it at all costs? Recall that a central interpretive concern in *Rosemary's Baby* is whether these things are really happening or whether Rosemary is imagining them. Similarly, in *The Craft*, the results of the spells the girls cast can be interpreted either as evidence of supernatural power or as a series of coincidences into which they read such power based on their professed connection to the unseen order represented by modern Witchcraft. Of course, this kind of interpretive problem is hardly limited to modern Pagans. Religious folk of all kinds read the will of their god or gods into all manner of mundane events. Things are "meant to be," "God had a plan," "my prayers were answered," or not—versions of these are common across the religious spectrum. Here, though, Fleming is careful to render the supernatural interpretation ambiguous by providing a plausible alternative explanation for each of the events. Do Bonnie's prayers to Manon (their Pagan deity) cure the horrific scars on her back, or is it the experimental gene therapy she has been receiving? Does Rochelle's racist rival on the swim team lose her hair because of a revenge spell, or a combination of bleaching her hair blonde and spending too much time in heavily chlorinated water? Does Nancy cause the death of her mother's abusive boyfriend, or does he succumb to a lethal combination of obesity, smoking, and alcoholism? The girls interpret these events as evidence of their growing power, but the possibility of more prosaic explanations is left wide open. This, too, accurately reflects the way many Pagans interpret the reality of the world around them. When something happens, it does so because they have played some integral part in it. Pagan literature is filled with examples of magic being used to influence the physical world—everything from waving lilies at the sky to ward off rain (Telesco, 1998, June 17) to placing "a piece of tiger eye on top of your external modem" to increase your computer's communication speed. "The results are remarkable," notes the author (Morrison, 1996). Whether they are or not, they are certainly interpreted so.

Finally, there is the way in which *The Craft* has been interpreted by those who have either been influenced by it to explore Paganism, by those who critique it as an inaccurate representation of their religious tradition, or by those who see it as the latest foothold in Satan's war of spiritual domination. In terms of its influence, for example, it is hardly unimportant that the main characters are exceptionally attractive young women, just like the four *Charmed* ones (three of whom have been named to different magazines' "100 Sexiest Women in the World" lists, while the fourth has posed several times in *Playboy*). Try to imagine either production succeeding with a storyline about three young Druids played by Pauly Shore, Jack Black, and Pee-wee Herman. An unfair comparison, perhaps, but not unrealistic given Hollywood's obsession with an ideal of physical (and by implication sexual) perfection, and the effect that obsession has had on hundreds of millions of young men and women around the globe. Online Pagan discussion forums, for example, reveal a wide range of opinions about *The Craft*. Some participants love the film and see it as an accurate, though essentially admonitory portrayal of their religious beliefs and ritual practice. Others despise it, wanting to concentrate only on the salutary aspects of their faith and noting the positive influence of Lirio in the film. One Yahoo! discussion group even includes a "Cool Entertainment or Bad Idea" item in its new member questionnaire and lists both *The Craft* and *Charmed*. Participant profiles in that discussion community are shaped, however modestly, by their reaction to these particular media products. For many members, it is indeed "cool entertainment," though almost all point out what they consider its flaws. Once again, they focus only on the positive aspects of their faith, falling prey, as do so many other religious believers, to the "good, moral, and decent" fallacy that marks modern Paganism no less than any other tradition. This is, perhaps, most evident in a "statement of position" issued by The Witches' Voice (www.witchvox.com), one of the most extensive modern Pagan sites on the Internet. Shortly after seeing the film, Witches' Voice cofounder Wren Walker wrote that the presence of a Wiccan advisor on the film was little more than an act of "'tokenism' to lend credibility to an otherwise inaccurate portrayal of Witches":

> It would certainly not be clear to the general viewing public which parts of the film show actual practices of the Religion and which are Hollywood fabrications. Hiding behind the shroud of "showing actual rituals of Witchcraft," the media in fact is exploiting the term "Witch" for the sole purpose of increasing profits and has refused to use the opportunity to correct an injustice against the religious community of Witchcraft. (Walker, 1997)

Indeed, most of *The Craft*'s audience would be ill-equipped to make these distinctions.

Walker's own naïveté, though, which in this instance is no less than that of Christians who object to the presentation of their faith in cinema horror, comes through both in her apparent belief that Hollywood studios are under some obligation to "correct" the presentations of religious groups on film and her contention that "all Witches conduct themselves in a way that upholds the laws and ethical codes of the land" (Walker, 1997). The former is open to considerable debate—who gets to decide what constitutes an "accurate" portrayal and how is that authority appropriated?—while the latter is patent nonsense.

Drawing on a sociophobic hundreds of years old, there are also those who see in these films nothing more than thinly veiled Satanism—whether the participants actively worship the Devil or not. Writing for the countercult organization Watchman Fellowship, Jason Barker advises that it is spiritually dangerous even to watch these programs, let alone investigate their practices or teachings. "During the time a Christian spends focusing on plots concerning subjects that are condemned by God," he writes, adding an appropriate biblical proof-text, "that person is tacitly following the occult rather than God" (Barker, 2000). Although many evangelical and fundamentalist Christians are now careful to point out that modern Witchcraft neither implies nor equates to devil-worship, just as Puritan preacher Cotton Mather argued four hundred years ago in *The Wonders of the Invisible World*, they remain convinced that modern Witchcraft and Wicca are part of an overall Satanic plan for the world. They constitute, in fact, "Satan's little white lie" (Schnoebelen, 1990; cf. Abanes, 2002; Alexander, 2004; Baker, 2003; Mather, [1693] 1862).

In its own way, each of these films testifies not to the reality of the onscreen presentation of modern Paganism—however it is framed—but to the power of that presentation and the deeply rooted cultural fears into which it taps.

## OF THE FLESH AND THE POWERLESSNESS OF RELIGION

Let us return to the *Horror Hotel* in Whitewood, Massachusetts. In the hours before her sacrifice at the hands of Elizabeth Selwyn's coven, we see Nan Barlow as a demure, somewhat shy young woman. Certainly nothing about her indicates anything other than a serious devotion to her studies and perhaps a slightly prudish attitude toward her boyfriend, Bill. Lying on her hotel bed making notes from the treatise on devil-worship, she wears a padded house robe, fastened at the collar and falling below her knees. When Mrs. Newliss invites her to join a party in the hotel lobby, Nan gets up to change clothes. The dowdy house robe falls from her shoulders to reveal a strapless, black-lace merry widow, complete with garter and stockings. Over this icon of corset fetishism, however, which is set off against her pale skin and blonde hair, she pulls an ordinary white blouse and a simple a-line skirt that falls, once again, well below her knees. As I noted above, we see the merry widow again at the moment of Nan's death. Though Moxey may well have included it as part of a studio formula designed to titillate as many members of his potential audience as possible, this brief bit of incongruity epitomizes the complex and largely unexplored relationship between repressed sexuality and cinema horror. Because fear is one of the most basic human emotions and sex one of the most basic human drives, it make perfect sense that they would find a lustful union in scary movies.

Sex and fear couple in virtually all aspects of cinema horror, from vampire movies to witchcraft films, from such Universal monster features as *Creature from the Black Lagoon* and *The Mummy* to Italian *giallo* cannibal films and more recent American slasher/torture efforts. Whether hetero- or homosexual, most focus on the woman's body as the object of fascination and desire, the site of repression and aggression, and, often, the locus of evil and catastrophe. (For a tour-de-force discussion of this in nineteenth- and twentieth-century art, see Dijkstra, 1986, 1996.) Indeed, in many of these films, especially the nunsploitation films we will discuss below, it is as though Augustine and Tertullian—two principal architects of Christian misogyny—sat in on the script sessions, costume meetings, and principal photography.

Barely suppressed sexuality shading into overt eroticism has marked vampire cinema ever since poor, doomed Dwight Frye (Renfield) met Geraldine Dvorak, Cornelia Thaw, and Dorothy Tree (the three brides of Dracula), and Bela Lugosi hovered over the prone body of Frances Dade (Lucy Weston). It took Hammer Studios and the films of European directors such as Jean Rollin, however, to bring this eroticism into its own. Combining often lesbian encounters with an almost formulaic amount of female nudity, Rollin directed such horror classics as *Requiem pour un Vampire* (*Requiem for a Vampire*, which was also released as *Caged Virgins* and *Virgins and Vampires*); *La vampire nue* (*The Nude Vampire*); *Le Viol du vampire* (*The Rape of the Vampire*); and what many critics consider his most sophisticated if surreal entry into the field, *Le Frisson des Vampires* (*The Shiver of the Vampires*, also released as *Sex and the Vampire, Vampire Thrills,* and *Strange Things Happen at Night*). Not to be outdone, Hammer offered British audiences buxom scream queens like Ingrid Pitt in *Countess Dracula* (loosely based on the life of Hungarian serial killer, Erzsébet Báthory) and *The Vampire Lovers,* Caroline Munro in *Captain Kronos—Vampire Hunter,* and Yutte Stensgaard in *Lust for a Vampire,* a film Jack Hunter calls "a veritable orgy of black magic, lesbianism, bloodletting and, almost in passing, vampirism" (1994, 105). Since then, from films such as *Innocent Blood* and *Bram Stoker's Dracula* to *The Hunger* and the unutterably campy *Bordello of Blood,* eroticism and terror have been virtually inseparable in vampire cinema.

Fear of witches and the sexual power of women go back hundreds, if not thousands of years. By the Middle Ages, this fear had become so deeply embedded in Christian systematic theology that such works as *Malleus Maleficarum* and *Compendium Maleficarum* today read like pure studies in sexual repression and projection. Reinforced by journalistic "exposés" such as *Sex and the Occult* (Wellesley, 1973), *Sex and the Supernatural* (Walker, 1970), and *Sex in Witchcraft* (Paine, 1972), twentieth-century cinema horror has followed diligently in this wake. The advertising poster for Hammer's *The Witches*, for example, which relies on an unsteady amalgam of witchcraft, Vodou, and indeterminate occultism, reads ominously (but invitingly):

```
What does it have to do with sex?...
Why does it attract women?...
What does it do to the unsuspecting?...
Why won't they talk about it?...
What do the witches do after dark?
```

The message, of course, is "Come see the movie and we'll show you!" Tigon British Films, another of Hammer's competitors in the late 1960s and early 1970s, produced a couple of similar attempts: *The Curse of the Crimson Altar*, starring Barbara Steele as the deathless witch, Lavinia Morley, and *Virgin Witch*, an otherwise forgettable lesbian romp whose star, Vicki Michelle, is best known for her portrayal of Yvette Carte-Blanche in the long-running British comedy, *'Allo 'Allo*. Mario Mercier's ultra-low budget *Erotic Witchcraft* leaves nothing to the imagination (see Tohill and Tombs, 1994, 61), while on this side of the Atlantic, many films based on the premise of erotic witchcraft quickly devolved into little more than supernatural vehicles for softcore pornography. The cinematic association of witchcraft and overt sexuality even extends to such light comedies as *Bell, Book and Candle*. When Gillian (Kim Novak) is still a Witch, her dress is bohemian and alluring. When she falls in love with Shep Henderson (Jimmy Stewart) and loses her powers—when she is no longer a Witch—her costume also changes, from slinky pullovers, bare backs, and bare feet to a conservative, high-necked dress, and satin pumps.

In each of these subgenres of cinema horror, lust is clearly seen as one of the vehicles used by those who would subvert the dominant social or religious order. Whether willing or not, the victims are most often ordinary people—men and women who experiment with the occult, who fall in with those given to experimentation, or who are simply offered up as victims. When, on the other hand, religion is meant to provide an explicit framework for spiritual growth apart from the demands of the flesh, the fear that religious belief and practice will be powerless in the face of those demands takes center stage.

## Nunsploitation: Fear and the Fetishization of the Female Religious

Numerous writers have commented on the multivariate concept of repression—especially sexual repression—that lies at or near the heart of horror (see, e.g., Clemens, 1999; Freud, [1919] 2003; Hogan, 1986; Kristeva, 1982; Stephens, 2002; Wood, 1996). Whether psychological or sociological, though, nowhere is the complex of interrelated repressions seen more clearly than in so-called "nunsploitation" cinema, movies that exploit centuries of fascination with, fantasizing about, and fear of the Roman Catholic female religious. Low-budget and occasionally little more than loosely veiled pornography, nunsploitation films are regularly decried as the obscene detritus of cinema horror. Production values are poor, and basic stories are similar, often appealing to the most prurient and voyeuristic instincts among horror audiences. Yet, like other dismissals of cinema horror, this rejection ignores the reality that these films—most of which are produced in predominantly Roman Catholic Europe (though there is a thriving Japanese nunsploitation market)—are part of a religio-political tradition extending back hundreds of years and encompassing art, literature, and theology. In the United States, at least, it could be argued that they constitute part of what Robert Lockwood calls "the last refuge of legitimate bigotry"—open and accepted anti-Catholicism (2000, 5). They are of a piece with much of the "true confessional"—though largely fictitious—anti-Catholic literature that flourished in the eighteenth and nineteenth centuries, the most well-known example of which is the (in)famous *Maria Monk* (Monk, [1836] 1876). Dealing with questions of (and fears about) secrecy, power, and the unseen order, they ask: What's under the habit, and what happens behind the cloister walls? If one is really closer to God in the convent, is one a more tempting target for the Devil? Ostensibly exploring the repressed sexuality of Roman Catholic women religious, they disclose an ongoing fetishistic obsession with what lies beneath the veil.

Though nunsploitation has been taken to mean any film that features nuns in any way, from *Brides of Christ* (about a convent school in Australia) and *Black Narcissus* (about a Anglican mission in the Himalayas) to *Christina, the Devil Nun* (also released as *Our Lady of Lust*) and *Convent of the Sacred Beast* (do we really need to know more than that?), here we are concerned with those that fit more directly into the horror genre. Specifically, I would like to touch briefly on the subgenre using two films by prolific Italian directors Bruno Mattei (*The Other Hell*) and Lucio Fulci (*Demonia*), and one by Nigel Wingrove (*Sacred Flesh*), a relative newcomer to the field.

Bruno Mattei (1931–2007), who directed under a host of other names, including Vincent Dawn, Werner Knox, and Stefan Oblowsky, the pseudonym he used for *The Other Hell*, was a prolific B-grade filmmaker, directing everything from pornography and Nazi exploitation films to zombie movies and science fiction. Set in a Catholic convent, from the opening shots, *The Other Hell* appears to leave little to the imagination. Searching the convent crypt, a nun enters the embalming room where a half-naked corpse lies on the table. "The first thing to do in embalming a sinful nun," says the sister in charge of preparing the body, "is to cleanse her of evil, starting *there*!" Stabbing the dead woman in the vagina, she continues:

```
                    NUN
    That's the place. The evil starts
    there, between her legs. The evil which
```

> grows and consumes everything, even the spirit. The devil enters a woman there and devours her. [She cuts into the vagina.] The genitals are the door to evil. The vagina and the uterus, the womb -- the labyrinth that leads to hell. The devil's tools. Hell is within us.

Suddenly, she attacks and nearly kills the other nun before taking her own life. Like *Children of the Corn*, all this happens before the opening credits roll. Told in a disjointed, episodic, yet densely symbolic fashion, *The Other Hell* unreels like a bizarre cautionary tale about the dangers of sexual repression: infanticide, suicide, murder, insanity—all cloistered behind the convent walls, and all driven by the collision between what the spirit wants and the body demands.

Although Mattei's colleague in the Italian B-movie industry, Lucio Fulci (1927–1996), is best known for his zombie films, he also contributed to the nunsploitation genre. And, once again, before *Demonia*'s opening credits roll we know the score. Angry villagers with torches drag five screaming nuns into a room off the crypt in a Sicilian convent. Five crosses surround a small opening in the floor—an *oubliette*—and the nuns are crucified, each one finally killed with a nail through the breast. Five hundred years later, members of an archeological team from the University of Toronto fall prey to mysterious forces that haunt the ruined nunnery. When ominous warnings from the locals are ignored, members of the dig team die in typical *giallo* fashion, and even Interpol's Inspector Carter (Lucio Fulci) is at a loss to explain who did it or why. Only young archeology student Liza Harris (Meg Register), who is interested in the occult and fascinated by the convent, is able to learn the truth. Meeting with a local medium (Carla Cassola), she learns the secret of Santa Rosalia:

LILLA

It's been hundreds of years and yet
I can see it all, as if it happened
just yesterday. There were five nuns
in the convent, all of them young and
beautiful, and each of them had a
covenant with Satan. At least that's
what was said about them.

Intercut with flashbacks to the scenes she describes, the camera circles with Lilla around her small room, her head framed at one point by holy pictures, at another haloed in the blue-white light from the window.

LILLA

Back then, some townsfolk even talked
about certain wild orgies which were
supposed to have taken place beneath
the nunnery. No one was able confirm
the rumors. Those young men who were
supposed to have taken part in the
orgies vanished mysteriously. And just
as mysteriously the terrible fruit of
those infernal nights vanished.

The scene in Lilla's room shifts to one of the murderous nuns giving birth. Another nun takes the newborn away, wrapped in bloody swaddling clothes. Rushing through the convent with the crying infant, she throws the tiny bundle into a large brazier. Through the flames, we see a tiny fist close tightly.

In 1993 British video distributor Nigel Wingrove created Redemption Films to showcase a variety of European cinema horror from past decades. A few years later, he entered the nun-sploitation field as writer-director for *Sacred Flesh*, which was shot in eight days on digital video using a number of first-time actors

(Mathews, 2000). When it refers to the transubstantiated host, "sacred flesh" has a specific theological meaning for Roman Catholics; it is the body of Christ shared among the community of his followers. When it refers to those followers themselves, however, it becomes something of an oxymoron—the ideal concept for exploitation.

Sister Elizabeth (Sally Tremaine), the Mother Superior of a medieval English convent, is rumored to be possessed—whether by the Devil or her own lurid imagination is left unclear. Plagued by visions of Mary Magdalene (Kristina Bill), whom she now regards as an "unrepentant whore," and a dead nun, who appears in skeleton costume and threatens her with eternal damnation, Elizabeth carries on extended internal debates about the nature of celibacy, the place of the women in the church, and the desires of the flesh. The Magdalene is unimpressed.

> MARY MAGDALENE
> 
> You claim chastity and purity of
> thought. You clothe yourself from head
> to foot as though the merest glimpse of
> flesh will induce lust, and release what
> in the originator? Some of that latent
> carnality which seethes beneath your
> sisters' habits? Or perhaps it would
> just reveal the woman beneath the lies.

At one point, Sister Elizabeth despairs of the conflict between the requirements of her Church, the restraints of the convent system, and the insistent demands of her own body.

> SISTER ELIZABETH
> 
> Sexual purity is the apex of my
> spirituality . . . I yearn, and I hate
> myself for these thoughts. It's so
> unfair. Men fantasize about convents

```
full of languishing virgins, and they
mock us for our faith. And the pain we
suffer keeping chaste.
```

Though marketed as a horror film, there is nothing either overtly or viscerally frightening about the movie. Didactic and obvious, from the beginning it breaks the cardinal rule of the dramatics arts—"show, don't tell." It is, rather, an extended debate—punctuated by sequences of set piece softcore pornography—on the central conflict that drives nunsploitation films and the sociophobic that underpins that conflict, both within the convent and without. If the viewer can but for a few moments contemplate the depth of horror experienced by Roman Catholic religious at the thought that their most basic physical urges condemn them to an afterlife of eternal torment and separation from God, then the message of *Sacred Flesh* becomes horrifying indeed. Though clearly offered as a cheap exploitation vehicle, once again, Kyrou's words ring true—bad films have a sublimity to them that is often belied by their surface presentation.

Born of the most durable and misogynistic of Christian myths—that woman is a temptress at best, evil incarnate at worst—nunsploitation films are a late modern reflection and refraction of two linked obsessions that developed in many countries where the Roman Catholic Church established convents and monasteries: fear about what was popularly believed to take place behind their walls, and a fetishistic fascination with the women religious who lived cloistered within.

"We fear the papal religion," wrote an unnamed reader to the *Trumpet and Universalist Magazine* in 1836, "and if we have ever offered a heart-felt petition to heaven, it has been, that the atrocities of that religion may never exist among us" (Anonymous, 1836b, 22). Of course, it did exist, and less than two years earlier that fear had exploded in Charlestown, Massachusetts, when a mob of Protestants attacked and burned an Ursuline convent overlooking Boston Harbor (cf. Schultz, 2000).

In 1836 anti-Catholic hysteria was whipped to a fever pitch with the publication of a fictitious memoir, *Awful Disclosures of Maria Monk*, which was subtitled in good nineteenth-century fashion, a *Narrative of her Sufferings during Her Residence of Five Years as a Novice and Two Years as a Black Nun in the Hotel Dieu Nunnery, at Montreal, Ont*. Reviewed in newspapers, journals, and magazines throughout Canada and the United States, many praised the young woman for her courage at finally exposing "these unparalleled sinks of polluting corruption" ("Religious Lies," 1836, 22). Only the dissolution of the conventual system, argued a letter "From One Who Knows" in the *New York Evangelist*, would prevent further atrocities in "that abominable prison, blasphemously denominated the Hotel Dieu Nunnery" (1836, 59). Others were horrified that anyone could credence the account, calling the book, among other things, the "most impudent humbug" (Anonymous, 1836a, 1). Outraged that believers would turn on believers in this manner, the editors of the *Christian Register and Boston Observer*, which was published by the American Unitarian Association, could "conceive of nothing more infamous than pandering to the prurient curiosity of low and vulgar minds" (Editors, 1836b, 50)—an accusation that has been leveled at cinema horror more than once. Calling it "the fabrications of a notorious harlot, the inventions of combined lunacy and profligacy," Montréal residents posted handbills throughout the city denouncing the book (Editors, 1837, 125). For months, the debates raged, fuelling suspicion on both sides. Roman Catholics feared a wave of attacks like the one in Charlestown, while many Protestants worried that if something wasn't done about the "Romish" menace, a tide of "awful disclosures" would rise in their midst. While thousands of readers across the continent did not know what to believe, arguably the most troubling response came in the form of a review printed originally in the influential *New York Observer*, but which was quickly reprinted in a number of other newspapers and magazines. Whether the claims made by Maria Monk "are true or false," read the review, "our opinion of convents and of the confessional will remain the same. They undoubtedly afford great facilities for the commission of the crimes here alleged to have been perpetrated" (Editors, 1836a, 28). Reading between the lines: we believe it, whether it's true or not.

From beginning to end, the *Awful Disclosures of Maria Monk* is an encomium of anti-Catholic horror, at the center of which are the allegations of sexual immorality and infanticide that would reappear a century-and-a-half later in nunsploitation films like *Demonia*. "It will be recollected," she wrote, "that I was informed immediately after receiving the veil, that infants were occasionally murdered in the convent," and "I learnt through nuns, that at least eighteen or twenty infants were smothered and secretly buried in the cellar while I was a nun" (Monk, [1836] 1876, 135, 136).

Whether events like this ever took place, however, the author herself was a fraud. She was not a nun, but a promiscuous, mentally unstable young woman who was consigned by the police to an asylum for prostitutes that was operated by the Roman Catholic Church. Put out in 1834 when she became pregnant, she partnered with a virulent anti-Catholic preacher named William Hoyt, and together they produced the *Awful Disclosures*, one of the most popular pieces of anti-Catholic literature in the nineteenth century. Selling more than 300,000 copies before the Civil War, it joined a growing subgenre of putative conventual memoirs, including Rebecca Reed's *Six Months in a Convent* (1835), the story of her time in the ill-fated Ursuline community in Charlestown, and Edith O'Gorman's *Trials and Persecutions* (1871), the first-edition spine text for which reads: "Convent Life Unveiled." Indeed, nearly forty years after the *Awful Disclosures*, the editors of *Zion's Herald*, one of the oldest American Methodist publications, concluded their review of O'Gorman's book by calling Roman Catholicism "the vilest horror under the American sun," and saying that "nothing is a tithe as corrupt and dangerous as the conventual system of the Roman Catholic Church" (Editors, 1871, 150). Understood as nineteenth-century versions of the "true crime" story, conventual memoirs rendered as nonfiction popular anti-Catholic satire and erotica that had been around for well over a hundred years and ranged from Voltaire's *La Pucelle d'Orleans* (1730), a ribald account of Joan of Arc that went through numerous illustrated editions over the next century-and-a-half, to Denis Diderot's *The Nun* ([1780] 1968), many of the works of the Marquis de Sade, and Matthew Lewis' *The Monk* ([1796] 1998).

Thus, fear was not the only reaction provoked by the habits of the nuns. Forty years before the *Awful Disclosures*, Thomas Cogan, a doctor writing about his travels in Europe, published an article in the *New York Magazine* about his "Visit to the Cloister of Mount Sion" in the Duchy of Cleves. Asking "how many Nuns might be sequestered from the world within these walls," Cogan was astonished to learn that there were "only twenty-eight" (1797, 134). Cogan's reply is not a little instructive:

> My imagination immediately took fire—I contemplated them all as in the bloom of youth and beauty, formed to enjoy and communicate happiness, in civil life, and in the conjugal state! ... "Good God!" cried I, "*only* twenty-eight of the loveliest of the human species buried alive within this gloomy mansion? Do you say *only*, Madam?" (Cogan, 1797, 134-35)

Three hundred years later, in *Sacred Flesh,* Father Henry (Simon Hill) complains that "if God had wished women to remain chaste, he wouldn't have made them so desirable." And, not surprisingly, the young religious in the movie are eminently desirable. Young and beautiful, buxom, in full makeup with impeccable French-tipped fingernails, they are the epitome of the fetishized nun.

Just as anti-Catholic propaganda reinforced the fears many had of the Church, nuns and monks have occupied pride of place in literary and visual erotica since the Middle Ages. In the eighteenth and nineteenth centuries, with technological advances in mechanical reproduction, engravings, drawings, and paintings regularly appeared depicting Roman Catholic religious in all manner of situations, from autoeroticism, seduction, and consensual sex to cross-dressing, sadomasochism (both heterosexual and homosexual), and implied rape. Artists like the Belgian symbolist Félicien Rops (1833–1898) and surrealist Clovis Trouille (1889–1975) portrayed women as evil, either as seductresses, as slaves to their own temptation, or both. Rops' *The Temptation of St. Anthony* (1878) depicts the hermit cowering before a cross on which hangs a voluptuous young woman with the word "Eros" tacked above her. *Calvary*, on the other hand, shows a priapic satyr hanging on a cross, his legs wrapped around a nun who has flung open her habit to reveal her naked body. A small, untitled sketch depicts a nun—whom Nikolas and Zeena Schreck identify as St. Teresa of Avila (2002, 143)—naked but for her veil, masturbating, while yet another provides a densely symbolic reinterpretation of the story of Susannah and the Elders—old men looking in at a naked woman in her bath. Anticlerical to a fault, Trouille made the fetishized nun a central part of his art. Looking like an erotic postcard, *Italian Nun Smoking a Cigarette* (1944) depicts a beautiful young religious lounging on a convent porch, languorously smoking. Her habit is red and white, its skirt lifted to reveal sheer stockings and garters. In *Dialogue at the Carmel* (also 1944), Trouille follows a similar theme, but introduces a lesbian subtext. Religious books sit on the bench beside two nuns, but there is also a skull wearing a crown of thorns—an unsubtle indication of the relationship between sex and death.

Taking the concept of an unseen order in altogether different directions, nunsploitation films—from *The Convent* (zombie nuns), *Behind Convent Walls* (sex and death), and *Convent of Sinners* (an adaptation of Diderot's novel) to *The Demons* (possessed novices), *Holy Terror* (possessed nuns), and *The Sinful Nuns of St. Valentine* (possessed Mother Superior)—tap into our fears of those who have given themselves over to religion and of those over whom religion has no control.

# 8

## CURTAIN AND HOUSE LIGHTS
### Possibility Persists in the World Outside the Frame

*They are reading things in that were never there, or never intended to be there. But let's face it, that is their job. They've got to find things to make themselves clever or to build up their own form of readership and present their own identity. They are, in a way, creating their own films in their own minds.*

(Michael Carreras, Director, *The Curse of the Mummy's Tomb*)

*I hope, and certainly my intention is to make a film that provokes people to ask themselves what they believe, and what they believe about evil, what they believe about the demonic. And, inevitably, when you ask questions like that, you end up asking yourself what you think about God, and what you think about morality, and what you think about about the nature of memory and truth. And these things are very, very significant, and if you can get an audience to wonder about such things while completely entertaining them, as a filmmaker you've done your job.*

(Scott Derrickson, Director, *The Exorcism of Emily Rose*)

### OUTTAKE: *THE EXORCISM OF EMILY ROSE*

The final shot is a close-up of defense attorney Erin Bruner (Laura Linney) falling asleep. Unlike other times during the preceding 115 minutes of the film, her face is relaxed, her eyes gently closed, on her lips the slightest hint of a smile. She sleeps peacefully, secure that she has a place in the universe, that she is not alone. And neither, her attitude suggests, are we. *The Exorcism of Emily Rose* fades to black balanced on the belief that the monster has been dispatched, that the sacred order has been restored—if only for the moment. Despite the title's implication, though, the monster in this case is neither demon nor Devil, but rather the late modern rejection of an unseen order in which these things still actively contend with God for the souls of humanity. Told in a series of flashbacks framed through the narrative of a courtroom trial, *The Exorcism of Emily Rose* has its frightening moments, to be sure. Scott Derrickson's direction and cinematographer Tom Stern's handheld camerawork accentuate the disturbing images of the possession experience, while the calm, deliberate courtroom sequences seem almost serene by comparison, highlighting and counterpointing the horrific energy of Emily's possession and failed exorcism. Portraying Emily, Jennifer Carpenter is particularly compelling as we watch her sink into the hell of demonic attack and oppression—screaming, eating insects, clawing at walls, lashing out at those who love her and want to help. We are meant to jump at certain spots, perhaps to shriek or to gasp, but there is a more intellectual project at work than simply that. Like *The Wicker Man*, we are meant to think about what scares us, and why. Conditioned and guided by the vicissitudes of culture, the mind is the engine of fear, and horror the physical reaction to the cognitive experience—or expectation—of terror.

    Father Richard Moore (Tom Wilkinson) is a parish priest accused of negligent homicide when Emily dies several days after a failed attempt to exorcize a number of demons—including, apparently, Lucifer himself. Prosecuted by a church-going Methodist (Campbell Scott) and defended by Erin Bruner, who claims to be, at best, an agnostic, Moore's trial is a set piece battle between contested worldviews: the rational, scientific view that Emily was psycho-epileptic and died because she stopped taking the medications designed to control her condition, and the religious view, which has not closed itself off to the potential reality of the unseen order, but that the prosecutor persistently derides as "based on archaic, irrational superstition." Between flashback sequences of Emily's deepening possession, viewers are presented with an extended argument between these two explanations for her affliction. Though a Reuters reviewer contends that this approach renders the characters little more than "ciphers in a theological debate" (in Chattaway, 2005a), another way of interpreting the film is to suggest that this is precisely the point. Though the principal goal of a horror movie may be to scare its audience, as I have tried to demonstrate throughout this book, that hardly exhausts its potential as an artistic or didactic medium.

In a number of ways, a film like *The Exorcism of Emily Rose* brings us full circle. Derrickson's courtroom is the medical laboratory in *Hellraiser: Bloodline* where Dr. Auguste tells Phillipe the toymaker that he could not possibly have seen hell raised in the form of the demon, Angelique. It is the book-lined study in Victorian England and the ancient sands of Egypt, where men of science confidently declare to their metaphysically inclined colleagues that the dead no longer walk, that neither *Dracula* or *The Mummy* could possibly exist. It is a quiet bench on the picturesque Georgetown campus where *The Exorcist*'s Damien Karras explains to Chris MacNeil that her daughter could not possibly be possessed, that schizophrenia and epilepsy have cast out Belial and Lucifer, and that the *Diagnostic and Statistical Manual* is modernity's authoritative text, not the *Roman Ritual*. For each of these, certainty is the foundation of rationality, an unshakeable confidence that the unseen order can be both explained and explained away.

Possibility, on the other hand, is the door Derrickson leaves open throughout *The Exorcism of Emily Rose*. Like *Rosemary's Baby* and *The Craft*, whatever argument is presented, whether defense or prosecution, another option is always available to the audience. Are Emily's terrifying visions the result of demonic oppression or frontal lobe epilepsy? Is her preternatural strength a function of psychosis or possession? Are the wounds that appear on her hands truly stigmata, clear evidence of the grace of God amidst her suffering, or lacerations caused by grabbing the farm's barbed wire fence during a grand mal seizure? Unlike *The Exorcist*, which leaves no cinematic room for doubt about the reality of Regan's possession, Derrickson clearly encourages his audience to follow him down the path of possibility. When she accepts the case, for example, Erin is warned by Father Moore that there is far more to this trial than simply evidence, witnesses, and legal wrangling.

>                       MOORE
> There are forces surrounding this
> trial. Dark, powerful forces. Just be
> careful, Erin, watch your step.
>
>                       BRUNER
> I see. Look, Father, you don't have
> to worry about me. I'm an agnostic,
> remember?
>
>                       MOORE
> Demons exist whether you believe in
> them or not.

Despite her confident assertion, though, at this point she does not see what Father Moore fears. She does not understand. And isn't that really the issue—the sociophobic that underpins so much of religiously oriented cinema horror? Against the arrogance of a rationality that assumes absence of evidence equals evidence of absence, the possibility remains that some things exist whether we believe in them or not. By the film's end, possibility is the horizon to which Erin's experience during the trial has opened her. She is the onscreen guide—the cipher, if you will—in which Derrickson lodges his hopes for the audience's experience of the movie. In the end, whether she is finally convinced or not is also left open. In her closing arguments to the jury Erin still contrasts herself with the prosecutor, whom she calls "a man of faith":

> BRUNER
>
> I, on the other hand, am a woman of doubt. Angels and demons. God and the Devil. These things either exist or they do not exist. Are we all alone in this life? Or are we not alone? Either thought is astonishing.

For Erin, the key question has become: "Is it possible?" Whether they ever see the film or not, hundreds of millions of people worldwide would answer "Yes," and Derrickson's closing shot seems to add Erin Bruner to their company. Indeed, through Erin, far more than through Emily herself—for the film could easily be retitled "The Conversion of Erin Bruner"—the audience is encouraged to take *possibility* seriously, to unlearn, if only for the duration of the movie, what late modernity has taught us not to see.

Preparing her case late one night, aware that they are losing badly at the hands of the prosecution's expert medical testimony, Erin proposes an alternate strategy to her assistant, Ray (JR Bourne).

> BRUNER
>
> This book I'm reading, it's by an anthropologist. It's about contemporary cases of possession, mostly in the third world.
>
> RAY
>
> Of course, people there are still primitive and superstitious.
>
> BRUNER
>
> Maybe. Or maybe they see possession for what it really is. Maybe we've taught ourselves not to see it.

RAY

Are you saying you believe in this stuff?

BRUNER

No, I'm saying maybe we shouldn't just try to invalidate the prosecution's case by poking holes in the medical approach. Maybe we should also try to validate the alternative.

Maybe . . . maybe . . . maybe . . . maybe . . . the pulse of possibility beating at the heart of a story from which the potential for invasion by the unseen order has ostensibly been excluded. But why have they been shut out? Recall that, as sociologist Rodney Stark points out in the midst of his trilogy on the history and power of monotheism, "*evil* supernatural forces (such as Satan) are essential to the most rational conception of deity" (2001, 25). "And why not?" asks Derrickson, echoing scores of scary movies going back many decades. As Maya Larkin says to the skeptical priest in *Lost Souls*, "If you really believed in God, Father, why is it so inconceivable to you that his adversary could be just as real?"

Like *The Exorcist*, *The Exorcism of Emily Rose* has its origins in real events. Unlike Blatty, however, who remains coy about details of the exorcism that inspired his book, Derrickson's film is based on the well-documented possession and failed exorcism of a young German student named Anneliese Michel, whose story was told by anthropologist Felicitas Goodman a few years after the girl's death. In 1976, Anneliese died following an exorcism that lasted several months—not a few hours, as so many possession and exorcism films suggest—and included nearly seventy separate rituals. Both her parents and the two priests involved were arrested and charged with negligent homicide. Convicted, they were sentenced to prison terms and court costs that stunned even the prosecution. Unlike the young boy at the unseen center of Blatty's story, the record of Anneliese's ordeal was public and prolonged. Indeed, two years after her death, her grave was opened to ensure that "her body was decomposing properly because [that] was a sure sign she was no longer possessed" (Fryer, 2005, 56).

In Derrickson's film, in order to validate the possession experience before the court (and the audience), Erin calls Dr. Sadira Adani (Shohreh Aghdashloo)—a thinly veiled allusion to Goodman herself, despite the fact that she had no involvement in the original trial and published her book only years later. An anthropologist specializing in the cross-cultural study of possession states, Adani is the voice of an alternative rationality in the film, one who regards the possession experience, while not "typical," as "scientifically verified" and "culturally universal." In dialogue not merely inspired by, but taken almost verbatim from Goodman's book (1981, xiii; cf. Goodman, 1988), she explains:

ADANI

Possession is one term for a basic human experience, reported by a great number of people all around the world. In my fieldwork, I have seen many people who experience a sense of being invaded by an entity from the supernatural realm . . . I believe Emily Rose was a 'hypersensitive,' a person with an unusual connection to what Carlos Castaneda called 'a separate reality.'

While Castaneda's work has been called into question for many years (cf. de Mille, 1976, 2001; Fikes, 1993), his books sell well and have tremendous cultural resonance among those who believe late modernity has done little more than teach us to close our eyes to the wonders and dangers of the unseen order.

Like *The Exorcist*, reviews of *Emily Rose* were mixed, and, once again, at least as interesting as the film itself is what these reactions reveal about the sociophobic space in which it was produced. Clearly bored by the proceedings, for example, one reviewer thought there was "too much courtroom" and "too little demonic action" (Persall, 2005), while another, calling it a "film that aims for the brain, not the gut" (Butler, 2005), seemed happy to be engaged at a more intellectual level than simply screaming, shaking, and special effects. Unable to resist the pun, the *Globe and Mail*'s David Gilmour dubbed it a "pointless exorcise"; Roger Ebert called it "intriguing and perplexing," suggesting somewhat more thoughtfully than many of his colleagues that "maybe it is too faithful to the issues it raises to exploit them" (2005).

*Christianity Today*, the most popular conservative Christian magazine in the English language, printed a lengthy review and included a number of discussion points designed to open up what its reviewers saw as the central issues raised by the film (Chattaway, 2005a). Can Christians be possessed, for example, or does the existence of the Devil prove the existence of God? Though there is no indication of religious devotion in the MacNeil household, and *The Exorcist* rather unsubtly suggests that Regan's possession is the result of playing with an Ouija board, both the Rose family and especially Emily are portrayed from the opening scenes as the epitome of rural Catholic devotion. Asked near the trial's conclusion how he thinks Emily will be remembered, Father Moore answers, "I believe that one day Emily will be recognized as a saint." In a vision during the penultimate stages of her possession, Emily sees the Virgin Mary, who offers her a quick and easy release from her suffering, or the opportunity to endure, to die, but in dying to show people that "the realm of the spirit is real."

Talking about the problems inherent in creating special effects, Canadian horror director David Cronenberg once said, "You have to forget everything outside the frame, because it is only what's in the frame that is real, in your movie" (in Rodley, 1992, 47). While this may be true from certain aspects of a production standpoint, in terms of the particular story and the larger sociophobics of cinema horror, it is more accurate to say that the reality of what is inside the frame *only* matters because of what is outside. It is only because the writers, producers, and directors of cinema horror can tap into these rich sociophobic veins that scary movies have any cultural power at all—something that was not lost on those who produced and marketed *The Exorcism of Emily Rose*.

First, for example, few commentators missed the fact that Derrickson is a practicing Christian, a Presbyterian who one Catholic News Service report indicates is "'very close' to becoming Catholic. He said he is 'one (G. K.) Chesterton book away from crossing over'" (Pattison, 2005). Interviewed by *Christianity Today*, Derrickson defended his directorial choice, arguing that "the horror genre is a perfect genre for Christians to be involved with" (Chattaway, 2005b). "It's about admitting that there is evil in the world," he continues, "and recognizing that there is evil within *us*, and that we're not in control, and that things we are afraid of must be confronted in order for us to relinquish that fear" (Chattaway 2005b). Traditionally, the Christian audience—whether Protestant or Catholic—has been largely, though not completely, closed to cinema horror (recall, e.g., Burke, 1999; Stone, 2001). While he is clearly not advocating all types of horror movies, Derrickson just as clearly challenges his fellow believers to consider whether cinema horror is one way to ask important questions about what tens of millions of people consider basic spiritual issues and realities.

Second, promotional material for *The Exorcism of Emily Rose* recognized and exploited popular fear of the Devil, belief in the possibility of possession, and a growing demand in some countries for exorcisms, both official and unofficial (see, e.g., Amorth, 1999; Cuneo, 2001; Peck, 2005; Wilkinson, 2007). Like *The Exorcist* more than thirty years before, both *Emily Rose* and *Requiem*, a German version of Anneliese's story that was released a year later, propagated renewed interest in (and fear of) possession phenomena. "Possessed: The State of Modern Exorcism," read the banner headline of a four-color advertising insert included in newspapers across North America the month prior to *Emily Rose*'s arrival in theaters (Screen Gems, 2005). "The real-life practice of exorcism is on the rise worldwide," a subhead continued, and the insert contained articles about a class for potential exorcists offered at a "Vatican-recognized university," the three exorcisms performed by John Paul II during his papacy, fear that possession is on the rise in Mexico (headlined as "land of witchcraft, pagan rituals"), and a picture of a man accused of killing a Korean woman during an attempted exorcism in California. Three months before the film's debut at the Venice Film Festival, a young Romanian nun died during an exorcism at a remote village convent. Though diagnosed with schizophrenia, a priest and four members of her order chained her to a crucifix in an attempt to drive out what they believed were demons. Two years later, the four nuns were excommunicated and the priest sentenced to fourteen years in prison. Just a few months after the Romanian trial ended, a Phoenix, Arizona, man died after police used stun guns to stop him choking his granddaughter during an attempted exorcism.

"Publicity," writes John Berger in his highly influential *Ways of Seeing*, "needs to turn to its own advantage the traditional education of the average spectator-buyer. What he has learnt at school of history, mythology, poetry can be used in the manufacture of glamour" (1972, 140). Or, dare we say, the manufacture of fear. This is, of course, the principle of intertextuality that has informed our analysis from the beginning, and every culture, every social class has a different intertextual register, a different palette of referent and response to which programmers—whether glamour or horror—must appeal to ensure the success of their products. While Michael Carreras may see this as simple exploitation—cinema horror equals company profit—he has ignored the crucial aspect of intertextuality: not everyone participates in the same intertextual register, and both register and audience must coincide for a particular product to succeed. "Fear," as David Scruton reminds us, "is a social act that occurs within a cultural matrix" (1986, 10). Though they manifest physically and psychologically, though they are real in that sense, our fears remain socially constructed. Whether we believe in these profoundly varied visions of the unseen order or not, whether we support the actions of those who combat what they regard as supernatural invasion, clearly what is outside the cinematic frame matters a great deal to what filmmakers frame within. "We hate *message* films," Sir James Carreras, Michael's father and the founder of Hammer Studios, said in a 1959 interview, continuing, "We make *entertainment*" (as quoted in Brosnan, 1976, 117). But, with cinema horror so suffuse with religion, in the midst of entertainment, can messages be avoided?

## DENYING CATHARSIS: CINEMA HORROR AND THE PERSISTENCE OF POSSIBILITY

A misconception that is astonishingly common in film interpretation, even cinema horror, is that everything turns out all right in the end—a cinematic correlative, if you will, to the "good, moral, and decent" fallacy discussed in chapter 1. According to Stephen King, for example, beyond the *frisson*, the shiver of fear in front of the cinematic campfire, one of the chief pleasures of horror is "that magic moment of reintegration and safety at the end" (1981, 14). Regan MacNeil's childhood restored as they leave Georgetown forever. The mummy returned to his tomb; the vampire staked in her crypt. The toymaker's box closed once again, and with it the doorway between our world and the unseen order of the Cenobites. Erin Bruner's smile as she falls asleep. In the face of all that has gone before, these moments provide a feeling of catharsis, of release, indications that the world is exactly as it should be. "However bad the situation of the characters may be at various points in the story," writes John Lyden, as part of his argument that "film itself functions as a religion" (2003, 34), "by the end all will be tidy and we will be reassured that all is well with the world" (2003, 46). While he is not talking about horror movies specifically, Darrol Bryant concurs, suggesting that "the profoundly spiritual significance of film" is "an experience of order and harmony that stands in counterpoint to the experience of the everyday world" (1982, 112). That is, these films are, in some way, cathartic. We have come through pain and fear into release and reintegration. King does point out, though, however venerable and not without its uses, the term *catharsis* "has been used rather too glibly by some practitioners in my field to justify what they do" (1981, 13). Catharsis, of course, suggests a cleansing, as King puts it, a "lancing," relief that does not come without cost, without effort, and, often in cinema horror, that does not last for long. Whether the unseen order is inversive, invasive, or renders insignificant the gods to whom we pray, for example, that "magic moment" is fleeting and unstable at best.

Many of the films we have considered suggest that cinema horror thrives on the power of the sequel, and that its appeal lies less in its ability to provide a cathartic experience for the audience than its unwillingness to let the cathartic process go to its conclusion. The sociophobics that give rise to different types of horror films—from fear of the dead and of the places where we hope and pray the dead stay buried, to fear both of religion's power and of its impotence in the face of stronger, more primal urges—still exist once the credits have rolled, the house lights come up, and we make our way through the darkened parking lot. Like the ghost stories *The Fog*'s Captain Machen tells the children gathered around him on the beach near Spivey Point, cinema horror is fantasy—however artfully brought to life for a couple of hours. Many of the fears on which those fantasies feed, however, are not. They continue to haunt us, awaiting only the arrival of the sequel to reflect them back to us once again.

In many cases, economic incentive invokes the denial of catharsis through the structural vehicle of the sequel itself. Audiences paid money to see one film, and filmmakers bet the success of a sequel on a similar willingness. Cinema history is filled with directors and producers who have explicitly programmed audiences in terms of sequels, whether as direct continuations of the original story (certain of the Universal *Mummy* films, the first three entries in the *Alien* cycle, *The Omen* trilogy, the first three *Exorcist* films), or, as is more common in cinema horror, as shared world sequels that build on, but may not continue, the original (the numerous *Dracula* or *Frankenstein* films, the *Hellraiser*, *Wishmaster*, or *The Prophecy* franchises). Once an audience has been established for a particular set of characters, an accepted framework of action, and an outline of narrative expectations and responsibilities, it is considerably easier to serve up more of the same than to risk the invention of entirely new cinematic worlds.

The sequel's structural aspects keep audiences coming back for more by continually attempting to offer us more to come back for. Although fans are often disappointed by sequels, they continue to be scripted, financed, produced, filmed, and distributed. They are marketed as an integral, indeed indispensible, menu item on the cinematic buffet, and viewers continue to line up at theaters and video stores. But this dynamic of availability only succeeds when there is a predisposition for it. In terms of cinema horror, this means when the sociophobic on which the films depend is still viable and resonant. The fear remains, no matter how many demons exorcized or monsters dispatched.

The narrative denial of catharsis, the second level at which cinema horror refuses to provide anything but temporary relief, is based on two opposing forces—the exploitation of familiarity and the expectation of difference—two sociocultural pressures that, when properly balanced, leave the audience with a sense of satisfaction that the updated version has done its job. Building on the investment audiences have in particular characters, themes, and narrative relationships, the exploitation of familiarity means that writers, producers, and directors can rely on audience familiarity to fill many of the gaps in the story left unexplained by the overall narrative. The power of these emerging mythologies, however, these alternate visions of the unseen order, often require the proactive extension of storylines and back stories. *Hellraiser: Bloodline*, for example, was an attempt to extend and present a more sophisticated version of the Cenobite mythology, to explore their unseen order in a more coherent way. Kevin Yagher's initial treatment called for Pinhead to be introduced much later in the film than studio executives wanted, however. They believed the audience would demand more of the head Cenobite, that fans had come to associate the evolving mythology with him, and interfered with production to the point where Yagher finally withdrew his name from the film. In this case, though, the final product disappointed audiences, and this installment is considered one of the worst in the series.

The expectation of difference, on the other hand, means that studios cannot simply produce the same film over and over, however similar many films may look to one another. Recall, for example, that, in order to cut production costs, a number of Universal's *Mummy* sequels used footage from the original film—a device that would not work today, though the occasional filmmaker still tries. Both audience reactions on fan sites and critical reviews of sequels indicate clearly that viewers do pay attention to the coherence of the storyline, they are invested in the mythologies developing in cinema horror franchises, and they are quick to point out flaws in continuity or consistency. While some franchises attempt to carry on coherent intertextual narratives, others, such as *The Mummy*, *Dracula*, and the *Hellraiser* series, rely simply on the identifiability of the main horrific characters for their commercial (and narrative) strength. The expectation of difference in the sequel demands that some new facet of these characters be revealed with each new installment of the series. Because they explicitly rely on the concept of the unfinished story, both the exploitation of familiarity and the expectation of difference contribute to the denial of catharsis and the persistence of possibility. Chaos may have been set aside for the moment, but it has not been defeated.

The deepest level at which the denial of catharsis occurs, though, is the existential, the realm of belief and imagination that exists apart from the screen, the fears we have that ghost stories are real, that devils and demons do exist, that the unseen orders pressing in around us do not evaporate when the projector is switched off. We don't forget any of this simply because the movie is over. Here, once again, we are back to the sociophobic of the "true story," whether manifest in advertising inserts designed to boost ticket sales (*The Exorcism of Emily Rose*) or religious rituals deeply embedded in popular culture (*Ju-On*). In many ways, these films are the cultural expressions of cognitive dissonance, as I noted in the introduction, the direct collision between what we hope to be true about the world and what we fear may be the reality.

Because filmmakers are bricoleurs, crafting their stories from a variety of sources and responding to a range of artistic, economic, and cultural influences—including the religious—their craft reflects those sources as much as it contributes to them. Writers, directors, and producers choose the cultural strands that they believe will resonate with their target audiences, and that will translate into meaningful films and profitable bottom lines. The economic incentive and willingness to exploit the familiar aside, much of cinema horror's love affair with the sequel is bound up with the unsettled feeling we have that evil is never really defeated, the monster never really destroyed, and chaos never permanently subjugated by cosmos.

Indeed, at some level, we know this; we know it isn't really over, and that's a significant part of the horror experience. Certainly, in the world around us there is little empirical evidence that the monsters are destroyed forever, or that the battles we fight ever bring the wars to an end. This is the dark beyond our collective headlights. The monster may have been vanquished for the moment, and order restored for a time, but we know that resolution is brief and that other monsters wait in the shadows. We may leave the theater or turn off the DVD player, and the angels, demons, vampires, ghosts, or mummies that haunted our present darkness may retreat for a time. But the larger demons, the ones that populate the darkness outside the theater, still remain. We know that, though our immediate fears may be temporarily allayed, the existential reasons that brought those fears to the surface in the first place—or the sociophobic reasons that allowed the horror stylist to surface them—are still out there.

Technology has not banished fear of the dark—candles burn down, batteries go flat (that is, they "die," and so often the characters in horror cinema die with them), and flashlights inevitably refuse to work just when we need them most (witness the terrifying end of Captain Dallas [Tom Skerritt] as he hunts for the creature in *Alien*). No matter how powerful our halogen headlights, the darkness and all the fears that live within it still exist on the ragged edge of the light we use to keep them at bay. Moreover, even while we keep it at bay, even as we use all our technological resources to pierce the darkness, we can still see it out there. We have, in fact, done nothing more than prick it, because in the context of the pitifully small segment of the electromagnetic spectrum to which we have visual access, darkness is our natural condition. Light is the intruder, a temporary island of relative security in a larger, largely uncharted, ocean of dark.

# FILMOGRAPHY

| Title | Date | Director |
|---|---|---|
| *13 Ghosts* | 1960 | William Castle |
| *28 Days Later* | 2002 | Danny Boyle |
| | | |
| *Abby* | 1974 | William Girdler |
| *Alien* | 1979 | Ridley Scott |
| *Alien Dead, The* | 1980 | Fred Olen Ray |
| *Alien³* | 1992 | David Fincher |
| *Aliens* | 1986 | James Cameron |
| *Amityville Horror, The* | 1979 | Stuart Rosenberg |
| *Apostate, The* | 1998 | William Gove |
| | | |
| *Bedazzled* | 1967 | Stanley Donen |
| *Bedazzled* | 2000 | Harold Ramis |
| *Beetlejuice* | 1988 | Tim Burton |
| *Behind Convent Walls* | 1978 | Walerian Borowczyk |
| *Believers, The* | 1987 | John Schlesinger |
| *Bell, Book and Candle* | 1958 | Richard Quine |
| *Bewitched* | 2005 | Nora Ephron |
| *Beyond, The* | 1981 | Lucio Fulci |
| *Beyond Re-Animator* | 2003 | Brian Yuzna |
| *Bio Cops* | 2000 | Wai-Man Cheng |
| *Biohazardous* | 2001 | J. Michael Hein |
| *Bio-Zombie* | 1998 | Wilson Yip |

| Title | Date | Director |
|---|---|---|
| *Black Narcissus* | 1947 | Michael Powell & Emeric Pressburger |
| *Black Sunday* | 1960 | Mario Bava |
| *Blacula* | 1972 | William Crain |
| *Blade* | 1998 | Stephen Norrington |
| *Blade: Trinity* | 2004 | David S. Goyer |
| *Blade II* | 2002 | Guillermo del Toro |
| *Blair Witch Project, The* | 1999 | Daniel Myrick & Eduardo Sánchez |
| *Bless the Child* | 2000 | Chuck Russell |
| *Blob, The* | 1958 | Irvin S. Yeaworth, Jr. |
| *Blood from the Mummy's Tomb* | 1971 | Seth Holt |
| *Bone Collector, The* | 1999 | Phillip Noyce |
| *Bone Snatcher, The* | 2003 | Jason Wulfsohn |
| *Book of Shadows: Blair Witch 2* | 2000 | Joe Berlinger |
| *Bordello of Blood* | 1996 | Gilbert Adler |
| *Braindead* | 1992 | Peter Jackson |
| *Bram Stoker's Dracula* | 1992 | Francis Ford Coppola |
| *Bride of Re-Animator* | 1999 | Brian Yuzna |
| *Brides of Christ* | 1991 | Ken Cameron |
| *Brides of Dracula, The* | 1960 | Terence Fisher |
| *Cape Canaveral Monsters* | 1960 | Phil Tucker |
| *Captain Kronos— Vampire Hunter* | 1974 | Brian Clemens |
| *Carnival of Souls* | 1962 | Herk Harvey |
| *Carrie* | 1976 | Brian De Palma |
| *Cat People* | 1943 | Jacques Tourneur |
| *Cell, The* | 2000 | Tarsem Singh |
| *Children, The* | 1980 | Max Kalmanowicz |
| *Children of the Corn* | 1984 | Fritz Kiersch |
| *Children of the Damned* | 1963 | Anton Leader |

| Title | Date | Director |
|---|---|---|
| *Children Shouldn't Play with Dead Things* | 1972 | Bob Clark |
| *Christina, the Devil Nun* | 1972 | Sergio Bergonzelli |
| *City of the Living Dead* | 1980 | Lucio Fulci |
| *Clueless* | 1995 | Amy Heckerling |
| *Constantine* | 2005 | Francis Lawrence |
| *Convent, The* | 2000 | Mike Mendez |
| *Convent of Sinners* | 1986 | Joe D'Amato |
| *Convent of the Sacred Beast* | 1974 | Norifumi Suzuki |
| *Countess Dracula* | 1970 | Peter Sasdy |
| *Craft, The* | 1999 | Andrew Fleming |
| *Creature from the Black Lagoon* | 1954 | Jack Arnold |
| *Cult of Fury* | 2001 | Yossi Wein |
| *Curse of the Blair Witch* | 1999 | Daniel Myrick & Eduardo Sánchez |
| *Curse of the Crimson Altar* | 1968 | Vernon Sewell |
| *Curse of the Mummy's Tomb, The* | 1964 | Michael Carreras |
| *Dagon* | 2001 | Stuart Gordon |
| *Damien: Omen II* | 1978 | Don Taylor |
| *Dark Water* | 2005 | Walter Salles |
| *Dawn of the Dead* | 1978 | George A. Romero |
| *Day of the Beast* | 1995 | Álex de la Iglesia |
| *Day of the Dead* | 1985 | George A. Romero |
| *Dead Creatures* | 2001 | Andrew Parkinson |
| *Dead Don't Die, The* | 1975 | Curtis Harrington |
| *Dead Life* | 2005 | William Victor Schotten |
| *Dead Men Don't Die* | 1991 | Malcolm Marmorstein |
| *Dead Next Door, The* | 1988 | J. R. Bookwalter |
| *Demonia* | 1990 | Lucio Fulci |
| *Demons* | 1985 | Lamberto Bava |
| *Demons, The* | 1972 | Jess Franco |

| Title | Date | Director |
|---|---|---|
| Devil and Daniel Webster, The | 1941 | William Dieterle |
| Devil Rides Out, The | 1968 | Terence Fisher |
| Devil's Daughter, The | 1972 | Jeannot Szwarc |
| Devil's Nightmare, The | 1971 | Jean Brismée |
| Die Hard | 1988 | John McTiernan |
| Dogma | 1999 | Kevin Smith |
| Dracula A.D. 1972 | 1972 | Alan Gibson |
| Dracula Has Risen from the Grave | 1968 | Freddie Francis |
| Dracula, Prince of Darkness | 1966 | Terence Fisher |
| Dracula III: Legacy | 2005 | Patrick Lussier |
| Dracula II: Ascension | 2003 | Patrick Lussier |
| Dracula 2000 | 2000 | Patrick Lussier |
| Dunwich Horror, The | 1970 | Daniel Haller |
| | | |
| Earth Dies Screaming, The | 1964 | Terence Fisher |
| El Fantasma del Convento | 1934 | Fernando de Fuentes |
| El Signo de la Muerta | 1939 | Chano Urueta |
| End of Days | 1999 | Peter Hyams |
| Erotic Witchcraft | 1972 | Mario Mercier & Bepi Fontana |
| Exorcism of Emily Rose, The | 2005 | Scott Derrickson |
| Exorcist, The | 1973 | William Friedkin |
| Exorcist: The Beginning | 2004 | Renny Harlin |
| Eyes of the Mummy, The | 1918 | Ernst Lubitsch |
| | | |
| Fantasma del Convento, El | 1934 | Fernando de Fuentes |
| Fear dot Com | 2002 | William Malone |
| Fog, The | 1979 | John Carpenter |
| Fog, The | 2005 | Rupert Wainwright |
| Frankenstein | 1931 | James Whale |
| Frankenstein Must Be Destroyed | 1969 | Terence Fisher |
| Friday the 13$^{th}$ | 1980 | Sean S. Cunningham |
| Friday the 13$^{th}$, Part 3 | 1982 | Steve Miner |

| Title | Date | Director |
|---|---|---|
| *Ghost* | 1990 | Jerry Zucker |
| *Ghost Ship* | 2002 | Steve Beck |
| *Ghostbusters* | 1984 | Ivan Reitman |
| *Ghoul, The* | 1975 | Freddie Francis |
| *Ghoul School* | 1990 | Timothy O'Rawe |
| *Ghouls, The* | 2004 | Chad Ferrin |
| *Gin Gwai (The Eye)* | 2002 | Oxide Pang Chun & Danny Pang |
| *Godzilla* | 1998 | Roland Emmerich |
| *Gojira* | 1954 | Inoshiro Honda |
| *Good Against Evil* | 1977 | Paul Wendkos |
| *Grapes of Death, The* | 1978 | Jean Rollin |
| *Grudge, The* | 2004 | Takashi Shimizu |
| *Grudge 2, The* | 2006 | Takashi Shimizu |
| *Halloween* | 1978 | John Carpenter |
| *Halloween III: Season of the Witch* | 1982 | Tommy Lee Wallace |
| *Halloween II* | 1981 | Rick Rosenthal |
| *Haunted Cop Shop* | 1987 | Jeff Lau Chun-Wai |
| *Haunted Jail House* | 1990 | Sai Hung Fung & Jing Wong |
| *Haunted Karaoke* | 1997 | Hin Sing "Billy" Tang |
| *Haunted Mansion* | 1998 | Dickson To |
| *Haunted Palace, The* | 1963 | Roger Corman |
| *Haunting, The* | 1963 | Robert Wise |
| *Haunting, The* | 1999 | Jan de Bont |
| *Heathers* | 1989 | Michael Lehmann |
| *Hellbound: Hellraiser II* | 1988 | Tony Randel |
| *Hellraiser* | 1987 | Clive Barker |
| *Hellraiser: Bloodline* | 1996 | Alan Smithee (Kevin Yagher) |
| *Hellraiser III: Hell on Earth* | 1992 | Anthony Hickox |
| *Highlander* | 1986 | Russell Mulcahy |

| Title | Date | Director |
|---|---|---|
| *Holy Terror* | 2002 | Massimiliano Cerchi |
| *Honogurai mizu no soko kara* (*Dark Water*) | 2002 | Hideo Nakata |
| *Horror Hotel* | 1960 | John Llewellyn Moxey |
| *Hotel* | 1981 | Shyam Ramsay & Tulsi Ramsay |
| *House by the Cemetery, The* | 1981 | Lucio Fulci |
| *House of Re-Animator* | 2008 | Stuart Gordon |
| *House on Skull Mountain, The* | 1974 | Ron Honthamer |
| *Hunger, The* | 1983 | Tony Scott |
| *I Walked with a Zombie* | 1943 | Jacques Tourneur |
| *I Was a Teenage Zombie* | 1987 | John Elias Michalakis |
| *I Was a Zombie for the F.B.I.* | 1982 | Marius Penczner |
| *In the Mouth of Madness* | 1995 | John Carpenter |
| *Indiana Jones and the Temple of Doom* | 1984 | Steven Spielberg |
| *Innocent Blood* | 1992 | John Landis |
| *Invaders from Mars* | 1953 | William Cameron Menzies |
| *Invaders from Mars* | 1986 | Tobe Hooper |
| *Invasion of the Body Snatchers* | 1956 | Don Siegel |
| *Invasion of the Body Snatchers* | 1978 | Philip Kaufman |
| *Invisible Invaders* | 1959 | Edward L. Cahn |
| *Isle of the Dead* | 1945 | Mark Robson |
| *Isle of the Snake People* | 1971 | Juan Ibáñez & Jack Hill |
| *John Carpenter's Vampires* | 1998 | John Carpenter |
| *Ju-on* | 2000 | Takashi Shimizu |
| *Ju-on: The Grudge* | 2003 | Takashi Shimizu |
| *King Kong* | 1933 | Merian C. Cooper & Ernest B. Schoedsack |

| Title | Date | Director |
|---|---|---|
| Lair of the White Worm, The | 1988 | Ken Russell |
| Land of the Dead | 2005 | George A. Romero |
| Lara Croft: Tomb Raider | 2001 | Simon West |
| Last Man on Earth, The | 1964 | Ubaldo Ragona |
| Last Temptation of Christ, The | 1988 | Martin Scorsese |
| Lifeforce | 1985 | Tobe Hooper |
| Little Mermaid, The | 1989 | Ron Clements & John Musker |
| Living Dead at Manchester Morgue, The | 1974 | Jorge Grau |
| Living Dead Girl, The | 1982 | Jean Rollin |
| Logan's Run | 1976 | Michael Anderson |
| Lord of Illusions | 1995 | Clive Barker |
| Lord of the Dead | 2000 | Greg Parker |
| Lost Souls | 2000 | Janusz Kaminski |
| Lust for a Vampire | 1971 | Jimmy Sangster |
| Maplewoods | 2003 | David B. Stewart III |
| Mary Shelley's Frankenstein | 1994 | Kenneth Branagh |
| Mean Girls | 2004 | Mark Waters |
| Messiah of Evil | 1973 | Willard Huyck |
| Metropolis | 1927 | Fritz Lang |
| Midnight Mass | 2003 | Tony Mandile |
| Mists of Avalon, The | 2001 | Uli Edel |
| Mr. Vampire | 1985 | Ricky Lau |
| Mr. Vampire IV | 1988 | Ricky Lau |
| Mummy, The | 1932 | Karl Freund |
| Mummy, The | 1959 | Terence Fisher |
| Mummy, The | 1999 | Stephen Sommers |
| Mummy, The | 2001 | Stephen Sommers |
| Mummy Dearest | 1999 | David J. Skal |
| Mummy's Curse, The | 1944 | Leslie Goodwins |
| Mummy's Ghost, The | 1944 | Reginald Le Borg |
| Mummy's Hand, The | 1940 | Christy Cabanne |

| Title | Date | Director |
|---|---|---|
| Mummy's Shroud, The | 1967 | John Gilling |
| Mummy's Tomb, The | 1942 | Harold Young |
| Mutation | 1999 | Timo Rose & Marc Fehse |
| Nang Nak | 1999 | Nonzee Nimibutr |
| Necronomicon: Book of the Dead | 1993 | Brian Yuzna, Shusuke Kaneko & Christophe Gans |
| Night of the Comet | 1984 | Thom Eberhardt |
| Night of the Creeps | 1986 | Fred Dekker |
| Night of the Living Dead | 1968 | George A. Romero |
| Night of the Zombies | 1981 | Joel M. Reed |
| Nightmare on Elm Street, A | 1984 | Wes Craven |
| Ninth Gate, The | 1999 | Roman Polanski |
| Nude Vampire, The | 1970 | Jean Rollin |
| Ode to Billy Joe | 1976 | Max Baer Jr. |
| Omen, The | 1976 | Richard Donner |
| Omen, The | 2006 | John Moore |
| Omen Legacy, The | 2001 | Brent Zacky |
| Omen III: The Final Conflict | 1981 | Graham Baker |
| Operation Condor | 1991 | Jackie Chan |
| Order, The | 2003 | Brian Helgeland |
| Other Hell, The (L'altro inferno) | 1980 | Bruno Mattei |
| Ouanga | 1936 | George Terwilliger |
| Outbreak | 1995 | Wolfgang Petersen |
| Plague of the Zombies, The | 1966 | John Gilling |
| Plan 9 from Outer Space | 1959 | Edward D. Wood Jr. |
| Planet of Blood | 1966 | Curtis Harrington |
| Planet of the Vampires | 1965 | Mario Bava |
| Poltergeist | 1982 | Tobe Hooper |
| Practical Magic | 1998 | Griffin Dunne |

| Title | Date | Director |
|---|---|---|
| *Prince of Darkness* | 1987 | John Carpenter |
| *Prophecy: Forsaken, The* | 2005 | Joel Soisson |
| *Prophecy 3: The Ascent* | 2000 | Patrick Lussier |
| *Prophecy II, The* | 1998 | Greg Spence |
| *Prophecy: Uprising, The* | 2005 | Joel Soisson |
| *Psycho* | 1960 | Alfred Hitchcock |
| *Pulp Fiction* | 1994 | Quentin Tarantino |
| *Q* | 1982 | Larry Cohen |
| *Quatermass 2* | 1957 | Val Guest |
| *Raiders of the Lost Ark* | 1981 | Steven Spielberg |
| *Rape of the Vampire, The* | 1967 | Jean Rollin |
| *Re-Animator* | 1985 | Stuart Gordon |
| *Requiem* | 2006 | Hans-Christian Schmid |
| *Requiem for a Vampire* | 1971 | Jean Rollin |
| *Resident Evil* | 2002 | Paul W. S. Anderson |
| *Resident Evil: Apocalypse* | 2004 | Alexander Witt |
| *Resident Evil: Extinction* | 2007 | Russell Mulcahy |
| *Resurrected, The* | 1992 | Dan O'Bannon |
| *Return of the Living Dead, The* | 1985 | Dan O'Bannon |
| *Revenge of the Living Dead Girls, The* | 1987 | Pierre B. Reinhard |
| *Revenge of the Zombies* | 1943 | Steve Sekely |
| *Revolt of the Zombies* | 1936 | Victor Halperin |
| *Ring, The* | 2002 | Gore Verbinski |
| *Ringu* | 1998 | Hideo Nakata |
| *Rocky Horror Picture Show, The* | 1975 | Jim Sharman |
| *Rosemary's Baby* | 1968 | Roman Polanski |
| *Runaway Bride* | 1999 | Garry Marshall |
| *Rush Hour 3* | 2007 | Brett Ratner |
| *Sacred Flesh* | 2000 | Nigel Wingrove |
| *Satanic Rites of Dracula, The* | 1973 | Alan Gibson |

| Title | Date | Director |
|---|---|---|
| *Saw* | 2004 | James Wan |
| *Scream, Blacula, Scream* | 1973 | Bob Kelljan |
| *Serpent and the Rainbow, The* | 1988 | Wes Craven |
| *Seventh Sign, The* | 1988 | Carl Schultz |
| *Seventh Victim, The* | 1943 | Mark Robson |
| *Shaun of the Dead* | 2004 | Edgar Wright |
| *Shining, The* | 1980 | Stanley Kubrick |
| *Shining, The* | 1997 | Mick Garris |
| *Shiver of the Vampires, The* | 1971 | Jean Rollin |
| *Shivers* | 1975 | David Cronenburg |
| *Shock Waves* | 1977 | Ken Wiederhorn |
| *Sinful Nuns of St. Valentine, The* | 1974 | Sergio Grieco |
| *Sister Act* | 1992 | Emile Ardolino |
| *Sister Luna's Confession* | 1976 | Masaru Konuma |
| *Sixth Sense, The* | 1999 | M. Night Shyamalan |
| *Sleeper* | 1973 | Woody Allen |
| *Splash* | 1984 | Ron Howard |
| *Stigmata* | 1999 | Rupert Wainwright |
| *Strange Invaders* | 1983 | Michael Laughlin |
| *Sugar Hill* | 1974 | Paul Maslansky |
| | | |
| *Taste the Blood of Dracula* | 1970 | Peter Sasdy |
| *Texas Chain Saw Massacre, The* | 1974 | Tobe Hooper |
| *Thirteen Ghosts* | 2001 | Steve Beck |
| *Tingler, The* | 1959 | William Castle |
| *Titanic* | 1997 | James Cameron |
| *To the Devil... a Daughter* | 1976 | Peter Sykes |
| *Toxic Zombies* | 1980 | Charles McCrann |
| *Trainspotting* | 1996 | Danny Boyle |
| *Tsui Hark's Vampire Hunters* | 2002 | Wellson Chin |
| *Twister* | 1996 | Jan de Bont |
| | | |
| *Undead* | 2003 | Michael & Peter Spierig |
| *Underworld* | 2003 | Len Wiseman |

| Title | Date | Director |
|---|---|---|
| *Underworld: Evolution* | 2006 | Len Wiseman |
| *Unnamable, The* | 1988 | Jean-Paul Ouellette |
| *Unnamable II: The Statement of Randolph Carter, The* | 1988 | Jean-Paul Ouellette |
| | | |
| *Vampire Lovers, The* | 1970 | Roy Ward Baker |
| *Vampirella* | 1996 | Jim Wynorski |
| *Vengeance of Egypt, The* | 1912 | Unknown |
| *Village of the Damned* | 1960 | Wolf Rilla |
| *Virgin Witch* | 1972 | Ray Austin |
| *Visitation, The* | 2006 | Robby Henson |
| *Voodoo Dawn* | 1990 | Steven Fierberg |
| | | |
| *War of the Worlds, The* | 1953 | Byron Haskin |
| *War of the Zombies* | 1964 | Giuseppe Vari |
| *White Noise* | 2005 | Geoffrey Sax |
| *White Zombie* | 1932 | Victor Halperin |
| *Wicker Man, The* | 1973 | Robin Hardy |
| *Wicker Man, The* | 2006 | Neil LaBute |
| *Wishmaster* | 1997 | Robert Kurtzman |
| *Witches, The* | 1966 | Cyril Frankel |
| *Witches of Eastwick, The* | 1987 | George Miller |
| *Wolf Man, The* | 1941 | George Waggner |
| | | |
| *Yeogo goedam* (*Whispering Corridors*) | 1998 | Ki-hyeong Park |
| *Yeogo goedam II* (*Memento Mori*) | 1999 | Tae-Yong Kim & Kyu-Dong Min |
| | | |
| *Zombie '90: Extreme Pestilence* | 1991 | Andreas Schnaas |

# BIBLIOGRAPHY

Abanes, Richard. (2002). *Fantasy and Your Family: Exploring The Lord of the Rings, Harry Potter, and Modern Magick*. Camp Hill, Penn.: Christian Publications.

Ackermann, Hans-W., and Jeanine Gauthier. (1991). "The Ways and Nature of the Zombi." *Journal of American Folklore* 104 (414): 466–94.

A.D.S. (1933). "Life after 3,700 years." *The New York Times* (7 January): 11.

Addiss, Stephen, ed. (1985). *Japanese Ghosts & Demons: Art of the Supernatural*. New York: George Braziller.

Adler, Renata. (1968). "The Screen: 'Rosemary's Baby,' a Story of Fantasy and Horror." *The New York Times* (13 June): 57.

Alexander, Brooks. (2004). *Witchcraft Goes Mainstream*. Eugene, Ore.: Harvest House.

Almond, Jocelyn, and Keith Seddon. (2004). *Egyptian Paganism for Beginners*. St. Paul, Minn.: Llewellyn Publications.

Amorth, Gabriele. (1999). *An Exorcist Tells His Story*. San Francisco: Ignatius Press.

Anonymous. (1836a). "Maria Monk, the Nun-Such." *Atkinson's Saturday Evening Post* (13 August): 1, col. 5.

———. (1836b). "Roman Catholic Editor." *Trumpet and Universalist Magazine* (30 July): 22.

AP [Associated Press]. (1974). "20 Books on Occult Burned." *Washington Post* (25 January): D14.

AP [Associated Press]. (1980). "62 Animals Rescued From Cult Rites." *Los Angeles Times* (8 June): A27.
———. (1989). "Movie Linked To Alleged Cult Slayers." *Washington Post* (16 April): A21.
———. (1999). "Antichrist Is Alive, And a Male Jew, Falwell Contends." *The New York Times* (16 January): A8.
Armstrong, Rod. (1999). "Review of *Lost Souls*"; www.reel.com, accessed 27 March 2006.
Austen, Jane. ([1818] 2006). *Northanger Abbey*. Cambridge: Cambridge University Press.
Baker, Tim. (2003). *Dewitched: What You Need to Know about the Dangers of Witchcraft and Wicca*. Nashville: Thomas Nelson.
Barber, Paul. (1988). *Vampires, Burial, and Death: Folklore and Reality*. New Haven: Yale University Press.
Barker, Clive. (1986). *The Hellbound Heart*. New York: Harper Paperbacks.
Barker, Elaine. (1984). *The Making of a Moonie: Choice or Brainwashing?* London: Basil Blackwell.
Barker, Jason. (2000). "Youth-Oriented TV and the Occult"; www.watchman.org/occult/youthandoccult.htm, accessed 7 August 2007.
Barner-Barry, Carol. (2005). *Contemporary Paganism: Minority Religions in a Majoritarian America*. New York: Palgrave Macmillan.
Bataille, George. (1962). *Erotism: Death and Sensuality*. Translated by Mary Dalwood. San Francisco: City Lights Books.
Baylor Religion Survey. (2006). *American Piety in the 21$^{st}$ Century: New Insights into the Depth and Complexity of Religion in the U.S.* Waco, Tex.: Baylor Institute for Studies of Religion.
BBC News. (2007). "Country Profile: Haiti"; www.bbc.co.uk, accessed 26 April 2007.
Beal, Timothy. (2002). *Religion and Its Monsters*. New York: Routledge.
Beck, Melinda, and Susan Frakar. (1978). "The World of Cults." *Newsweek* (4 December): 78.

Bellin, Joshua David. (2005). *Framing Monsters: Fantasy Film and Social Alienation*. Carbondale: Southern Illinois University Press.

Benét, Stephen Vincent. (1937). *The Devil and Daniel Webster*. New York: Farrar & Rinehart.

Bennett, Tony, and Janet Woollacott. (1987). *Bond and Beyond: The Political Career of a Popular Hero*. New York: Methuen.

Benshoff, Harry M. (2000). "Blaxploitation Horror Films: Generic Reappropriation or Reinscription?" *Cinema Journal* 39 (2): 31–50.

Berger, John. (1972). *Ways of Seeing*. London: Penguin Books.

Berger, Peter L. (1967). *The Sacred Canopy: Elements of a Sociological Theory of Religion*. New York: Anchor Books.

Berger, Peter, and Thomas Luckmann. (1966). *The Social Construction of Reality: A Treatise in the Sociology of Knowledge*. Harmonsworth, U.K.: Penguin Books.

Best, Joel, James T. Richardson, and David G. Bromley. (1991). *The Satanism Scare*. New York: de Gruyter.

Biskind, Peter. (1983). *Seeing is Believing: How Hollywood Taught Us to Stop Worrying and Love the Fifties*. New York: Owl Books.

Black, Art. (2003). "Coming of Age: the South Korean Horror Film." In *Fear Without Frontiers: Horror Cinema Across the Globe*. Edited by Steven Jay Schneider, 185–203. Godalming, U.K.: FAB Press.

Blain, Jenny, and Robert J. Wallis. (2004). "Sacred Sites, Contested Rites/Rights: Contemporary Pagan Engagements with the Past." *Journal of Material Culture* 9 (3): 237–61.

Blatty, William Peter. (1971). *The Exorcist*. New York: Book-of-the-Month Club.

———. (1976). Review of *Hostage to the Devil*, by Malachi Martin. *Los Angeles Times* (29 February): P1, 13, 14.

Bondeson, Jan. (2001). *Buried Alive: The Terrifying History of Our Most Primal Fear*. New York: W. W. Norton.

Bonsal, Stephen. (1909). "At the Shrine of the Little Serpent of Haiti." *New York Times Saturday Magazine* (7 March): 8.

Boot, Andy. (1993). *Fragments of Fear: An Illustrated History of British Horror Films*. London: Creation Books.

Bourguignon, Erika. (1959). "The Persistence of Folk Belief: Some Notes on Cannibalism and Zombis in Haiti." *Journal of American Folklore* 72 (283): 36–46.

Boyer, Paul S. (1992). *When Time Shall Be No More: Prophecy Belief in Modern American Culture*. Cambridge: Belknap Press, Harvard University Press.

Brandon, George. (1993). *Santeria from Africa to the New World: The Dead Sell Memories*. Bloomington: Indiana University Press.

Breznican, Anthony. (1999). "Artful Deception of 'Blair Witch' Turning Some Viewers into Believers." AP (28 July).

Brooks, Ann Page. (1981). "*Mizuko Kuyō* and Japanese Buddhism." *Japanese Journal of Religious Studies* 8 (3–4): 119–47.

Bromley, David G., and J. Gordon Melton, eds. (2002). *Cults, Religion, and Violence*. Cambridge: Cambridge University Press.

Bromley, David G., and James T. Richardson, eds. (1983). *The Brainwashing/Deprogramming Controversy: Sociological, Psychological, Legal, and Historical Perspectives*. New York: Edwin Mellen Press.

Bromley, David G., and Anson D. Shupe Jr. (1981). *Strange Gods: The Great American Cult Scare*. Boston: Beacon Press.

Brosnan, John. (1976). *The Horror People*. New York: St. Martin's Press.

Brottman, Mikita. (1998). *Hollywood Hex: Death and Destiny in the Dream Factory, An Illustrated History of Cursed Movies*. New York: Creation Books.

Brown, Dan. (2000). *Angels & Demons*. New York: Atria Books.

———. (2003). *The Da Vinci Code*. New York: Doubleday.

Brown, David D. (2003). *Santeria Enthroned: Art, Ritual, and Innovation in an Afro-Cuban Religion*. Chicago: University of Chicago Press.

Brown, Karen McCarthy. (2001). *Mama Lola: A Vodou Priestess in Brooklyn*. Rev. ed. Berkeley: University of California Press.

Brown, Rebecca. (1992a). *He Came to Set the Captives Free*. New Kensington, Penn.: Whitaker House.

———. (1992b). *Prepare for War*. Rev. ed. New Kensington, Penn.: Whitaker House.

Browning, Norma Lee. (1968). "Storm Wakes 'Baby,' While Mia . . . ?" *Chicago Tribune* (31 July): B2.

Browning, Robert. (1980). *Robert Browning's Poetry*. Edited by James F. Loucks. New York: W. W. Norton.

Brunvard, Jan Harold. (1981). *The Vanishing Hitchhiker: American Urban Legends and Their Meanings*. New York: W. W. Norton.

Bryant, M. Darrol. (1982). "Cinema, Religion, and Popular Culture." In *Religion in Film*. Edited by John R. May and Michael Bird, 101–14. Knoxville: University of Tennessee Press.

Burke, Ron. (1999). "Review of *Stigmata*, directed by Rupert Wainwright." *Journal of Religion and Film* 3 (2); www.unomaha.edu/jrf/stigmata.htm, accessed 5 October 2005.

Butler, Richard K. (2005). "An Exorcism Film that Aims for the Brain, not the Gut." *Philadelphia Inquirer* (9 September): W04.

Canby, Vincent. (1973). "Blatty's 'The Exorcist' Comes to the Screen." *The New York Times* (27 December): sec. L, 46.

Canfield, Tom. (1999). "It's Not Like The Movies . . . Thank Goddess!"; www.witchvox.com, accessed 4 August 2007.

Cannon, Walter B. (1942). "'Voodoo' Death." *American Anthropologist*, n.s. 44 (2): 169–81.

Carroll, Noël. (1990). *The Philosophy of Horror, or Paradoxes of the Heart*. New York: Routledge.

Carus, Paul. ([1900] 1996). *The History of the Devil and the Idea of Evil*. New York: Gramercy Books.

Carver, Mrs. ([1799] 2006). *Horrors of Oakendale Abbey*. Edited by Curt Herr. Camarillo, Calif.: Zittaw Press.

Champlin, Charles. (1968). "'Rosemary's Baby' on Crest Screen." *Los Angeles Times* (14 June): H11.

———. (1973). "Hypnotic Spell of 'Exorcist' Based on Fact." *Los Angeles Times* (30 December): H1.

Chappetta, Robert. (1969). "Rosemary's Baby." *Film Quarterly* 22 (3): 35–38.
Chattaway, Peter T. (2005a). "The Exorcism of Emily Rose." *Christianity Today* (9 September); www.christianitytoday.com/movies/reviews/exorcismofemilyrose.html, accessed 9 September 2007.
———. (2005b). "Horror: The Perfect Christian Genre." *Christianity Today* (30 August); www.christianitytoday.com/movies/interviews/scottderrickson.html, accessed 9 September 2007.
Chick, Jack T. (1988). *The Death Cookie*. Chino, Calif.: Chick Publications.
———. (1994). *Last Rites*. Chino, Calif.: Chick Publications.
Clark, Rosemary. (2003). *The Sacred Magic of Ancient Egypt: The Spiritual Practice Restored*. St. Paul, Minn.: Llewellyn Publications.
Clemens, Valdine. (1999). *The Return of the Repressed: Gothic Horror from* The Castle of Otranto *to* Alien. Albany: State University of New York Press.
Clover, Carol J. (1992). *Men, Women, and Chain Saws: Gender in the Modern Horror Film*. Princeton: Princeton University Press.
Cogan, Thomas. (1797). "Visit to the Cloister at Mount Sion." *The New York Magazine* (March): 134–40.
Cohen, Gary G. (1974). *Civilization's Last Hurrah*. Chicago: Moody Press.
Collectanea. (1916). "Burial Face Downward to Prevent the Return of the Ghost." *Folklore* 27 (2): 224–25.
Cowan, Douglas E. (2003a). *Bearing False Witness? An Introduction to the Christian Countercult*. Westport, Conn.: Praeger Publishers.
———. (2003b). *The Remnant Spirit: Conservative Reform in Mainline Protestantism*. Westport, Conn.: Praeger Publishers.
———. (2005). *Cyberhenge: Modern Pagans on the Internet*. New York: Routledge.
———. (2007). "Intellects Vast and Cool and Unsympathetic: Science, Religion, and *The War of the Worlds*." *Journal of Religion and*

*Film* 11 (1); www.unomaha.edu/jrf/vol11no1/CowanWarWorlds htm, 12 January 2008.

Cowan, Douglas E., and David G. Bromley. (2008). *Cults and New Religions: A Brief History*. Oxford: Blackwell.

Crane, Jonathan Lake. (1994). *Terror and Everyday Life: Singular Moments in the History of the Horror Film*. Thousand Oaks, Calif. Sage Publications.

Crooke, W. (1902). "An Indian Ghost Story." *Folklore* 13 (3) 280–83.

Crouch, Ben, and Kelly Damphouse. (1991). "Law Enforcement and the Satanic Crime Connection: A Survey of 'Cult Cop.s'" In *The Satanism Scare*. Edited by James T. Richardson, Joe Best, and David G. Bromley, 191–204. New York: de Gruyter.

Cumbey, Constance. (1985). *A Planned Deception: The Staging of a New Age "Messiah."* Detroit: Pointe Publishing.

Cuneo, Michael W. (1997). *The Smoke of Satan: Conservative and Traditionalist Dissent in Contemporary American Catholicism*. Baltimore: The Johns Hopkins University Press.

———. (2001). *American Exorcism: Expelling Demons in the Land of Plenty*. New York: Doubleday.

"Curse of Pharaoh denied by Winlock." (1934). *The New York Times* (26 January): 19–20.

Davis, Mitch. (2003). "The Rain beneath the Earth: An Interview with Nonzee Nimibutr." In *Fear Without Frontiers: Horror Cinema Across the Globe*. Edited by Steven Jay Schneider, 61–66. Godalming, U.K.: FAB Press.

Davis, Wade. (1985). *The Serpent and the Rainbow*. New York: Touchstone.

———. (1988). *Passage of Darkness: The Ethnobiology of the Haitian Zombie*. Chapel Hill: University of North Carolina Press.

Dawson, Lorne L. (1989). "Otto and Freud on the Uncanny and Beyond." *Journal of the American Academy of Religion* 57: 283–311

———. (2006). *Comprehending Cults: The Sociology of New Religious Movements*. Rev. ed. Oxford: Oxford University Press.

Dawson, Warren R. (1929). Review of *The Magic Island*, by William B. Seabrook. *Man* 29 (154–55): 198–99.

Day, Jasmine. (2006). *The Mummy's Curse: Mummymania in the English-speaking World*. New York: Routledge.

Dayan, Joan. (1995). *Haiti, History and the Gods*. Berkeley: University of California Press.

de Camp, L. Sprague. (1975). *Lovecraft: A Biography*. Garden City. N.Y.: Doubleday.

de Mille, Richard. (1976). *Castaneda's Journey: The Power and the Allegory*. Santa Barbara: Capra Press.

———, ed. (2001). *The Don Juan Papers: Further Castaneda Controversies*. Lincoln, Neb.: Authors Guild.

de Sade, Marquis ([1791] 1965). *Justine, Philosophy in the Bedroom and Other Writings*. Translated by Richard Seaver and Austryn Winhouse. New York: Grove Press.

Dempsey, Michael. (1974). Review of *The Exorcist*. *Film Quarterly* 27 (4): 61–62.

Desmangles, Leslie. (1992). *The Faces of the Gods: Vodou and Roman Catholicism in Haiti*. Chapel Hill: University of North Carolina Press.

Diamond, Sara. (1989). *Spiritual Warfare: The Politics of the Christian Right*. Boston: South End Press.

Diderot, Denis. ([1780] 1968). *The Nun*. Translated by Eileen B. Hennesy. Los Angeles: Holloway House.

Dijkstra, Bram. (1986). *Idols of Perversity: Images of Feminine Evil in Fin-de-Siècle Culture*. New York: Oxford University Press.

———. (1996). *Evil Sisters: The Threat of Female Sexuality in Twentieth-Century Culture*. New York: Owl Books.

Douglas, Mary. (1966). *Purity and Danger: An Analysis of Concepts of Pollution and Taboo*. New York: Praeger.

"Dr. Lucas, Survived 'Pharaoh's Curse.'" (1945). *The New York Times* (10 December): 21.

du Boulay, Juliet. (1982). "The Greek Vampire: A Study of Cyclical Symbolism in Marriage and Death." *Man*, n.s. 17 (2): 219–38.

du Plessix Gray, Francine. (1976). Review of *Hostage to the Devil*, by Malachi Martin. *The New York Times* (14 March): BR3.
Dubois, Laurent. (2001). "Vodou and History." *Comparative Studies in Society and History* 43 (1): 92–100.
Duffus, R. L. (1929). "A Book on Haiti That Dips Below The Surface Controversies." *The New York Times* (6 January): 70.
Dundes, Alan. (1998a). "The Vampire as Bloodthirsty Revenant: A Psychoanalytic Post Mortem." In *The Vampire: A Casebook*. Edited by Alan Dundes, 159–75. Madison: University of Wisconsin Press.
———, ed. (1998b). *The Vampire: A Casebook*. Madison: University of Wisconsin Press.
Ebert, Roger. (1973). "The Exorcist" (26 December); www.rogerebert.com, accessed 5 May 2007.
———. (2005). "The Exorcism of Emily Rose" (9 September); www.rogerebert.com, accessed 12 September 2007.
Editors. (1836a). "Awful Disclosures." *Boston Recorder* (12 February): 28.
———. (1836b). "Awful Disclosures of Maria Monk." *Christian Register and Boston Observer* (25 March): 50.
———. (1837). "Maria Monk's Awful Disclosures." *Niles' Weekly Register* (22 April): 125.
———. (1871). "The Convent Horror." *Zion's Herald* (30 March): 150.
Eliade, Mircea. (1954). *Cosmos and History: The Myth of the Eternal Return*. Translated by Willard R. Trask. New York: Harper & Row.
Eliade, Mircea. (1959). *The Sacred and the Profane: The Nature of Religion*. Translated by Willard R. Trask. San Diego: Harvest/HBJ Books.
———. (1964). *Shamanism: Archaic Techniques of Estasy*. Translated by Willard R. Trask. New York: Pantheon Books.
Ellis, Bill. (2000). *Raising the Devil: Satanism, New Religions, and the Media*. Lexington: University of Kentucky Press.

Fackre, Gabriel J. (1982). *The Religious Right and Christian Faith*. Grand Rapids: Eerdmans.

Farrar, Janet, and Stewart Farrar. (1984). *The Witches' Way: Principles, Rituals and Beliefs of Modern Witchcraft*. Custer, Wash.: Phoenix Publishing.

Faulkner, R.O., trans. (1985). *The Ancient Egyptian Book of the Dead*. Edited by Carol Andrews. Rev. ed. Austin: University of Texas Press.

Fikes, Jay Courtney. (1993). *Carlos Castaneda, Academic Opportunism and the Psychedelic Sixties*. Victoria, B.C.: Millenia Press.

"Film, 'White Zombie,' On Capitol Bill." (1932). *Hartford Courant* (20 August): 16.

Fisher, G. Richard, and M. Kurt Goedelman. (1996). "The Curse of Curse Theology: The Return of Rebecca Brown, M.D." *Personal Freedom Outreach*; www.pfo.org/curse-th.htm, accessed 15 May 2007.

Fisher, Lucy. (1992). "Birth Traumas: Parturition and Horror in *Rosemary's Baby*." *Cinema Journal* 31 (3): 3–18.

Fishwick, Marshall W. (2005). "Popular Witchcraft: Right from the Witch's Mouth." *Journal of American Culture* 28 (3): 334–35.

Fiske, Edward B. (1974). "'Exorcist' Adds Problems For Catholic Clergymen." *The New York Times* (28 January): 1, 15.

Forbes, Bruce David, and Jeanne Halgren Kilde, eds. (2004). *Rapture, Revelation, and the End Times: Exploring the* Left Behind *Series*. New York: Palgrave Macmillan.

Freeland, Cynthia A. (2000). *The Naked and the Undead: Evil and the Appeal of Horror*. Boulder: Westview Press.

Freud, Sigmund. ([1913] 1950). *Totem and Taboo: Some Points of Agreement between the Mental Lives of Savages and Neurotics*. Translated by James Strachey. New York: W. W. Norton.

———. ([1919] 2003). *The Uncanny*. Translated by David Mclintock. New York: Penguin Books.

From One Who Knows. (1836). "Maria Monk and Her Awful Disclosures." *New York Evangelist* (9 April): 59.

Fryer, Jane. (2005). "Satan's Schoolgirl." *Daily Mail* (London; 8 December): 56.

Frykholm, Amy Johnson. (2004). *Rapture Culture: "Left Behind" in Evangelical America*. New York: Oxford University Press.

Fuller, Robert C. (1995). *Naming the Antichrist: The History of An American Obsession*. New York: Oxford University Press.

Gallup, George H., Jr. (2003). "Public Gives Organized Religion Its Lowest Rating" (7 January); www.gallup.com, accessed 21 December 2004.

———. (2004). "Gallup Religion Index Up From Record Low" (13 January); www.gallup.com, accessed 21 December 2004.

Gardner, Gerald B. ([1954] 2004). *Witchcraft Today*. New York: Citadel Press.

———. ([1959] 2004). *The Meaning of Witchcraft*. New York: Citadel Press.

Garrett, Susan R. (1989). *The Demise of the Devil: Magic and the Demonic in Luke's Writings*. Minneapolis: Fortress.

Geertz, Clifford. (1973). *The Interpretation of Cultures: Selected Essays*. New York: Basic Books.

Germain, David. (1999). "'Blair Witch' Success Holds Hope for Independent Filmmakers." AP (3 August).

Gilmour, David. (2005). "A Pointless Exorcise." *Globe and Mail* (9 September): R17.

Godbeer, Richard. (1992). *The Devil's Dominion: Magic and Religion in Early New England*. Cambridge: Cambridge University Press.

Goldberg, Ruth, and Steven Jay Schneider. (2003). "Sex and Death, Cuban Style: The Dark Vision of Jorge Molina." In *Fear Without Frontiers: Horror Cinema Across the Globe*. Edited by Steven Jay Schneider, 81–90. Godalming, U.K.: FAB Press.

Golding, William. (1954). *Lord of the Flies*. New York: G. P. Putnam.

Goleman, Daniel. (1994). "Proof Lacking for Ritual Abuse by Satanists." *The New York Times* (31 October): A13.

Goodman, Felicitas D. (1981). *The Exorcism of Anneliese Michel.* Eugene, Ore.: Resource Publications.

———. (1988). *How About Demons? Possession and Exorcism in the Modern World.* Bloomington: Indiana University Press.

Goodrick-Clarke, Nicholas. (1992). *The Occult Roots of Nazism: Secret Aryan Cults and Their Influence on Nazi Ideology.* Rev. ed. New York: New York University Press.

———. (2002). *Black Sun: Aryan Cults, Esoteric Nazism and the Politics of Identity.* New York: New York University Press.

Gorney, Cynthia. (1988). "Ritual Abuse: A Perplexing Pattern of Reports." *Washington Post* (17 May): B2.

Graham, Billy. (1975). *Angels: God's Secret Agents.* New York: Doubleday.

Grant, Barry Keith, ed. (1996). *The Dread of Difference: Gender and the Horror Film.* Austin: University of Texas Press.

Gray, Elmon T., et al. (1992). *Report of the Virginia State Crime Commission Task Force Study of Ritual Crime.* House Document no. 31. Richmond: Commonwealth of Virginia.

Greene, Richard, and K. Silem Mohammad, eds. (2006). *The Undead and Philosophy: Chicken Soup for the Soulless.* Chicago: Open Court.

Guazzo, Francesco Maria. ([1608] 1988). *Compendium Maleficarum.* Edited by Montague Summers. Translated by E. A. Ashwin. New York: Dover Publications.

Hadden, Jeffrey K. (1988). "Desacralizing Secularization Theory." In *Secularization and Fundamentalism Reconsidered.* Edited by Jeffrey K. Hadden and Anson Shupe, 3–26. New York: Paragon House.

Haiven, Judith. (1984). *Faith, Hope, No Charity: An Inside Look at the Born Again Movement in Canada and the United States.* Vancouver, B.C.: New Star Books.

Halberstam, Judith. (1995). *Skin Shows: Gothic Horror and the Technology of Monsters.* Durham, N.C.: Duke University Press.

Hankiss, Elemér. (2001). *Fears and Symbols: An Introduction to the Study of Western Civilization*. Budapest, Hungary: Central European University Press.

Hardacre, Helen. (1997). *Marketing the Menacing Fetus in Japan*. Berkeley: University of California Press.

Harrington, Curtis. (1952). "Ghoulies and Ghosties." *The Quarterly of Film, Radio and Television* 7 (2): 191–202.

Hearn, Lafcadio. (1887). *Some Chinese Ghosts*. Boston: Roberts Brothers.

———. (1899). *In Ghostly Japan*. Boston: Little, Brown.

———. (1904). *Kwaidan: Stories and Studies of Strange Things*. Boston: Houghton, Mifflin.

Hertenstein, Mike, and Jon Trott. (1993). *Selling Satan: The Evangelical Media and the Mike Warnke Scandal*. Chicago: Cornerstone Press.

Hicks, Robert D. (1991). "The Police Model of Satanism Crime.' In *The Satanism Scare*. Edited by James T. Richardson, Joel Best, and David G. Bromley, 175–90. New York: de Gruyter.

Hindson, Ed. (1998). *Is the Antichrist Alive and Well: 10 Keys to His Identity*. Eugene, Ore.: Harvest House Publishers.

Hinson, Hal. (1987). "Schlesinger's Bizarre 'Believers.'" *Washington Post* (10 June): C1, C3.

Hogan, David J. (1986). *Dark Romance: Sexuality in the Horror Film*. Jefferson, N.C: McFarland.

Hornblower, G.D. (1931). "The Laying of a Ghost in Egypt." *Man* 31 (August): 164.

Hoshowsky, Robert. (1998). "Cults, The Next Wave: Almost Everyone is Vulnerable." *Homemaker's Magazine* (March): 54–60.

Howe, Desson. (1987). "Unbelievable 'Believers.'" *Washington Post* (12 June): A1.

Hudson, Elizabeth. (1989). "Spring Break Reveler Met Grisly End: Cultists Believed To Have Killed Teen." *Washington Post* (13 April): A3.

Hunt, Dave. (1994). *A Woman Rides the Beast: The Catholic Church and the Last Days*. Eugene, Ore.: Harvest House Publishers.

Hunt, Dave, and T. A. McMahon. (1938). *America: The Sorceror's New Apprentice*. Eugene, Ore.: Harvest House Publishers.

Hunter, Jack. (1994). *House of Horror: The Complete Hammer Films Story*. Rev. ed. London: Creation House.

Hurston, Zora Neale. ([1938] 1966). *Tell My Horse: Voodoo and Life in Haiti and Jamaica*. New York: Harper Perennial.

Ingebretsen, Edward J. (2001). *At Stake: Monsters and the Rhetoric of Fear in Public Culture*. Chicago: University of Chicago Press.

Ireland, William-Henry. ([1799] 2006). *The Abbess*. Edited by Jeffrey Kahan. Camarillo, Calif.: Zittaw Press.

———. ([1805] 2005). *Gondez the Monk: A Romance of the Thirteenth Century*. Edited by Jeffrey Kahan. Camarillo, Calif.: Zittaw Press.

Irwin, John T. (1980). *American Heiroglyphics: The Symbol of the Egyptian Hieroglyphics in the American Renaissance*. Baltimore & London: The Johns Hopkins University Press.

Ivakhiv, Adrian J. (2001). *Claiming Sacred Ground: Pilgims and Politics at Glastonbury and Stonehenge*. Bloomington: Indiana University Press.

Iversen, Erik. (1961). *The Myth of Egypt and Its Hieroglyphs in European Tradition*. Princeton: Princeton University Press.

Iwasaka, Michiko, and Barre Toelken. (1994). *Ghosts and the Japanese: Cultural Experience in Japanese Death Legends*. Logan: Utah State University Press.

Jackson, Shirley. ([1959] 2006). *The Haunting of Hill House*. New York: Penguin Books.

Jahoda, Gustav. (1969). *The Psychology of Superstition*. Harmondsworth, U.K.: Penguin Books.

James, William. ([1902] 1999). *The Varieties of Religious Experience*. New York: Modern Library.

Jancovich, Mark. (1996). *Rational Fears: American Horror in the 1950s*. Manchester, U.K.: Manchester University Press.

Jenkins, Philip. (2003). *The New Anti-Catholicism: The Last Acceptable Prejudice*. Oxford: Oxford University Press.
Johnson, Malcolm L. (1976). "Peck Dignifies 'Omen.'" *Hartford Courant* (27 June): 18F.
Jones, Darryl. (2002). *Horror: A Thematic History in Fiction and Film*. London: Arnold Publishers.
Joshi, S. T. (1999). "Explanatory Notes." In *The Call of Cthulhu and Other Weird Stories*, by H. P. Lovecraft. Edited by S. T. Joshi, 361–420. New York: Penguin Books.
———. (2001). "Explanatory Notes." In *The Thing on the Doorstep and Other Weird Stories*, by H. P. Lovecraft. Edited by S. T. Joshi, 367–443. New York: Penguin Books.
———. (2005). "Introduction." In *Count Magnus and Other Ghost Stories*, by M. R. James. Edited by S. T. Joshi, vii–xvii. New York: Penguin Books.
Kalat, David. (2007). *J-Horror: The Definitive Guide to* The Ring, The Grudge *and Beyond*. New York: Vertical.
Kamen, Henry. (1997). *The Spanish Inquisition: A Historical Revision*. New Haven: Yale University Press.
Kane, Paul. (2006). *The* Hellraiser *Films and Their Legacy*. Jefferson, N.C.: McFarland.
Keesing, Roger M. (1982). *Kwaio Religion: The Living and the Dead in a Solomon Island Society*. New York: Columbia University Press.
Kendrick, Walter. (1991). *The Thrill of Fear: 250 Years of Scary Entertainment*. New York: Grove Press.
Kennedy, Tammie. (2005). "(Re)Presenting Mary Magdalene: A Feminist Reading of *The Last Temptation of Christ*." *Journal of Religion and Popular Culture* 9; www.usask.ca/relst/jrpc/art9-scorsesemisogynist.html, accessed 5 August 2005.
Kilday, Gregg. (1974). "'Exorcist'—A View from Catholic Church People are getting 'the hell scared out of them.'" *Los Angeles Times* (21 January): E1.
King, Stephen. (1978). "Children of the Corn." In *Night Shift*, by Stephen King. New York: Signet.

King, Stephen. (1981). *Danse Macabre*. New York: Berkeley.
Kirban, Salem. ([1974] 1998). *Countdown to Rapture*. 3d ed. Chattanooga, Tenn.: Future Events Publications.
Knelman, Martin. (1973a). "The Exorcist: Do You Have to be Possessed to Dig It?" *The Globe and Mail* (31 December): 10.
———. (1973b). "Mean Streets: A Great Vision of Evil." *The Globe and Mail* (28 December): 10.
Kramer, Heinrich, and James Sprenger. ([1486] 1971). *The Malleus Maleficarum of Heinrich Kramer and James Sprenger*. Edited and translated by Montague Summers. New York: Dover Publications.
Kristeva, Julia. (1982). *Powers of Horror: An Essay on Abjection*. Translated by Leon S. Roudiez. New York: Columbia University Press.
Krogh, Marilyn C., and Brooke Ashley Pillifant. (2004). "The House of Netjer: A New Religious Community Online." In *Religion Online: Finding Faith on the Internet*. Edited by Lorne L. Dawson and Douglas E. Cowan, 205–19. New York: Routledge.
Kyrou, Adonis. (1963). *Le surréalisme au cinéma*. Paris: Le terrain vague.
LaFleur, William R. (1994). *Liquid Life: Abortion and Buddhism in Japan*. Princeton: Princeton University Press.
Lanning, Kenneth. (1992). *Investigator's Guide to Allegations of Ritual Child Abuse*. Quantico, Va.: National Center for the Analysis of Violent Crime, Federal Bureau of Investigation.
Lant, Antonia. (1997). "The Curse of the Pharoah, or How Cinema Contracted Egyptomania." In *Visions of the East: Orientalism in Film*. Edited by Matthew Bernstein and Gaylyn Studlar, 69–98. New Brunswick, N.J.: Rutgers University Press.
Larson, Bob. (1989). *Satanism: The Seduction of America's Youth*. Nashville: Thomas Nelson Publishers.
———. (1996). *In the Name of Satan*. Nashville: Thomas Nelson Publishers.

---. (1997). *UFOs and the Alien Agenda: Uncovering the Mystery Behind UFOs and the Paranormal*. Nashville: Thomas Nelson.

---. (1998a). "First Ever Live Public Exorcism in Calgary." Seminar presented at the Sheraton-Cavalier Hotel, Calgary, Canada, 7 August.

---. (1998b) "Let Me Help You Demon-Proof Your Life." Fundraising letter (May).

---. (1999). *Larson's Book of Spiritual Warfare*. Nashville: Thomas Nelson.

Lehner, Mark. (1997). *The Complete Pyramids: Solving the Ancient Mysteries*. London: Thames & Hudson.

Lewis, James R. (1996). "Works of Darkness: Occult Fascination in the Novels of Frank E. Peretti." In *Magical Religion and Modern Witchcraft*. Edited by James R. Lewis, 339–50. Albany: State University of New York Press.

---. (2002). "Diabolical Authority: Anton LaVey, *The Satanic Bible* and the Satanist 'Tradition.'" *Marburg Journal of Religion* 7 (1); http://web.uni-marburg.de/religionswissenschaft/journal/mjr/pdf/2002/lewis2002.pdf, accessed 24 May 2007.

Lewis, Matthew. ([1796] 1998). *The Monk*. Edited by Howard Anderson. Oxford: Oxford University Press.

Lex, Barbara W. (1974). "Voodoo Death: New Thoughts on an Old Explanation." *American Anthropologist*, n.s. 76 (4): 818–23.

Lindsey, Hal, with C. C. Carlson. (1970). *The Late Great Planet Earth*. Grand Rapids: Zondervan.

Lockwood, Robert P., ed. (2000). *Anti-Catholicism in American Culture*. Huntingdon, Ind.: Our Sunday Visitor.

"Lore of Haiti." (1938). Review of *Tell My Horse: Voodoo and Life in Haiti and Jamaica*. *The New York Times* (23 October): 100.

Lovecraft, H. P. ([1919] 1999). "Dagon." In *The Call of Cthulhu and Other Weird Stories*, by H. P. Lovecraft. Edited by S. T. Joshi, 1–6. New York: Penguin Books.

---. ([1920] 1999). "The Statement of Randolph Carter." In *The Call of Cthulhu and Other Weird Stories*, 7–13.

Lovecraft, H. P. ([1922] 1999). "Herbert West—Reanimator." In *The Call of Cthulhu and Other Weird Stories*, 50–88.

———. ([1925] 2004). "The Unnamable." In *The Dreams in the Witch House and Other Weird Stories*, by H. P. Lovecraft. Edited by S. T. Joshi, 82–89. New York: Penguin Books.

———. ([1927] 2000). *The Annotated Supernatural Horror in Literature*. Edited by S. T. Joshi. New York: Hippocampus Books.

———. ([1928] 1999). "The Call of Cthulhu." In *The Call of Cthulhu and Other Weird Stories*, 139–69.

———. ([1929] 2001). "The Dunwich Horror." In *The Thing on the Doorstep and Other Weird Stories*, by H. P. Lovecraft. Edited by S. T. Joshi, 206–45. New York: Penguin Books.

———. ([1931] 1999). "The Whisperer in Darkness." In *The Call of Cthulhu and Other Weird Stories*, 200–67.

———. ([1936] 1999). "The Shadow over Innsmouth." In *The Call of Cthulhu and Other Weird Stories*, 268–335.

———. [1936] 2001). "At the Mountains of Madness." In *The Thing on the Doorstep and Other Weird Stories*, 246–340.

———. ([1941] 2001). "The Case of Charles Dexter Ward." In *The Thing on the Doorstep and Other Weird Stories*, 90–205.

Lovecraft, H. P., with Zealia Bishop. ([1930?] 2001). "The Mound." In *Black Seas of Infinity: The Best of H. P. Lovecraft*, selected by Andrew Wheeler, 329–93. Garden City, N.Y.: SFBC Science Fiction.

Lucas, Phillip Charles. (2007). "Constructing Identity with Dreamstones: Megalithic Sites and Contemporary Nature Spirituality." *Nova Religio: The Journal of Alternative and Emergent Religions* 11 (1): 31–60.

Lyden, John. (2003). *Film as Religion: Myths, Morals, and Rituals*. New York: New York University Press.

Lyons, Linda. (2005a). "One-Third of Americans Believe Dearly May Not Have Departed." *The Gallup Poll*® (12 July); www.gallup.com, accessed 12 February 2006.

———. (2005b). "Paranormal Beliefs Come (Super) Naturally to Some." *The Gallup Poll®* (1 November); www.gallup.com, accessed 12 February 2006.

Mank, Gregory W. (1981). *It's Alive! The Classic Cinema Saga of Frankenstein*. San Diego: A.S. Barnes.

———, ed. (2000). *The Mummy's Curse (including the original shooting script)*. Absecon, N.J.: Magic Image Filmbooks.

Mars, Louis P. (1945). "The Story of Zombi in Haiti." *Man* 45 38–40.

Martin, Malachi. (1976). *Hostage to the Devil: The Possession and Exorcism of Five Americans*. New York: Reader's Digest.

———. (1987). *The Jesuits: The Society of Jesus and the Betrayal of the Roman Catholic Church*. New York: Touchstone Books.

———. (1992). "Preface to the New Edition: Possession and Exorcism in America in the 1990s." In *Hostage to the Devil: The Possession and Exorcism of Five Americans*, by Malachi Martin, xi–xxvi. New York: HarperSanFrancisco.

———. (1996). *Windswept House: A Vatican Novel*. New York: Doubleday.

Mason, Heather. (2004). "Divine Subjects: Canadians Believe, Britons Skeptical." Gallup Poll News Service (November 16); www.gallup.com, accessed 21 December 2005.

Massaro, John J. (1974). "'Exorcist' Like Prank of Children." *Hartford Courant* (14 February): 4.

Mather, Cotton. ([1693] 1862). *The Wonders of the Invisible World: Being an Account of the Tryals of Several Witches Lately Executed in New England*. London: J. R. Smith.

Mathews, Tom Dewe. (2000). "Flesh Wars"; www.homecinemachoice.com, accessed 11 August 2007.

McCabe, Bob. (1999). *The Exorcist: Out of The Shadows, The Full Story of the Film*. London: Omnibus Press.

McGinn, Bernard. (1994). *Antichrist: Two Thousand Years of the Human Fascination with Evil*. New York: HarperSanFrancisco.

McNeil, W. K. (1978). "Lafcadio Hearn, American Folklorist." *Journal of American Folklore* 91 (362): 947–67.

Medved, Michael. (1992). *Hollywood vs America*. New York: HarperPerennial/Zondervan.

Medway, Gareth J. (2001). *Lure of the Sinister: The Unnatural History of Satanism*. New York: New York University Press.

Melton, J. Gordon. (1999). *The Vampire Book: The Encyclopedia of the Undead*. Rev. ed. Detroit: Visible Ink Press.

Merry, Robert. (1974). "Once possessed, vicar is now a busy exorcist." *Chicago Tribune* (20 January): 1, 14.

Métraux, Alfred. ([1959] 1972). *Voodoo in Haiti*. Translated by Hugo Charteris. New York: Schocken Books.

Meyer, Birgit. (2003). "Pentecostalism, Prosperity, and Popular Cinema in Ghana." In *Representing Religion in World Cinema: Filmmaking, Mythmaking, Culture Making*. Edited by S. Brent Plate, 121–43. New York: Palgrave Macmillan.

Migliore, Andrew, and John Strysik. (2006). *Lurker in the Lobby: A Guide to the Cinema of H. P. Lovecraft*. San Francisco: Night Shade Books.

Monk, Maria. ([1836] 1876). *Awful Disclosures of Maria Monk, as Exhibited in a Narrative of her Sufferings during Her Residence of Five Years as a Novice and Two Years as a Black Nun in the Hotel Dieu Nunnery, at Montreal, Ont*. Rev. ed. New York: The Truth Seeker.

Moore, David W. (2005). "Three in Four Americans Believe in Paranormal." *The Gallup Poll*® (15 June); www.gallup.com, accessed 12 February 2006.

Morris, Wesley. (2004). "'Ju-on' is cursed by unanswered questions." *Boston Globe* (17 September): Arts, C8.

Morrison, Dorothy. (1996). "Magical Aids for Cyberspace Travel." *Circle Network News* 62 (Winter): 21.

Mulhern, Sherrill. (1991). "Satanism and Psychotherapy: A Rumor in Search of an Inquisition." In *The Satanism Scare*. Edited by James T. Richardson, Joel Best, and David G. Bromley, 145–72. New York: de Gruyter.

Naha, Ed. (1975). *Horrors: From Screen to Scream*. New York: Flare Books.
Nathan, Debbie. (1991). "Satanism and Child Molestation: Constructing the Ritual Abuse Scare." In *The Satanism Scare* Edited by James T. Richardson, Joel Best, and David G. Bromley, 75–94. New York: de Gruyter.
Nathan, Debbie, and Michael Snedecker. (1995). *Satan's Silence Ritual Abuse and the Making of a Modern American Witchhunt* New York: Basic Books.
*New York Times, The*. (1976). Display advertisement for *Hostage to the Devil*, by Malachi Martin. *The New York Times* (29 February): 217.
Newell, William W. (1888). "Myths of Voodoo Worship and Child Sacrifice in Hayti." *Journal of American Folklore* 1 (1): 16–30.
———. (1889). "Reports of Voodoo Worship in Hayti and Louisiana." *Journal of American Folklore* 2 (4): 41–47.
Newport, Frank, and Maura Strausberg. (2001). "Americans' Belief in Psychic and Paranormal Phenomena is up over Last Decade" (8 June); www.gallup.com, accessed 24 December 2005.
O'Brien, Daniel. (2003). *Spooky Encounters: A Gwailo's Guide to Hong Kong Horror*. Manchester, U.K.: Critical Vision.
O'Gorman, Edith. (1871). *Trials and Persecutions of Edith O'Gorman Otherwise Sister Teresa de Chantal, of St. Joseph's Convent, Hudson City, N.J.* Hartford: Connecticut Publishing.
O'Leary, Stephen D. (1994). *Arguing the Apocalypse: A Theory of Millennial Rhetoric*. New York: Oxford University Press.
Oesterreich, T. K. (1966). *Possession: Demoniacal & Other*. New York Dell.
Olmos, Margarite Fernández, and Lizabeth Paravisini-Gebert (1997). *Sacred Possessions: Vodou, Santería, Obeah, and the Caribbean*. New Brunswick, N.J.: Rutgers University Press.
Otto, Rudolf. ([1923] 1950). *The Idea of the Holy*. Translated by John W. Harvey. London Oxford University Press.
Paffenroth, Kim. (2006). *Gospel of the Living Dead: George Romero's Visions of Hell on Earth*. Baylor, Tex.: Baylor University Press.

Page, Clarence. (1974). "6 Who Saw 'Exorcist' under Care." *Chicago Tribune* (18 January): 1.

Pagels, Elaine. (1995). *The Origin of Satan*. New York: Vintage Books.

Paine, Lauren. (1972). *Sex in Witchraft*. New York: Taplinger Publishing.

Paris, Edmund. (1983). *The Secret History of the Jesuits*. Chino, Calif.: Chick Publications.

"Paris Prophetess Has a Theory." (1923). *The New York Times* (6 April): 3.

Passantino, Bob, Gretchen Passantino, and Jon Trott. (1990). "Satan's Sideshow: The True Lauren Stratford Story." *Cornerstone* 18 (90): 23–28.

———. (1999). "Lauren Stratford: From Satanic Ritual Abuse to Jewish Holocaust Survivor." *Cornerstone* 28 (117): 12–16, 18.

Pattison, Mark. (2005). "Director of 'Emily Rose' Hopes Film Prompts Viewers to Examine Faith." *Catholic Online News* (9 September); www.catholic.org, accessed 9 September 2007.

Pattison, O. R. B. (1969). *The Undelivered*. Old Tappan, N.J.: Fleming H. Revell.

Paul, William. (1994). *Laughing Screaming: Modern Hollywood Horror and Comedy*. New York: Columbia University Press.

Peck, M. Scott. (2005). *Glimpses of the Devil: A Psychiatrist's Personal Accounts of Possession, Exorcism and Redemption*. New York: Free Press.

Peretti, Frank E. (1986). *This Present Darkness*. Wheaton, Ill.: Crossway Books.

———. (1989). *Piercing the Darkness*. Westchester, Ill.: Crossway Books.

———. (1995). *The Oath*. Dallas, Tex.: Word Publishing.

Pérez-Reverte, Arturo. (1993). *The Club Dumas*. Translated by Sonia Soto. New York: Vintage International.

Perlmutter, Dawn. (2004). *Investigating Religious Terrorism and Ritualistic Crimes*. Boca Raton, Fla.: CRC Press.

Persall, Steve. (2005). "Too Much Courtroom, Too Little Demonic Action." *St. Petersburg Times* (8 September): 10W.
Peters, Edward. (1988). *Inquisition*. Berkeley: University of California Press.
Petersen, Clarence. (1974). "'Exorcist' Not Like Its Image." *Chicago Tribune* (22 May): 18.
Pinedo, Isabel Cristina. (1997). *Recreational Terror: Women and the Pleasures of Horror Film Viewing*. Albany: State University of New York Press.
Poe, Edgar Allan. ([1845] 1975). "Some Words with a Mummy." In *The Complete Tales and Poems of Edgar Allan Poe*, 535–48. New York: Vintage Books.
Polidori, John. ([1819] 1990). *The Vampyre*. Oxford: Woodstock Books.
Pratt, Ambrose. (1910). *The Living Mummy*. Toronto: McLeod & Allen.
Pritchard, James B. (1958). *The Ancient Near East*. Vol. 1: *An Anthology of Texts and Pictures*. Princeton: Princeton University Press.
Prothero, Stephen. (2007). *Religious Literacy: What Every American Needs to Know—and Doesn't*. New York: HarperSanFrancisco.
Radcliffe, Ann. ([1794] 1987). *The Mysteries of Udolpho: A Romance*. Edited by Devendra P. Varma. London: Folio Society.
Ravaisson-Mollien, François. (1975). *Archives de la Bastille*, vol. 6. Genève: Slatkine-Megariotis Reprints.
Ravenscroft, Trevor. (1973). *The Spear of Destiny: The Occult Power Behind the Spear Which Pierced the Side of Christ*. Toronto: Bantam Books.
RavenWolf, Silver. (1998). *Teen Witch: Wicca for a New Generation* St. Paul, Minn.: Llewellyn Publications.
Reed, Rebecca. (1835). *Six Months in a Convent, or, the Narrative of Rebecca Theresa Reed, Who Was under the Influence of the Roman Catholics about Two Years, and an Inmate of the Ursuline Convent on Mount Benedict, Charlestown, Mass., Nearly Six Months, in the Years 1831–2*. Boston: Russell, Odiorne & Metcalf.

Reed, Rex. (1973). "Filming of 'The Exorcist'—It Was Hell." *Los Angeles Times* (18 November): U28.
Reizler, Kurt. (1944). "The Social Psychology of Fear." *American Journal of Sociology* 49 (6): 489–98.
Relfe, Mary Steward. (1981). *When Your Money Fails: The "666 System is Here*. Prattville, Al.: League of Prayer.
"Religious Lies." (1836). *Zion's Herald* (10 February): 22.
Reuters. (1974). "'Exorcist' Sadistic, Says Soviet Press." *Los Angeles Times* (9 February): A7.
Rhodes, Gary D. (2003). "Fantasma del cine Mexicano: The 1930s horror film cycle of Mexico." In *Fear Without Frontiers: Horror Cinema across the Globe*. Edited by Steven Jay Schneider, 93–103. Godalming, U.K.: FAB Press.
Rhodes, Ron. (1998). *Alien Obsession*. Eugene, Ore.: Harvest House Publishers.
Richardson, James T., Joel Best, and David G. Bromley, eds. (1991). *The Satanism Scare*. New York: de Gruyter.
Richman, Paula. (1991). "Introduction: The Diversity of the *Ramayana* tradition." In *Many Ramayanas: The Diversity of a Narrative Tradition in South Asia*. Edited by Paula Richman, 3–21. Berkeley: University of California Press.
Rigby, Jonathan. (2002). *English Gothic: A Century of Horror Cinema*. Rev. ed. London: Reynolds & Hearn.
Robison, Jennifer. (2003). "The Devil and the Demographic Details" (25 February); www.gallup.com, accessed 21 December 2004.
Rodley, Chris, ed. (1992). *Cronenberg on Cronenberg*. London: Faber & Faber.
Ross, Colin A. (1995). *Satanic Ritual Abuse: Principles of Treatment*. Toronto: University of Toronto Press.
Rowe, Laurel, and Gray Cavender. (1991). "Cauldrons Bubble, Satan's Trouble, But Witches Are Okay: Media Constructions of Satanism and Witchcraft." In *The Satanism Scare*. Edited by James T. Richardson, Joel Best, and David G. Bromley, 263–75. New York: de Gruyter.

Russell, Jamie. (2005). *Book of the Dead: The Complete History of Zombie Cinema*. Godalming, U.K.: FAB Press.
Russell, Jeffrey Burton. (1977). *The Devil: Perceptions of Evil from Antiquity to Primitive Christianity*. Ithaca: Cornell University Press.
———. (1981). *Satan: The Early Christian Tradition*. Ithaca: Cornell University Press.
———. (1984). *Lucifer: The Devil in the Middle Ages*. Ithaca: Cornell University Press.
———. (1986). *Mephistopheles: The Devil in the Modern World*. Ithaca: Cornell University Press.
Russell, M. E. (2004). "A Scary Nonlinear Curse." *The (Portland) Oregonian* (20 August): Arts and Living, 33.
Sakheim, David K., and Susan E. Devine. (1992). *Out of Darkness: Exploring Satanism and Ritual Abuse*. San Francisco: Jossey-Bass.
Satter, David. (1974). "Billy Graham Talks about Demons, Faith." *Chicago Tribune* (3 March): 14.
Scheuer, Philip K. (1959). "'Tingler' Gimmick Picture." *Los Angeles Times* (29 October): C8.
Schnoebelen, William. (1990). *Wicca: Satan's Little White Lie*. Chino, Calif.: Chick Publications.
Schreck, Nikolas. (2000). *The Satanic Screen: An Illustrated History of the Devil in Cinema, 1869–1999*. New York: Creation Books.
Schreck, Nikolas, and Zeena Schreck. (2002). *Demons of the Flesh: The Complete Guide to Left Hand Path Sex Magic*. New York: Creation Books.
Schroeder, Caroline T. (2003). "Ancient Egyptian Religion on the Silver Screen: Modern Anxieties about Race, Ethnicity, and Religion." *Journal of Religion and Film* 7 (2); www.unomaha.edu/jrf/Vol7No2/ancientegypt.htm, accessed 12 October 2006.
Schultz, Nancy Lusignan. (2000). *Fire and Roses: The Burning of the Charlestown Convent, 1834*. New York: The Free Press.
Scott, Vernon. (1974). "Mishaps, Tragedies Beset 'Exorcist' Cast." *Hartford Courant* (13 January): 13F.

Screen Gems. (2005). "Possessed: The State of Modern Exorcism" (Summer). Newspaper advertising insert.

Scruton, David L. (1986). "The Anthropology of an Emotion." In *Sociophobics: The Anthropology of Fear*. Edited by David L. Scruton, 7–49. Boulder: Westview Press.

Seabrook, William B. ([1929] 1989). *The Magic Island*. New York: Paragon House.

Shales, Tom. (1976). "A Deadly Thriller." *Washington Post* (26 June): C1, C4.

Shelley, Mary. ([1818] 1996). *Frankenstein*. Edited by J. Paul Hunter. New York: W. W. Norton.

Shermer, Michael. (1998). "Talking Twaddle with the Dead: The Tragedy of Death—The Farce of James van Praagh." *The Skeptic* 6 (1): 48–53.

———. (2000). *How We Believe: Science, Skepticism, and the Search for God*. 2d ed. New York: W. H. Freeman/Owl Books.

Showers, Renald E. (1999). "Revival of the Roman Empire." In *Countdown to Armageddon: The Final Battle and Beyond*. Edited by Joe Jordan and Tom Davis, 53–62. Eugene, Ore.: Harvest House Publishers.

Shuck, Glenn W. (2005). *Marks of the Beast: The Left Behind Novels and the Struggle for Evangelical Identity*. New York: New York University Press.

Siskel, Gene. (1973a). "'Fallout' Predicted." *Chicago Tribune* (28 December): sec. 2, A1.

———. (1973b). "Friedkin's 'The Exorcist': Brutal in Its Brilliance." *Chicago Tribune* (28 December): sec. 2, A1.

———. (1976). "'The Omen' Another Shocker Based on 'Sound' Principle." *Chicago Tribune* (29 June): sec. 3, B5.

Skal, David J. (1994). *The Monster Show: A Cultural History of Horror*. New York: Penguin Books.

Slater, Jay, ed. (2002). *Eaten Alive! Italian Cannibal and Zombie Movies*. London: Plexus.

Smith, Greg M. (2001). "'It's Just a Movie': A Teaching Essay for Introductory Media Classes." *Cinema Journal* 41 (1): 127–34.

Smith, Jonathan Z. (1982). *Imagining Religion: From Babylon to Jonestown*. Chicago: University of Chicago Press.
———. (1987). *To Take Place: Toward Theory in Ritual*. Chicago University of Chicago Press.
Smith, Margaret. (1993). *Ritual Abuse: What It Is, Why It Happens, How to Help*. New York: HarperSanFrancisco.
Smith, Michelle, and Lawrence Pazder. (1980). *Michelle Remembers* New York: Congdon & Lattes.
Sobchak, Vivian. (1987a). "Bringing It All Back Home: Family Economy and Generic Exchange." In *American Horrors: Essays on the Modern American Horror Film*. Edited by Gregory A. Waller, 175–94. Urbana: University of Illinois Press.
———. (1987b). *Screening Space: The American Science Fiction Film*. Rev. ed. New York: Ungar.
Southgate, Jeanette. (2007). "I Live with a Ghost in my House." *Beyond Magazine* 6 (June): 56–57.
Spong, John Shelby. (1991). *Rescuing the Bible from Fundamentalism: A Bishop Rethinks the Meaning of Scripture*. New York: HarperSanFrancisco
Stark, Rodney. (2001). *One True God: Historical Consequences of Monotheism*. Princeton: Princeton University Press.
Stark, Rodney, and William Sims Bainbridge. (1987). *A Theory of Religion*. New Brunswick, N.J.: Rutgers University Press.
Steakley, John. (1990). *Vampire$*. New York: ROC.
Stephens, Walter. (2002). *Demon Lovers: Witchcraft, Sex, and the Crisis of Belief*. Chicago: University of Chicago Press.
Stern, D. A. (1999). *The Blair Witch Project: A Dossier*. New York: Onyx Books.
Stoker, Bram. ([1897] 1998). *Dracula*. Edited by Glennis Byron. Peterborough, Canada: Broadview Press.
———. ([1903] 1996). *The Jewel of Seven Stars*. Oxford: Oxford University Press.
———. ([1911] 1998). *Lair of the White Worm*. Polegate, U.K.: Pulp Fictions.

Stone, Bryan. (2001). "The Sanctification of Fear: Images of the Religious in Horror Films." *Journal of Religion and Film* 5 (2); www.unomaha.edu/~wwwjrf/sanctifi.htm, accessed 28 January 2003.

Stratford, Lauren. (1988). *Satan's Underground*. Eugene, Ore.: Harvest House Publishers.

Strinati, Dominc (2000). *An Introduction to Studying Popular Culture*. London: Routledge.

Summers, Montague. ([1928] 1960). *The Vampire: His Kith and Kin*. New Hyde Park, N.Y.: University Books.

———. (1964). *Gothic Bibliography*. New York: Russell & Russell.

Telesco, Patricia. (1998). *365 Goddesses: A Daily Guide to the Magic and Inspiration of the Goddess*. New York: HarperSanFrancisco.

Terry, Clifford. (1968). "'Rosemary's Baby' Mixture of Obstetrics, Occult." *Chicago Tribune* (28 July): F7.

Thomas, Keith. (1971). *Religion and the Decline of Magic: Studies in Popular Belief in 16th and 17th Century England*. London: Weidenfeld & Nicolson.

Thomas, Paul. (2004). "Re-Imagining Inanna: The Gendered Reappropriation of the Ancient Goddess in Modern Goddess Worship." *The Pomegranate: The International Journal of Modern Pagan Studies* 6 (1): 53–69.

Thompson, Gary. (1997). *Rhetoric Through Media*. Boston: Allyn & Bacon.

Tohill, Cathal, and Pete Tombs. (1994). *Immoral Tales: European Sex and Horror Movies 1956–1984*. New York: St. Martin's Griffin.

Tombs, Pete. (2003). "The Beast from Bollywood: A History of the Indian Horror Film." In *Fear Without Frontiers: Horror Cinema Across the Globe*. Edited by Steven Jay Schneider, 243–53. Godalming, U.K.: FAB Press.

Topley, Marjorie. (1955). "Ghost Marriages among the Singapore Chinese." *Man* 55 (February): 29–30.

———. (1956). "Ghost Marriages among the Singapore Chinese: A Further Note." *Man* 56 (May): 71–72.

Trott, Jon. (1993). "Bob Larson's Ministry Under Scrutiny." *Cornerstone* 21 (100): 18, 37, 41–42.
Tsutsui, William. (2004). *Godzilla on My Mind: Fifty Years of the King of Monsters*. New York: Palgrave Macmillan.
Tudor, Andrew. (1989). *Monsters and Mad Scientists: A Cultural History of the Horror Movie*. London: Basil Blackwell.
Twitchell, James B. (1985). *Dreadful Pleasures: An Anatomy of Modern Horror*. New York: Oxford University Press
UPI [United Press International]. (1974a). "Tunisia Bans 'Exorcist.' *Los Angeles Times* (25 February): A18.
———. (1974b). "Waves from 'Exorcist' Roll On in Boston." *Hartford Courant* (16 February): 17.
———. (1980a). "Cult Mixing Voodoo and Christianity Believed Flourishing in Miama Area." *Washington Post* (26 June): A26.
———. (1980b). "Two Refugees Shot After Cult Mass." *Los Angeles Times* (18 November): A23.
Vaughan, Genevieve. (1998). "My Journey with Sekhmet, Goddess of Power and Change." *SageWoman* 42: 18–23.
Victor, Jeffrey S. (1991). "The Dynamics of Rumor—Panics About Satanic Cults." In *The Satanism Scare*. Edited by James T. Richardson, Joel Best, and David G. Bromley, 221–36. New York: de Gruyter.
———. (1993). *Satanic Panic: The Creation of a Contemporary Legend*. Chicago: Open Court.
Viser, William C. (1994). *The Darkness among Us: A Look at the Sinister Growth of the Occult and How Dangerously Close It Is To You*. Nashville: Broadman & Holman.
Volsky, George. (1987). "Religion From Cuba Stirs Row In Miami." *The New York Times* (29 June): A15.
Voltaire. ([1730] 1757). *La Pucelle d'Orleans*. A. Amsterdam.
Walker, Benjamin. (1970). *Sex and the Supernatural*. N.p.: Castle Books.
Walker, Wren. (1997). "Sony's *The Craft*"; www.witchvox.com, accessed 20 July 2007.

Waller, Gregory A. (1986). *The Living and the Undead: From Stoker's* Dracula *to Romero's* Dawn of the Dead. Urbana: University of Illinois Press.

———. (1987). "Introduction." In *American Horrors: Essays on the Modern American Horror Film*. Edited by Gregory A. Waller. Urbana: University of Illinois Press.

Wallis Budge, E. A. ([1899] 1971). *Egyptian Magic*. New York: Blom.

———. ([1900] 1959). *Egyptian Religion: Egyptian Ideas of the Future Life*. New York: University Books.

Warnke, Mike. (1972). *The Satan Seller*. Plainfield, N.J.: Logos International.

Watson, Sydney. ([1910] 1933). *In the Twinkling of an Eye*. Old Tappan, N.J.: Spire Books.

———. ([1918] 1933). *The Mark of the Beast*. Old Tappan, N.J.: Spire Books.

Weaver, James B., III, and Ron Tamborini, eds. (1996). *Horror Films: Current Research on Audience Preferences and Reactions*. Mahwah, N.J.: Lawrence Erlbaum Associates.

Weldon, John, and James Bjornstad. (1984). *Playing with Fire*. Chicago: Moody Press.

Weldon, John, with Zola Levitt. (1975). *UFO's: What on Earth is Happening: The Coming Invasion*. Irvine, Calif.: Harvest House Publishers.

Wellesley, Gordon. (1973). *Sex and the Occult*. New York: Bell Publishing.

Welter, Barbara. (1987). "From Maria Monk to Paul Blanschard: A Century of Protestant Anti-Catholicism." In *Uncivil Religion: Interreligious Hostility in America*. Edited by Robert Bellah and Frederick Greenspahn, 43–72. New York: Crossroad.

Westbrook, Bruce. (2004). "Retro chill factor; Japanese film takes the boo out of a twisted monster tale." *Houston Chronicle* (10 September): Star, 3.

Wexman, Virginia Wright. (1987). "The Trauma of Infancy in Roman Polanski's *Rosemary's Baby*." In *American Horrors: Essays on the Modern American Horror Film.* Edited by Gregory A. Waller. Urbana: University of Illinois Press.

Wharton, David Michael. (2003). "Crucified to the Machine: Religious Imagery in Fritz Lang's *Metropolis. Strange Horizons* (6 January); www.strangehorizons.com/2003/20030106/metropolis.shtml, accessed 5 October 2005.

Wheatley, Dennis. (1953). *To the Devil—A Daughter.* London: Hutchinson.

"White Zombie Is Coming to the Capitol." (1932). *Hartford Courant* (14 August): A7.

Whitehead, Henry S. ([1931] 1990). "Passing of a God." In *Weird Tales: A Selection, in Facsimile, of the Best from the World's Most Famous Fantasy Magazine.* Edited by Peter Haining, 115–28. New York: Carroll & Graf Publishers.

W. H. R. (1893). "Worshippers of the Voodoo: How Southern Negroes Propitiate the Spirit of Evil." *The New York Times* (25 June): 5.

Wilkinson, Tracy (2007). *The Vatican's Exorcists: Driving Out the Devil in the 21st Century.* New York: Warner Books.

Wilson, Colin. (1971). *The Occult.* London: Granada.

———. (1978). *Mysteries: An Investigation into the Occult, the Paranormal, and the Supernatural.* London: Granada.

Wilson, Jeffrey. (2008). *Mourning the Unborn Dead: American Uses of Japanese Buddhist Post-Abortion Rituals.* Oxford: Oxford University Press.

Wilson, Katharina M. (1985). "The History of the Word 'Vampire.'" *Journal of the History of Ideas* 46 (4): 577–83.

Wilson, P. W. (1926). "Pharaoh's Curse Clings to His Tombs." *New York Times Saturday Magazine* (11 April): 3, 16.

Wimbish, David. (1990). *Something's Going On Out There: Visitors from Space: Friendly or Fiendish?* Old Tappan, N.J.: Fleming H. Revell.

Winseman, Albert L. (2004a). "Eternal Destinations: Americans Believe in Heaven, Hell" (25 May); www.gallup.com, accessed 21 December 2004.

———. (2004b). "Faith Renewed? Confidence in Religion Rises" (22 June); www.gallup.com, accessed 21 December 2004.

Wojcik, Daniel. (1997). *The End of the World As We Know It: Faith, Fatalism, and Apocalypse in America*. New York: New York University Press.

Wolhowe, Cathe. (1974). "Bedeviled by Film, Curious go to GU." *Washington Post* (10 January): C1.

Wood, Robin. (1996). "Buring the Undead: The Use and Obsolescence of Count Dracula." In *The Dread of Difference: Gender and the Horror Film*. Edited by Barry Keith Grant, 364–78. Austin: University of Texas Press.

Woods, Richard. (1971). *The Occult Revolution: A Christian Meditation*. New York: Herder & Herder.

———. (1973). *The Devil*. Chicago: Thomas More Press.

Worland, Rick. (1997). "OWI Meets the Monsters: Hollywood Horror Films and War Propaganda, 1942 to 1945." *Cinema Journal* 37 (1): 47–65.

World Values Survey. (2006a). "United Kingdom," Association of Religion Data Archives; www.TheARDA.com, accessed 7 March 2007.

———. (2006b). "United States (General)," Association of Religion Data Archives; www.TheARDA.com, accessed 7 March 2007.

Wyndham, John. (1957). *The Midwich Cuckoos*. New York: Ballantine Books.

Zablocki, Benjamin, and Thomas Robbins, eds. (2001). *Misunderstanding Cults: Searching for Objectivity in a Controversial Field*. Toronto: University of Toronto Press.

Zillman, Dolf, and James B. Weaver III. (1996). "Gender-Socialization Theory of Reactions to Horror." In *Horror Films: Current Research on Audience Preferences and Reactions*. Edited by James B. Weaver, III, and Ron Tamborini, 81–101. Mahwah, N.J.: Lawrence Erlbaum Associates.

# INDEX

*28 Days Later*, 93–94, 95, 155

*Alien*, 7, 32, 261, 264
*Aliens*, 18
*Alien³*, 42
angels, 65, 68–71, 85, 91–92, 105, 106, 177, 202, 263; fallen, 157, 174, 176
Antichrist, 27–30, 46, 189, 190–95, 198, 216
atheism, 36–38
*Awful Disclosures of Maria Monk*, 240, 245–47

Barker, Clive, 84, 85
Barner-Barry, Carol, 53
Beal, Timothy, 74, 76, 91, 99
Beck, Steve, 8, 30, 33, 127
*Bedazzled*, 125
*Believers, The*, 8, 114, 209–13 passim
*Bell, Book and Candle*, 221, 238
Benshoff, Harry M., 41
Berger, John, 258

Berger, Peter, 11, 64, 66, 91, 92
black mass, 76, 79, 104, 113, 164, 179, 222
*Blair Witch Project, The*, 9, 115–16, 118
Blatty, William Peter, 42, 172, 178, 183, 254–55
blaxploitation, 41, 157
*Bless the Child*, 44, 90, 104–5, 217
*Bone Snatcher, The*, 17–18
*Bram Stoker's Dracula*, 21, 135, 237
*Brides of Dracula, The*, 8, 39
Brosnan, John, 57–58, 259
Brunvard, Jan Harold, 114

Carnarvon, Lord, 108–9, 143, 145
Carpenter, John, 2, 5–6, 65, 12, 94
Carroll, Noël, 18–19, 171
Carter, Howard, 108–9, 143, 145
Castle, William, 19, 127
catharsis, 259–64
cemeteries, 12, 80–81, 97, 102, 106 118, 122, 130, 224, 226; *see also* graveyards

Cenobites (*Hellraiser*), 7, 61, 84–89 *passim*, 92, 259, 261, 262
*Charmed*, 221, 233, 234
Charon, 8, 33, 34
*Children of the Corn*, 217–21, 241
*Children of the Damned*, 102, 120–22
Church of Jesus Christ of Latter-day Saints, The, 143
clergy, 7, 179; *see also* ministers, priests
Coppola, Francis Ford, 21, 135
Corman, Roger, 76
*Craft, The*, 53, 221, 229–35, 251
Crane, Jonathan Lake, 41
*Cult of Fury*, 201–2, 204, 206, 219
cults, 14–15, 35, 77, 82, 105, 146–47, 201–4, 207–29 *passim*

*Dagon*, 76, 81–84, 209
Davis, Wade, 35, 163
*Dawn of the Dead*, 95, 152, 154
de Sade, Marquis, 79, 247
death, fear of, 39, 45, 51–52, 59, 96, 123–65 *passim*
*Demonia*, 9, 240–42, 246
demons and demonic forces, 6, 65, 76, 90, 91, 150, 158; fear of, 20, 54, 56, 258, 261, 262; in films, 26–28, 46, 48, 62–63, 71, 85, 87–88, 89, 168–69, 170, 172–84 *passim*, 189, 192, 195, 198, 205, 206, 250–53, 263
Dempsey, Michael, 42

Derrickson, Scott, 250–54, 255, 257
Devil, 9, 27, 48, 125, 167, 168–70, 172, 174–78, 184–85, 195, 204, 208 210, 214, 240–41, 243, 250, 253, 256; belief in, 53–54, 181–82, 197–98, 257; *see also* Lucifer, Satan
*Devil Rides Out, The*, 105, 112, 213, 214
*Devil's Nightmare, The*, 204–7
Donner, Richard, 191, 192, 195, 197
*Dracula 2000*, 39, 137–38
*Dracula*, 21, 34, 62, 63, 89, 101, 133, 251, 261, 262
*Dracula Has Risen from the Grave*, 25, 35–39, 103, 104, 135
*Dunwich Horror, The*, 76–81, 83, 209

Egypt and Egyptian religion, 98, 108–9, 112, 127, 141–42, 191; in film, 8, 98, 100, 102, 105, 107, 108, 110–11, 140–41, 145, 146–47, 157, 209, 251; popular fascination with, 13, 67, 98, 107, 143–44, 145–46, 150–51
Eliade, Mircea, 195–196, 199
*End of Days*, 29, 44, 67, 189
exorcism, 27, 36, 48, 136, 168–69, 172–84 *passim*, 188, 250–51, 254, 257–58; *see also* possession
*Exorcism of Emily Rose, The*, 249–58, 263

*Exorcist, The*, 13, 27, 41, 42, 44, 47–48, 62, 63, 72, 90, 102, 114, 167–71, 172–74, 177–78, 183–84, 185, 186, 192–93, 196, 216, 251, 252, 254, 256, 257

Falwell, Jerry, 29, 190
Fisher, Lucy, 41, 186
Fisher, Terence, 105, 107, 110, 111, 147, 157, 213
*Fog, The*, 2–7, 33, 75, 94, 260
Freeland, Cynthia, 47–48, 85
Frankenstein, 8, 107, 123–25, 133, 139, 261
Freud, Sigmund, 15, 46, 74, 76, 129, 138, 186
Freund, Karl, 13, 109, 139
*Friday the 13th, Part 3*, 49–50
Friedkin, William, 42, 173, 175, 178, 192, 196
Fulci, Lucio, 9, 152, 157, 240–41

Gardner, Gerald, 223
ghosts and ghost stories, 6, 40, 52, 54, 55, 75, 97, 107, 126, 140, 152, 171–72, 174, 176; fear of, 12, 20, 23, 24, 262; in film, 2–4, 32, 68, 126–33, 134, 263
*Ghost Ship*, 8, 25, 30–35
gods and goddesses, 14, 16, 29, 58, 64, 75–76, 100, 112, 119, 138, 153, 175, 188–89, 240, 260; fear of, 22, 24, 52–53, 213; in film, 8, 38, 67, 69–70, 77, 79–83 *passim*, 84, 86–90 *passim*, 98, 101, 105–6, 140, 142–43, 148, 150–51, 198, 219–20, 225, 228–29, 232, 244
good, moral, and decent fallacy, 15–16
Goodman, Felicitas, 254–55
Gordon, Stuart, 81
Graham, Billy, 68, 173, 178
graveyards, 99, 106, 107, 122, 137, 223; *see also* cemeteries
*Grudge, The*, 128–33; *see also Ju-on*

Haller, Daniel, 76–81 *passim*
Halperin, Victor, 8, 106, 156, 160, 162, 164
Hammer Studios, 21, 35, 37, 45, 67, 98, 103, 104, 105, 108, 110, 112, 113, 140, 142, 146, 150, 188, 214, 221, 237, 238, 259
Hankiss, Elemér, 22
Hardy, Robin, 8, 105, 224, 226
Harrington, Curtis, 40
haunted house, 24, 33, 56, 92, 127
hell, belief in, 53–54, 177, 184
*Hellbound: Hellraiser II*, 87
*Hellraiser*, 7, 40, 61, 84, 85, 92, 261, 262
*Hellraiser: Bloodline*, 51, 61–63, 88, 106, 251, 261
*Hellraiser III: Hell on Earth*, 87–88, 102
horror, defined, 17–22; metataxis of, 7, 30, 67–68, 85, 165
*Horror Hotel*, 8, 9, 118, 221–24, 236

Hunt, Dave, 30, 212

*In the Mouth of Madness*, 65–66
Ingebretsen, Edward, 40
intertextuality, cultural, 11–12, 72, 113, 202, 206, 213, 220, 231, 258, 262

Jahoda, Gustav, 54–55
James, William, 15
Jancovich, Mark, 40
Jesus Christ, 137, 174–75, 220
J-horror, 128–33
*John Carpenter's Vampires*, 12, 39, 67, 136–37
Jones, Daryl, 41
Joshi, S. T., 76, 97
*Ju-on*, 128–33; see also The Grudge

Kaminski, Janusz, 8, 11, 25, 26
Karloff, Boris, 106, 107, 123–24
King, Stephen, 10, 127, 217, 259, 260
Krueger, Freddy, 5, 170
*kyonsi* (hopping corpses), 107, 127
Kyrou, Adonis, 78, 206, 244

*Lair of the White Worm, The*, 8, 34, 98
Lang, Fritz, 8
Larson, Bob, 181–83
LaVey, Anton, 79, 172, 179, 196–97
Lee, Christopher, 35, 103, 105, 111, 113, 188–89, 213–14, 226–28

Lewis, Matthew, 79, 97, 247
Lindsey, Hal, 29, 192, 194
*Lost Souls*, 8, 11, 25, 26–30, 35, 44, 68, 114, 188, 254
Lovecraft, H. P., 45, 65, 75–84 *passim*, 97, 98, 114, 129, 156, 223
Lucifer, 69, 190, 221, 250, 251; see also Devil, Satan
Luckmann, Thomas, 11
Lugosi, Bela, 45, 160, 164, 237

Mandile, Tony, 67, 102
Mattei, Bruno, 9, 240–41
Medved, Michael, 42–43, 46, 57
Méliès, Georges, 8
*Metropolis*, 8
Michel, Anneliese, 254–55
*Midnight Mass*, 67, 102, 134
minister, 6, 10, 170, 174, 217, 218, 227; see also clergy, priest
Molina, Jorge, 12
Moxey, John Llewellyn, 8, 118, 223, 236
mummies, 6, 174, 176; fear of, 114, 127, 171; in film, 13, 20, 67–68, 98, 100–101, 102, 105, 106, 107–12, 126, 139–51 *passim*, 153, 157, 162, 259, 262, 263
mummification, 141–42, 144, 145
*Mummy, The*, 13, 67, 101, 106, 107, 109–12, 139–40, 145, 147–50, 209, 236, 251, 262
*Mummy's Curse, The*, 100–1, 142
*Mummy's Ghost, The*, 8, 100, 142, 146–47

*Mummy's Hand, The,* 100, 110, 140, 142, 147

*Necronomicon,* 77, 114
*Night of the Living Dead,* 45, 95, 152, 155, 162
*Nightmare on Elm Street, A,* 5
*Ninth Gate, The,* 214
Nunsploitation, 9, 237, 239–48

occult and occultism, 8, 54, 55, 62–63, 79–80, 102, 104, 108–9, 110, 182–83, 185, 197, 204, 235, 238–39, 241
*Omen, The,* 29, 41, 172, 189, 191–95, 197–99, 216, 261
*Order, The,* 71–74, 137
*Other Hell, The,* 9, 68, 240–41
Otto, Rudolf, 22–24, 52

Paffenroth, Kim, 154
Pagans and Paganism, 53, 73, 101–2, 106, 144, 187, 208, 224–35 *passim*
Paoli, Dennis, 81, 82
Peoples Temple, 207, 208, 211
Petronius, 22
Polanski, Roman, 41, 46–47, 185–86, 196–97, 214
*Poltergeist,* 107, 114, 217
possession, 27–29, 48, 54, 56, 63, 158, 168–69, 171, 172–84 *passim,* 188, 196, 216, 250–58 *passim; see also* exorcism

priestess, 84, 106, 113, 140, 142, 148
priest, Anglican, 177; Catholic, 10, 12, 30, 35, 36, 38–39, 48, 71, 83, 87–88, 94, 135, 136, 138, 157, 169-70, 173, 177, 178, 183, 192, 205-6, 232, 250, 254, 258; Episcopal, 3, 191; Egyptian, 8, 98, 100–101, 107, 109, 139, 140, 142, 143, 145, 150, 209; Israelite, 51; Orthodox, 135; Santerían, 210; Satanic, 180, 188, 192, 198; Taoist, 107, 127; *see also* clergy, minister
*Prophecy, The,* 69–71, 85, 106, 261
Protestantism, Evangelical and Fundamentalist, 10, 27, 29, 42–43, 48, 64, 119, 172, 178–79, 212, 216, 244, 257
*Psycho,* 6
pulps, 78, 98, 99, 146, 159, 222

Quinn, Seabury, 98, 99, 146

*Re-Animator,* 45, 75, 156
religion, ambivalence toward, 7, 9, 51, 53, 75, 90, 93–121 *passim,* 124, 135, 138, 139, 154, 158, 178; defined, 14–16
*Resident Evil,* 45, 94, 156
*Resident Evil: Apocalypse,* 93–95
*Return of the Living Dead, The,* 106, 156
*Ring, The,* 128, 199

Rollin, Jean, 237
Roman Catholicism, 11, 13, 16, 27, 29–30, 41, 48, 67, 71–74, 82–83, 85, 86, 87, 94, 119, 136–37, 157, 170, 176–79, 184, 210, 231–32, 239–48 *passim*, 256, 257
Romero, George, 45, 95, 152, 156
*Rosemary's Baby*, 27, 29, 46–48, 77, 114, 172, 184–89, 196–97, 213, 214, 232, 251
Russell, Jamie, 152, 153, 154

*Sacred Flesh*, 240, 242–44, 247
sacrifice, 18, 26, 143; ritual, 8, 16, 44, 77, 80, 81, 83, 98, 105, 112–13, 158–59, 210, 212–23, 218, 220, 222–24, 228–29, 236
Santería, 209–13
Satan, 26, 28, 91, 164, 179–84 *passim*, 188–89, 204, 206, 214, 223, 233, 254; Church of, 79, 172, 179, 196, 197; *see also* Devil, Lucifer
satanic panic, 48, 78, 113, 174, 177, 180, 213
*Satanic Rites of Dracula, The*, 112–13
Satanism, 46–47, 56, 105, 163, 179–81, 184–85, 188, 196–97, 235
Schlesinger, John, 8, 209, 210, 212
Scruton, David, 58–59
Seabrook, William, 158–65 *passim*
secularization, 50–51, 54, 62, 90
Seltzer, David, 191, 193, 194, 195, 198

*Serpent and the Rainbow, The*, 35, 163
*Seventh Victim, The*, 214–16
sex and sexuality, 41, 204–7, 236–48 *passim*
Shelley, Mary, 123–24
Shimizu, Takashi, 128–29, 131
Smith, Jonathan Z., 15–16, 95–96
Smith, Joseph, 143
Sobchak, Vivian, 21, 186, 189
sociophobics, 9, 25, 54, 56–59, 78, 89, 96, 97, 100, 106, 111, 114, 117, 122, 124, 125, 129–31, 134, 135, 140, 164, 171–72, 174, 177, 182–84, 185, 187–88, 193, 195, 196, 198, 208, 209, 211, 215, 216, 220, 223, 235, 244, 252, 256–57, 260, 261, 263, 264; defined, 58–59
soul, 5, 6, 24, 32–34, 68, 69, 72, 124–26, 136, 138, 139, 141, 189, 250
Spielberg, Steven, 26
spirits, 6, 52, 55, 126–29 *passim*, 132, 138, 140, 141, 142, 153, 162, 171, 183
spiritualism, 55, 64, 182
Stark, Rodney, 91, 254
*Stigmata*, 8, 44, 67
Stoker, Bram, 21, 34, 36, 39, 98, 133, 135, 138, 145
Stone, Bryan, 43–45, 46, 50, 57, 220
supernatural, 6, 17, 28, 44, 48, 50, 62–63, 89, 157, 231; fear of, 9, 24,

162, 167–99 *passim*; persistence of belief in, 53–56, 90, 116, 127
superstition, 50, 54–55, 62, 63, 133, 158, 161, 163, 223, 251

taphophobia, 140–41
*Taste the Blood of Dracula*, 103–4
Tate, Sharon, 196–97
temptation, 9, 51, 89, 175–76, 205, 244, 248
Thatcher, Margaret, 5
*Tingler, The*, 19–20
*Touched by an Angel*, 69
Twitchell, James, 19, 41, 46, 153
*To the Devil . . . a Daughter*, 29, 68, 102
Tudor, Andrew, 56
Tutankhamen, 108–9, 114, 143, 145

Universal Studios, 67, 98, 100, 105, 110–11, 139, 140, 142, 145, 147, 236, 260, 262

vampires, 6, 7, 8, 12, 56, 84, 98, 126, 174, 176; eroticism of, 13, 137, 153, 236, 237; in film, 36–40, 62, 63, 104, 106, 107, 127, 133–39, 140, 162, 171, 259, 263; origins of, 133–39
*Village of the Damned*, 120, 217
Vodou, 35, 46, 141, 157–59, 163, 177, 209, 212, 238, ; in film (as "Voodoo"), 45–46, 157–59, 163–64, 210–212

Wainwright, Rupert, 5, 8
Waller, Gregory, 9, 41
Weaver, James, 48–50, 57
werewolves, 6, 56, 63, 134
Wexman, Virginia, 46–48, 50, 57, 186, 187
*White Zombie*, 8, 45, 106, 160, 163–64
Wicca, 53, 163, 223, 229–35
*Wicker Man, The*, 8, 105–6, 112, 221, 224–29, 231, 250
Wilson, Colin, 150–51
Wingrove, Nigel, 240, 242–43
*Witches, The*, 112–13, 238
Witches and Witchcraft, 9, 56, 113, 115–16, 163, 176, 187–88, 208, 221–24, 229–38 *passim*, 258
*Wolf Man, The*, 62, 63
Woods, Richard, 183–84
Worland, Rick, 40, 146–47

*X-Files, The*, 11, 55, 117

Yagher, Kevin, 88, 262

Zillman, Dolf, 48–50, 57
zombies and zombiism, 35, 45; fear of, 12, 20, 171, 174, 176, 177; in film, 45–46, 93–95, 106, 126, 127, 151–65 *passim*, 217, 240, 241, 248